The First Rasta

Leonard Howell and the Rise of Rastafarianism

by Hélène Lee

translated by Lily Davis

edited and with an introduction by Stephen Davis

T0159228

Lawrence Hill Books

Chicago

Library of Congress Cataloging-in-Publication Data

Lee, Hélène.
[Premier Rasta. English]
The first Rasta : Leonard Howell and the rise of Rastafarianism / by
Hélène Lee ; translated by Lily Davis and Hélène Lee ; edited and with
an introduction by Stephen Davis.
  p.   cm.
Includes bibliographical references and index.
  ISBN 1-55652-466-8
  1. Maragh, G. G.   2. Rastafari movement—History.
I. Davis, Stephen, 1947–   II. Title.

BL2532.R37 L44513   2003
299'.676—dc21   2002153774

Jacket design: Joan Sommers Design
Jacket photograph: © Susanne Moss/Selah Photo
Interior design: Pamela Juárez

Originally published in 1999 by Flammarion, France, as *Le Premier Rasta*

Contents

Give Thanks

To Prof. Robert Hill, with respect. To Donovan Philips, who could have written this book. To the Brethren who accepted and encouraged me, and patiently answered my questions: Mortimer Planno, Bongo Puru, Bongo Sheffan, The Mystic Revelation of Rastafari, Jah Youth, Johnny "Dizzy" Moore, Bro Manny, Bro Sam, David Elliott, Bernard "Satta" Collins, Cedric "Im" Brooks, and all the others. Jah Love! To the elders of Tredegar Park: Miss Amy, Miss Vinette, Chi-chi Boy, and the queen—Miss Gertrude Campbell. To Jimmy Cliff. To Ras Miguel Lorne for his work on the diffusion of Rasta thought. To the Jamaica Institute, the National Archives of Jamaica in Spanish Town, the Schomburg Center in New York, the University of the West Indies, and to Profs. Ajai and Laxmi Mansingh, Prof. Barry Chevannes, and Mrs. Dunn. To Sister Ignatius, Joe Watt, Hartley Neita, Dicky Jobson, Winston Chang, and Miss Lucy Lovelace. To Sharon and Gladdy, for their patience. To Perry, Sally, and Jason—guardian angels, without whom . . . To David Marchand, spiritual artist. To Stephen Davis and Lily Davis. To Francis Falceto. To Bruno Bayon who had the idea for this book, and to Bernard Loupias who belived it. To Yuval Taylor and Lawrence Hill Books. To my lovely and brave daughter Melanie ("Sometimes I wish I had a mother like all the others") and everyone who supported me. To the entire Howell family: Avinel Taylor, Patrick, "Son" and Lesford, Daphney, Kathleen, Curlyn, Rosie, and their children. Special thanks to Monty and Blade.

Fools saying in their hearts, "Rasta, your god is dead." But I and I know . . . Jah live!

—Bob Marley

Leonard Howell.

Introduction

When Bob Marley began his reggae crusade in 1972, he came armed not just with the best street poet's songbook since Bob Dylan, but with a strange new spiritual nationality as well. The first time I interviewed Bob, in Boston the following year, he was much more interested in talking about being a Rastafarian than he was about selling reggae music, which was beginning to catch fire with its own irresistible momentum. Sitting in a Beacon Street motel room amid lounging members of his band and the aroma of cooking vegetables, Marley quietly said that he and the band thought that the Ethiopian emperor, Haile Selassie I, was a living god. Taking off his wool cap and shaking out his dreadlocks, the twenty-eight-year-old singer looked me in the eye and quoted the lyric he and Peter Tosh were singing every night to ecstatic audiences in small clubs around America: "We know and we over-stand, Almighty God is a living man."

Not many of the rock stars I wrote about for *Rolling Stone* in the 1970s arrived with such unshakeable belief in a spiritual manifesto. And it wasn't just the Wailers. Most of the hot new reggae stars emerging from Jamaica—Burning Spear, Big Youth, Max Romeo, the Heptones—also wore flamboyant, ropy dreadlocks and sported the signifying red, green, and gold colors of the Rastas. All were careful to warn against the assumption that Rasta was just a fad or a hairstyle. The worst that could be said about such a person was "Him have locks on him head, but not in him heart."

As Marley's fame spread through the Wailers' early albums and their incandescent performances, journalists literally lined up to speak with Bob. His record company imported them to Kingston in packs. Reggae and the cultural shock wave pulsing outward from Jamaica was the best story most of them had ever seen. For the next three years, Bob Marley fenced with his many interviewers about his deeply held faith. Yes, he told them, Haile Selassie was *"Jah, Rastafari*, who liveth and reigneth I-tinually." Marley spoke and sang in a Rasta jargon that was quick to catch on, and his words were punctuated with jabs of a burning marijuana spliff the size of a cigar. Reggae's popularity grew even faster when music fans on both sides of the Atlantic were made to understand that marijuana— called *ganja* in Jamaica—was a sacrament to the Rastas.

Many of the journalists sent to interview Bob were openly skeptical about the divinity of the emperor, especially after Selassie was overthrown in a 1974 coup amid terrible famine and civil war in Ethiopia. Bob Marley remained adamant in his faith. Few of the writers who argued with him realized that Bob was on a personal crusade, and indeed had been dispatched on a dangerous international mission by important Rasta elders in Jamaica, who assured him that his ambitious pursuit of planetary renown was part of the plan to spread the word that a Black King had come to redeem the world, if only the world could be made to take heed.

When I next spent time with Bob Marley, at his house in Kingston in 1976, he was obviously tiring of the repetitive rigors of marketing Rasta to the world, but his belief in the power of Jah was no less diminished. He was performing his intense anthems and modern psalms in front of huge cloth backdrops depicting Selassie in his glory, and recording new songs like "Jah Live" and "Exodus," which spoke of the metaphoric desire of Africans in the West to return to an African Zion represented by modern Ethiopia.

"Yeah, mon," he told me one night, bored with my skepticism. "Rasta must go home to Africa. I know it sound funny to some people some time. Sometimes sound like a mad t'ing. But it is our real desire to go home to Africa. Certain things that happened a long time ago must be revealed," he said with a cryptic smile and a pull on his spliff. "Until that happens, I and I still in captivity." At the end of a long conversation, I asked Bob whether Rastas could be rebels too, and he just laughed. "Many more will have to suffer, and many more will have to die, no ask me why. But Rasta not violent, y'know? Rasta *physical*!" Then he turned the defense of Rasta over to his young keyboard player, Tyrone Downie, and spent the rest of the interview smoking and listening, leaning against his silver BMW as Tyrone preached the Rasta gospel of the Twelve Tribes of Israel, the powerful new alliance of Rastafarians that Bob and his friends supported.

Bob Marley had five years left at that point, and he didn't waste them. He toured constantly, wrote new songs every day, and gradually turned into a world champion of human rights. He put one of Haile Selassie's most passionate anti-imperialist speeches to a reggae-rockers rhythm and called it "War." He used his moral authority and Rasta neutrality to try to end Jamaica's murderous political strife. After performing at Zimbabwe's independence ceremonies in 1980, Marley traveled to Ethiopia and visited the fertile valley that Selassie had set aside for black Americans who wished to return to Africa. In London, Bob met with Selassie's grandson, who gave him a special ring that had been owned by the emperor. Bob wore it until the day he died in 1981, and he wears it still, in his tomb in the hills of the parish where he was born.

So Bob Marley spread the message of a new religion through his music, and over time it became a worldwide, star-quality alternative spiritual identity. It took only thirty years for Rastafarian culture and ideas to colonize a world through the power of Bob's music, attitude, and image; to permeate modern communications through radio, television, and even advertising. The Beatles are unknown in China and India, but one sees Bob Marley T-shirts from Shanghai to Calcutta, from Marrakech to Brazzaville, from Jakarta to Recife. "*Jah Live*"—indeed. The little half-breed singer from Trench Town did what the Rasta leaders had asked of him, and much more. No one expected it would happen, except for Bob Marley himself.

Many of us who closely followed Jamaican culture were surprised that, when Bob died, his widow handed his funeral over to the almost unknown Ethiopian Orthodox Church. This was the western legatee of the ancient Coptic Christian church, the one in which Selassie himself worshipped. It later came out that Bob had helped pay for the church's tabernacle in Kingston. At his mother's urging, Bob had even been baptized by an Orthodox bishop, in a New York hotel room, after he collapsed while on his final tour in 1980.

The state funeral in Kingston thus proceeded as an Orthodox service, replete with hymns in Amharic and Geez, burning incense, and lines of richly robed and bearded priests carrying heavy silver crosses. A dramatic moment occurred when Bob's friend Allan Cole, a Jamaican soccer star who supported the spurned Twelve Tribes organization, strode up to the lectern and shouldered aside the presiding Coptic priest. Cole delivered a short eulogy on behalf of the Rastafarians, one decidedly not on the printed schedule. This "capture of ceremonies," as it was later called, was the first time I realized how differentiated were the various Jamaican branches of the Rastafarians. Some believed Selassie was god. Some believed him a messiah, an incarnation of the Christ energy. Others saw him as a powerful leader whose words were divinely inspired. The Ethiopian Orthodox Church seemed to think the Rastas were pagans and idolaters.

This made one think. Anyone who wanted to reduce the Rastas to their square roots was obviously in for a struggle. The old joke was always that Jamaica is a place without facts. I knew, even back then, that it would take a heroic effort on the part of some reporter, as well as years of archival stoop-labor, to really locate the loose threads of Rasta history going back a hundred years, and then weave them into a tricolored tapestry of inspiration and soul. Who could do this? Who had the time and the patience? I didn't think I knew anyone who could fill these shoes.

In 1982 I returned to Jamaica, at the invitation of Bob Marley's family, for a memorial concert to mark the first anniversary of his death. I rented a car in Kingston and drove for three hours up to Nine Miles, the tiny mountain hamlet in St. Ann parish on the north coast of the island, where Bob Marley was both born and buried. After an Orthodox priest chanted some prayers as night fell over the rolling green hills, the surviving Wailers and the I-Threes played a splendid set of Bob's songs for a few hundred friends and family members, plus a few media people who had worked with Bob during the glory years.

It was after midnight when I found my car in the pitch-black country night and headed down the rough gravel track toward the main road back to town. Leaving the village, I saw a young white woman, walking alone in the dark, trying to find a ride. My car was already full, so I motioned her to the car behind me, driven by my photographer, Peter Simon. A few miles down the road, we stopped at a tavern for some beer, and I learned that the hitchhiker was the legendary Paris-based writer Hélène Lee.

Hélène was and is the top French journalist covering black music. She first made her name writing about Bob Marley and the other reggae stars for the magazine *Rock & Folk*, and then branched out to cover Caribbean and African music in all its variations. She didn't just write about the music, she actually lived it. She has been married to two of the great superstars of modern African music, Salif Keita and Alpha Blondy, and helped launch their careers in Europe and America. Her first book, *Rockers d'Afrique* (Paris: Albin Michel, 1986), still stands as the best study of African popular musicians yet published. (Full disclosure: Hélène also translated two of my books on Jamaican music, *Reggae Bloodlines* and *Bob Marley*.) In 1979, just as the African music scene exploded in France, she began writing about black music for the Paris daily newspaper *Libération*, where she continues to work as one of the best music journalists in any language. She has also produced superb television documentaries on ahead-of-the-curve French bands like the brilliant reggaerai avatars, Orchestre National de Barbès. In other words, for the last twenty years Hélène has provided a voice, a viewpoint, and a context for the some of the most interesting music being made on the planet.

Most writers who covered reggae music during its international ascendancy in the 1970s abandoned Jamaica after Bob Marley died. The big story—Marley, Rastas, ganja, Jamaica's socialist experiments—seemed to be over, and reggae itself changed from an accessible, almost wholesome roots music to the coked-up, techno-driven, and often obscene style known as dancehall. But reggae and Rasta culture has had a much greater effect in Europe and in Africa than in North America, and Hélène Lee became one of the only cosmopolitan journalists to delve even deeper into the history and background of Jamaica's indispensable contribution to world consciousness. Hélène had a burning desire to learn how far back the Rastafarian movement went, who had started it, who sustained it against violent colonial oppression, and who transformed it from a despised cult on a small island into a spiritual nationality that has captivated two generations around the world.

Most foreign journalists working in Jamaica rent cars at the Kingston airport, move into one of the expensive uptown hotels, and speak to the same cast of experts from academia, the media, and the political milieu. Then they go home and write the same old boilerplate about the struggle between rich and poor under the tropical sun. Hélène Lee, traveling on a backpacker's budget, deploys a radically different approach. Instead of renting a car, she rides the crammed taxis and buses with ordinary Jamaicans. Instead of hotels, she stays with friends in some of the toughest slums in the Western Hemisphere. Instead of relying on the usual suspects, she walks in the footsteps of the people she's writing about, searches out their families, and gets her data from the invisible but articulate people who lived the story along with people like the first Rasta, Leonard Howell, and the most famous Rasta, Bob Marley. Hélène spent weeks researching the historical records in the archives in Spanish Town and the Jamaica Institute, and then in Harlem's Schomburg Center for Research in Black Culture. For the more crucial oral history, she traveled far and wide through rural and urban Jamaica, interviewing Rastafarian elders, various master musicians, people in politics and business, and especially the women who knew and, in some cases, loved the mysterious and shadowy founder of the movement, Leonard Howell.

The First Rasta is an extraordinary book, not just about the founding father of the Rastafarians, but about the last hundred years of Jamaican history. Hélène Lee writes not as an academic researcher but as a spiritual seeker herself. Her often lonely and grueling travels through the azure cane fields, lush valleys, and limestone mountains of Jamaica's interior read like a real-time adventure in ethnology and religious history. She digs for her story with unapologetic passion and first-person involvement, and then challenges the reader to separate the facts from the myths. Those who demand their "history" cut, dried, flash-frozen, and prepackaged can decide for themselves whether or not some of Hélène Lee's astonishing conjectures about modern Jamaican political history are on the mark. "Pick sense from nonsense," Bob Marley used to tell the writers who pestered him. In *The First Rasta*, Hélène Lee has picked a hell of a lot of sense from a murky and hidden river of memory, testimony, and even a bit of guesswork.

The First Rasta was published in Paris by Flammarion in 1999 and was an immediate sensation. Widely read, reviewed, and admired in France and in Francophone Africa, her book opened a window into a hidden world for thousands of curious readers. For this English edition, Hélène corrected and updated some of her data while living in the mud-walled desert city of Bamako, Mali. She translated her text into English with the help of Lily Davis, a Paris-based writer who produced the first mix of the manuscript. My own contribution is a simple edit and a few emendations for the convenience of an English-speaking readership. Whatever pleasure and knowledge the reader receives from this wonderful book is due solely to Hélène Lee's ardor, passion, and quest for meaning in a world gone awry with what our hero Bob Marley called "ism and schism." So take my advice and fasten your seatbelts. *The First Rasta* is a wild ride into the alternative history of our era. I'm extremely proud to be associated with Hélène's brave and provocative work.

—Stephen Davis

1

The Footsteps of a Spirit

A rusty placard at a bend in the road reads, "De la Vega Heights—Lots for Sale." It points toward a faded trail leading up into the hills. "This is the entrance to Pinnacle," the taxi driver says. I give him twenty dollars and walk toward the entrance. Behind me the Lada taxi lingers while the passengers' eyes follow me in silence. Not long before, as we were passing a house in the valley, the driver had knowingly commented, "Two pickney [children] from Pinnacle bury in this corner. And now dem build a house 'pon the grave." The lady squeezed in next to me scowls, "It full of duppy [spirits], this gully."

The road I'm walking on looks abandoned. The tar is gray and eaten up by plants at the edges, but it seems like it was built to last. Who built it? And where does it lead? There is nothing in sight for miles. . . . I tread on. The road winds into a maze of hills, right, left, right again, and after a while I lose my sense of direction. Under the tropic sun everything is silent; dried creepers hang limp from the trees. Is this really Pinnacle, the "promised land" of the Rastafarians?

Pinnacle. Every book about the Rasta movement mentions Pinnacle, but no one seems to know where it is, or what happened there. Was the most fascinating twentieth-century religion born here, in this brilliant chaos of green jungle and rugged limestone? Did the planetwide phenomenon of red, green, and gold culture—reggae, dreadlocks, and an international champion of human rights—spring from this very spot?

As I turn around I notice a woman standing in the middle of the road looking at me. From this distance I can't see her face, but she is wearing the long dress and head wrap of a Rasta woman. After a few seconds she turns away and disappears to the left into the bush. I walk back to the spot. A footpath leading uphill is barely visible. Looking closer, I see that it must have been an old stone road, the kind that slaves built up to the old plantation "great houses," wide enough for wagon traffic. Now I see only a vague flatness under the growth of wild bush.

A loud shriek from a bird makes me jump and look around. Perched on a hill, right at my back, an empty-eyed ruin stares at me. Farther up, an elegant arch of red brick rises between two rocks; it seems to support the sky. All around grow gigantic aloe spikes as large as spears. I walk past them and suddenly an incredible view opens beneath me, with every shade and tone of blue shimmering in the distance as far as the eye can see. Far below, Spanish Town, the old capital of Jamaica, sprawls out like an industrial wasteland. Farther to the left are Kingston and its upland suburbs against the misty line of the Blue Mountains. Southward lie the indigo blue expanse of sugar estates, the Hellshire Hills, and the sea. The view is dizzying, and I keep walking up the old road. There is not much left of the great house that used to stand on the top of the hill; all that remains is a stone platform and a red brick cistern with green weeds rotting in an inch of black water.

As I prepare to turn back, the woman with the long green dress materializes from behind the cistern, carrying something in her hand. She is much older than I had originally thought. I'd been misled by her slender body and swift movements.

The remains of Pinnacle's great house (2001). © HÉLÈNE LEE.

"You lookin' somethin'?"
"History . . . I'm trying to learn about Leonard Howell."
"Counselor Howell!"
"Do you know anything about Counselor Howell?"
"Well . . . not too much."

The woman squeezes her eyes shut in a silent laugh, then bends toward my ear. "He was a *powerful* man!" In her hand is an old red brick smoothed by age. She mutters, "He loved to walk barefoot. His feet have touched this stone." Opening up her old patched-up bag, she ceremoniously puts the brick inside, adding, "They say he is dead, but he is alive." She is still muttering, squinting in a smile. Then she looks straight into my eyes. "*You* believe he is alive?"

I am on the verge of answering a noncommittal "I understand," when I remember that Rastas do not like the word *under-stand*. They do not like to stand under anything, preferring to "over-stand," so I say instead, "I know he is alive. He brought me up here! Who else could have brought me to this place?"

She laughs and comes down the flight of steps. "So you want to learn about Counselor Howell. What do you want to know?"

"Anything."

"If you want to know, you have to come with me."

"Come where?" I think. "And who is she?" I follow her down the path, but suddenly, at a grove of flamboyants, she cuts left toward sheer cliffs that fall toward the Rio Cobre, far below. I try to keep up, but stumble and then lose sight of her. I want to call to her but don't know her name. A rock fall blocks my path. The sun is going down and her footprints vanish. I feel like I'm chasing a phantom or a spirit.

When Pinnacle, the first Rastafarian community, was burned to the ground in 1958, an estimated two thousand of its residents took refuge in Kingston. Ironically the Jamaican police had succeeded only in spreading the "Rasta Menace" they were trying to suppress. From then on, the preachers and disciples of this strange cult based their headquarters in the downtown ghettos of the capital, where they were feared and despised by the Jamaican establishment. The Rastas' poverty, their boldness of speech, and their wild looks were a contemptuous challenge to the colonial order. Jamaican educators and preachers realized that the Rastafarians could become a real threat to established religion in Jamaica. The rich and especially the middle class saw them as a rebel army crawling nearer to their uptown lawns. After eighteen years of peaceful relations within the boundaries of the Pinnacle community, thousands of Rastas had been thrown into western Kingston's hopeless maze of decrepit shanties. The terrible conditions in Trench Town and the other slums left them in a desperate struggle to survive.

And strangely enough, they were not the ones to start the war. On May 7, 1959, a dispute between a policeman and a city worker in Kingston's Coronation Market turned into a riotous brawl. The city worker had been sporting a beard, which was the distinctive sign of the Rasta in the days when dreadlocks were still scarce. The police blamed the Rastas for the violence and retaliated by descending on the ghettos, burning Rasta dwellings, beating them, and cutting their hair. Fifty-seven of them were thrown in jail.

Something had to be done. An articulate leader of the Rasta community, Mortimer Planno, managed to contact the head of the University of the West Indies in Kingston. Planno suggested to W. A. Lewis that he send a team of academic experts to the ghettos to investigate the Rasta problem. This commission's published conclusions, the famous 1960 "Report on the Rastafari Movement in Kingston," included a list of recommendations to the government.[1]

Among other things, the report advised the police to "leave innocent Ras Tafari brethren alone, stop cutting off their hair, stop moving them on, stop arresting them on minor pretexts, stop beating them up." The purpose of the report was not so much to research the origins of the cult as it was to end the confrontation and violence. It didn't begin to penetrate the history of the movement. It describes Leonard P. Howell, Pinnacle's founder, as "genuinely regarded as being the first to preach the divinity of Ras Tafari in Kingston," and "the most successful early preacher." But the few lines devoted to Howell prove only that no contact was made with him personally. The report states that he served in the British army that fought the Ashanti King Prempeh in West Africa in 1896, which would lead one to think that Howell was born before 1876. In 1960 he would have been at least eighty-four, a very old man indeed. If this was true, it was astonishing that the newspapers never mentioned the founding Rasta, and that the younger Rastas ignored him.

This assumption was misleading. In the 1960s, Leonard Howell was still alive and well. But he had become the victim of a conspiracy of silence and was in danger of being forgotten by history. When my fascination with this character began, I would try desperately to imagine how he looked. And when I met his son Blade many years later, my disappointment made him smile. Had I known his father, Blade hinted, I probably wouldn't have been so passionate in my research. But certain things do not happen by chance, and I felt compelled to learn more.

According to his birth certificate (No.1695 HK, Clarendon Register), Leonard Percival Howell was born June 16, 1898, eighteen months before the turn of the century. Coming of age at a crossroads in world history, between the old world and the new, between black and white, Marx and the Bible, Howell lit a spiritual spark whose explosion sent shock waves even to the remotest villages on the planet. To millions of youth across the earth, Jamaica is the land of Bob Marley and the Rastafarians.

But the reality of the island is far removed from the cliché. In Jamaica, Rastafarians still suffer for religious beliefs that society deems delusional. Police harassment continues to this day, since the Rasta sacrament of ganja, or marijuana, remains illegal. Female bank clerks are fired for growing locks. Rasta parents still have to go to court to demand that their children be enrolled into decent schools. Even history seems to conspire against them. No one has done any serious research on Leonard Howell, the first Rasta. In vain I looked up his name in the catalogs of university libraries; almost every single study refers to the University Report and accepts its vague approximations. After jailing Howell, wrecking his properties, stealing his money, arresting his disciples, and violating his rights in every possible manner, the establishment now strives to erase him from memory. His rich library was seized by the army and dispersed. His legal archives were burned. Only three pictures of him have been rescued; no recording of his voice, no film footage remain.

So who was the first Rasta?

Besides my burning curiosity, my only guide during my quest to learn more about this shadowy figure was an article published in the *Jamaica Journal* of February 1983 entitled "Leonard Howell and Millenarian Visions in Early Rastafari" by Professor Robert Hill of the University of California. I always carried a battered copy of this article at the bottom of my bag. Hill, a leading authority on Marcus Garvey, does not share the Jamaican disdain for the first Rasta. His article is a bubbling account of the ideas crisscrossing the politically and culturally tumultuous Caribbean of the 1930s. For me, it was a map to a fascinating treasure hunt.

But where to start? Look to a country place called Red Lands, Crooked River, Hill writes, for this is where Howell was born.

2

The Bird Hunter

Four graves rest in the tall grass. Each is a cement box, like a small coffin, sitting side by side. The two in the middle bear the names of Charles Howell (died 1935) and his wife Clementina Howell, born Bennett (died 1919)—Leonard's parents. The hexagonal grave on the right is his sister Morrios—"Died October 31, age 24." The inscription on the last grave reads ". . . my wife Diana . . ." but the date is blurred. Diana Walters was the second of Charles Howell's three wives; she raised Clementina's children and died circa 1932. A year later the old man took a third wife, named Loretta Henrietta Persey. Where is her grave, I wonder. Nearby, under a breadfruit tree, a strange building sits, a concrete airplane covered with graffiti. "This must be Loretta's grave," her nephew says.

I catch a country bus early in the morning at the Coronation Market bus stop. We pass Salt Lane, the old Rasta headquarters, nowadays a slum so dangerous that it turns into a ghost town after sunset. Three hours of traveling takes us to Crooked River in the Clarendon mountains. It is raining. I ask an old lady taking shelter under a porch if she knows any of the members of Howell's family. She takes me to a grocery store, saying the owner was born a Howell. Yes, the woman in the grocery knows the Red Land cousins and explains how to get there. "Me show you the way to Pumpkins," the old lady announces, stuffing her shopping bag and her cane into the crammed taxi.

"Pumpkins" is a river crossing with an old iron bridge. The narrow road winds up the red earth hill to the edge of a plateau. Patches of fog settle slowly down the steep gully banks covered with dark vegetation. Bamboos and cottonwood trees have replaced old citrus groves. Houses perch on the ridges. Past Red Lands, we reach Red Hills, where Howell's house stood on the plateau's rim with a splendid view. Nothing is left of the family house but a cement foundation surrounded by a stand of sickly yellow banana trees.

The history of the Howell family takes us back into colonial Jamaica. Seized at gunpoint from the Spaniards in 1665, Jamaica became a British colony and was quickly turned into an enormous sugar plantation. Exploiting the labor of thousands of African slaves, English cane planters built immense fortunes as refined sugar energized early modern Europe. But these landowners didn't bother settling on this "heathen" island with its deadly yellow fever and other tropical diseases. Instead they appointed overseers—mostly Scots—to run their plantations. Most of these overseers had little or no education; their manners were rough and their morality weak. Their mixed-race children got some education and became part of the ruling class of Jamaica, but the minimum quota of ten percent whites that the colonial administration tried to enforce was never reached, and the British lived in constant fear of slave insurrections.

Leonard Howell's grandfather was born around the time of Emancipation in 1834. Legally he was a free man, but he had no land, no education, and no rights. Under the "apprentice" system that replaced slavery, workers were entitled only to a small stipend. Some of them sought the aid of the churches, especially the Baptist churches that fought for emancipation and helped manumitted slaves to buy plots of land to farm.

As far as we know, Leonard's grandfather was a churchgoing Christian, owned a farm, married four times, and had many children. His granddaughter Daphney Howell remembers some of them: "Tartar," who went to Portland to raise cattle; the two aunties who used to sing in church "with voices like bells"; the one who could cook wonderful pea soup and corn pudding. The interesting thing was that this grandfather was not a Baptist but an Anglican— the planters' religion. A loyal subject of the Crown, he encouraged his sons to join the British colonial army. This was how some slaves had earned their freedom, leading to a military tradition in the Howell family—several of his sons, nephews, and grandchildren joined the ranks. Did Charles Howell, Leonard's father, fight for the British in the Ashanti War of 1896? It is possible, and could explain how his son Leonard knew of King Prempeh of the Gold Coast. Later Leonard would tell his followers the stories that he had heard from his father, some of which entered Leonard's own legend.

Charles Howell had a talent for making clothes. His nickname was "Tailor Howell," and his son inherited his taste for fine garments. But if in the off-season Charles indulged in tailoring, the rest of the year he and his family worked hard in the fields. Farming was the basis for his prosperity, especially during the banana boom of the first quarter of the twentieth century.

Bananas were introduced to Jamaica as early as the late 1500s, but the Jamaican banana industry only began late in the nineteenth century. Even then, the fruit ripened too fast to be shipped any farther than Florida until refrigerated cargo ships were invented. In 1901

the United Fruit Company of New Jersey began shipping Jamaican bananas to metropolitan markets. United Fruit steamers became the most common transportation for thousands of immigrants to the United States and England.

But in Jamaica the United Fruit Company met with some unusual resistance. Some smaller Jamaican planters refused to sell their crops at the standard prices fixed by United Fruit. Charles Howell's generation acted as their predecessors had when they first bought land—they got together and formed a cooperative, and by 1929 the members of the Banana Planters Association of Jamaica managed to carve out a decent share of the banana market for themselves.

This move brought about an important change. Some of the small planters began collecting substantial profits and became a political force. Charles Howell probably owed his prosperity to his mentality of self-reliance. By the end of his life he was said to have acquired a large portion of land, and he was also a justice of the peace. He had bought his wife a lady's saddle like those of the big planters' wives, and rode with her on his properties. This was, however, a rare display of elegance. Howell maintained his peasant ways for the greater part of his life. "The wagons could not come up the Red Lands road, so we had to bring the crops down on donkeys," remembers one of his grandchildren. He describes the heavy carts leaving for Old Harbor, where they were taken to ship by railroad. Claude McKay, the Jamaican voice of the Harlem Renaissance, described such a scene from his own childhood in his book *Banjo*: "Black draymen coming from the hilltops, singing loudly—rakish chants, whipping up the mules bearing loads of brown sugar and of green bunches of bananas, trailing along the winding chalky ways down to the port . . ."

With crop money, Howell's father bought more land, enough land for each of his children to inherit a sizeable plot. When he died, however, most of them sold their land and went to live in town.

Charles Theophilus ("Friend of God") Howell attended the Anglican church on the other side of the road in Red Lands several times a week. Eventually he was appointed a lay preacher. Monogamy—the missionary obsession—was now expected of Brother Howell. Daphney Howell recalls, "My grandfather kept saying that one should not have any children out of wedlock. He himself did not have any." But the Spanish Town Register records at least five children credited to one Charles Theophilus Howell between 1894 and 1920—beside the nine that he had with his wife. Could there have been another Charles Theophilus Howell? It seems doubtful. Avinel Taylor, the only survivor of the nine children, knew of at least one half-brother, Leslie.

Concerning her elder brother Leonard Percival, called "Percy," Avinel does not know much. When she was born in 1917, he had already left for America. When he returned in 1932, there was conflict with the family and he soon left the house. Avinel professes total scorn for Rastas—the contempt of an elderly coal seller who once saw her brother riding in his chauffeur-driven car. But it is too late to rewrite history, and Avinel is not particularly interested in the past. A better Howell family source about Percy might be Avinel's son Lesford. He admired his uncle and once wanted to join him at Pinnacle. Today Lesford sells medicinal herbs in front of the Rex movie theater in May Pen. Every morning you can find him there. Just ask for "Les" or "Kentucky"—this is how people know him.

Lesford is just a regular guy. His graying beard makes him look fiftyish, but his voice sounds like that of a child with a bad flu. He weakly complains, "Why not 'More?'" when people call him Les. But then, his uncle *was* the first Rasta. When I look straight into his eyes he recoils, troubled.

We walk together on mountain roads. At every step he picks up a leaf, telling me what it is good for. Nature is his capital. He collects rare medicinal plants, dries them, and sells them to his clients, mostly aging women. "Uncle Percy," as he calls Leonard Howell, "was a bush doctor too." Did he learn from him? No, Lesford says. The recipes have been in the family for ages; he also did some training with American alternative doctors. Modern ideas float in his magic. But yes, he says, Uncle Percy was a magician too—especially with women.

His niece Daphney has similar memories of Uncle Percy. She welcomes us into her upscale May Pen shop, full of fancy lamps and plastic chaise longues. "He was a gentleman, he knew how to dress," says the businesswoman with a dreamy smile. "I remember the slick black suit he used to wear, with his bow necktie and white spats. Big shoulders. Always dressed in style. And he did not lock up his hair, he kept it short, well-oiled, and combed . . ."

"Did the ladies love him?"

Daphney suppresses a smile.

"He was a baaad boy! He had *lots* of women."

Daphney is one of the few members of the family who kept in touch with Uncle Percy after Pinnacle was formed. She met Leonard through her father, Vivian, when he came back from the States. The image of the handsome man from New York is imprinted in her childhood memories. Does she know anything about what happened before he left? She definitely knew some of Percy's brothers, but has no idea of their ages. She was too young. But there is one thing she knows—the reason why Leonard Percival left Jamaica.

"There was a crime in the village, and Uncle Percy was the only witness. There was a path alongside the Howell land, planted with big trees. On the other side of the path lived a man and girlfriend—his concubine. They were *always* fighting. One day Percy was up in a tree—you know boys, always climbing trees, picking breadfruit or catching birds—and he saw the man running after the woman in the path—she was screaming pure murder—and then he stabbed her to death with his cutlass as Percy watched from above. Police wanted Percy's testimony, but he refused to give it. Maybe he felt sorry for the man, because the woman used to cheat on him. But there was a lot of pressure on the boy, and after a while his father decided that it was better to send him away."

When did this happen? How old was Percy?

Anthony Johnson, in his book about J. A. G. Smith, the "poor man's barrister" and star lawyer of the black man, states that Smith's "most celebrated victory" was precisely this case.

> For lack of records of the court proceedings, the fantastic case of Rex vs. Edward Rodney for the murder of his paramour Caroline remains part fact, part legend. It is a favorite tale of old-timers in the part of Clarendon where Rodney, who owned thirty-four acres of good land, lived with Caroline, who owned less than an acre nearby. The Crown alleged that he murdered her to gain her little plot—the murder being witnessed by Leonard Howell, a small boy in a nearby tree, who was so scared he ran away. This was the same Leonard Howell who years later founded the Rastafarian Movement. There are witnesses today to swear Jags got an acquittal while others swear he pleaded insanity with success.[2]

Johnson does not give a year for the trial, but J. A. G. Smith started his career in 1910, when Howell was twelve. At his 1934 trial, the first Rasta told H. M. Radcliffe, assistant attorney general representing the Crown, that he had left Jamaica in 1912; he would have been fourteen. That fits. A year later, with his strong physical appearance, he would not have been dubbed a "small boy." The case *Rex vs. Edwards* was probably one of the first Smith won. This throws a new light on the reason why Leonard's father sent him away to America—he did not want the boy to testify against J. A. G. Smith's client, for the lawyer was the champion of the black man and the poor. And it is of interest to note that J. A. G. Smith often argued against H. M. Radcliffe, winning his first case against him in 1910. Radcliffe probably never forgot how Howell refused to testify for the Crown in the Rodney case, and when he had to prosecute him in 1934, he may have been prejudiced.

My only hope to complete Howell's family tree is the National Archives, which reside on a red brick square, a relic of colonial classicism amid the sprawling ghettos of Spanish Town.

Spanish Town was the first capital of Jamaica. Back in the day, the sea came right up to the borders of the town, but eventually the swampy coast was drained and turned into cane plantations. Spanish Town was where the slave ships first landed on their voyages from Africa. It is said that the slave merchants dumped the most rebellious individuals in Jamaica, keeping the "good" ones for the States where they could sell them for a better price. Jamaican planters were not too fussy about the rebels. The island was small, the living rough, and the white population reduced to a bunch of half-literate overseers.

This aspect of their history could explain the famously indomitable temperament of Jamaicans. It is remarkable that the small island has given so many prophets and revolutionaries to the black consciousness movement. Boukman, who turned the St. Domingue voodoo against the white slave masters and launched the Haitian revolution, was born in Jamaica. (Writer/director Perry Henzell believes that Boukman owed his name to the fact that he could read books.) Marcus Garvey, father of African Repatriation, was Jamaican. The first Rasta was too, and so was Bob Marley. This circumstance could also account for the legendary toughness of the Jamaican maroons, the runaway slaves who fought a merciless war against the British redcoats in the hills and gullies of Cockpit Country. After eighty years of bitter war, they managed to obtain a semi-autonomous status within the country that still exists to this day, at least on paper.

At the National Archives, I am rerouted to a wire-fenced compound outside the city that houses the civil registers of Jamaica. After paying a small fee we are admitted to the hot, crowded register room for four hours. The hunt becomes a race against the clock. Huge leather volumes stand on shelves in approximate sequence. Ten registers are missing from the 1891–1920 period—the years when Charles Howell could have been having children. But the twenty remaining show fourteen children credited to Charles Theophilus or to Clementina Bennett (only one of the two parents is mentioned). This seems reasonable for the period. As a landowner, Charles Howell would have attracted any number of young "daughters" in search of a rich father for their babies. His son Leonard had the same problem. "Women are like that. When you treat them good, they don't want to leave," he once said to his own son Blade. All but one of Charles' nine lawful children are easy to spot: their survivors only remember their nicknames. Lennard (the register's spelling) Percival Howell was the first child of Clementina, born June 16, 1898. Vivian, father of Daphney, is probably Donard V. Howell, born in 1905. A year later Cordial V. was born, whom people remember as Cordy, or Cardiff. He became an employee of the coastal police in Jamaica, and spent a few years in New York. Hope, born in 1913, went to live in England and recently died there. Godman (Gady) also died in London. Hansford (Hansy) was the only one to work with Howell at Pinnacle. He ran the coal business from his house in the gully that lies above the entrance of the estate. With Morrios dead, there remains only one. Maybe this was Osbert, born in 1902. No one in the family knows anything about him.

So Lennard—or Leonard—went to the States, leaving behind his ancestral Jamaican paradise where a child can survive on wild fruit and snared birds, barefoot, in complete freedom. Daphney told us the story of his departure like one of those family legends that people tell a hundred times but no one can actually confirm. Chronologically challenged, it engenders more questions than it answers. How old was Leonard when he was hunting birds? Was he up there by chance, or did he already know that from up high he could learn some of the secrets of the world? In the 1940s he told a journalist that he "started his father's work at age six." What had happened to turn a six-year-old into a mystic—maybe this tragedy of love and death? And what did he learn about the means that the system uses to pressure a stubborn child? Whatever the case may be, Leonard Howell was able to keep his secret. And he grew to understand that, when one knows the secrets of society, one has a powerful tool to use against it.

3

En Route to New York

The only public account that Howell ever gave of his travels was to journalist John Carradine of the *Daily Gleaner*, Jamaica's national newspaper, published in Kingston. He claimed that he had "left Jamaica at the age of fourteen for the United States. [My] father wished to make a doctor of me, but I couldn't handle chemistry. When he learned this, my father abandoned me and cut off my allowance. I skipped from one job to another, until I came upon an American army colonel named Aites who happened to be a globe trotter. With Colonel Aites, I traveled over a large section of the inhabited world, from Asia across Europe where I witnessed scenes of horror in such places as Austria, as the war had just ended. After my travels and subsequent return to the United States, I became attracted to the Ras Tafarites and afterwards returned home to Jamaica to preach its tenets."[3]

Clearly this story, if not totally rearranged, is fairly limited and leaves out numerous episodes. Howell, like most of his comrades, rewrote his past. One thing is certain, however—he started his course in Colón, Panama, like many of his Caribbean contemporaries.

The turn of the twentieth century was an age of great migrations, one of the earliest and most influential of which led thousands of immigrants to Panama, where Ferdinand de Lesseps was orchestrating the construction of a new canal. The French company lost most of its employees to malaria, yellow fever, and other fatal illnesses and was inevitably forced to abandon the project. Caribbean immigrants, though altogether tougher than their European brethren, also died by the thousands. But many survivors stayed with the French and formed the first Caribbean community in Colón.

In 1904, Americans picked up the project where the French had left off, and a new wave of migrants flocked to Panama. Men dug, women cooked and washed or, in some cases, fell prey to human flesh merchants. But many workers did travel back home, carrying with them prideful economic independence and flashy fashions. As one Jamaican song goes, "Colón man-a-come/ Brass chain lick him belly bam bam bam/ But if you ask him fe de time/ Him look 'pon the sun!"

When Howell left Jamaica, the Panama scene was in full bloom. The canal was still being dug, the Jamaican community was big, and, resourceful as he was, Howell had no problem finding his way there. He made several visits to Panama, working there at different times. In 1924, when he decided to settle permanently in the United States, he declared to the immigration authorities that he came from Colón and had left his Jamaican wife, Myra, there.

Panama played an important role in the developing African American consciousness. It provided a haven for the exchange of information and ideas, and from there people boarded steamers headed for exotic destinations. Howell was not the only one of the early Rastas to visit Panama. Joseph Myers, whose name often appears in the petitions of the Jamaican Back-to-Africa movement, lived in Panama. According to the University Report, Joseph Nathaniel Hibbert, born in 1894, emigrated to Bocas del Toro in 1911; after staying several years in Costa Rica he went to live in Colón, where he was ordained Master of a Masonic society called the Ancient Mystic order of Ethiopia. In 1931, one year before Howell's return, Hibbert went back to Jamaica, where he was to become Howell's lieutenant. Archibald Dunkley, who is credited with researching the Bible for apposite quotations about the king of kings, also visited Panama while he was working for the Atlantic Fruit Company. He went back to Jamaica around the same time (December 1930). Three forerunners of the movement—Athlyi Rogers, Grace Jenkins, and Balintine Pettersburgh—appear to have met in Panama in 1924. But the most visible of all Jamaican migrants to Panama was, no doubt, Marcus Garvey.

Garvey was born ten years before Howell in St. Ann's Bay, a small town on the north coast of Jamaica. His father was a visionary like Howell's, but, unlike Charles Howell, Garvey's father lost all his land. A self-taught historian, he spent his life locked up in his private library and wasted his money on fruitless legal battles. Young Marcus Mosiah, his only surviving son, had to start small in life. In 1900 he became an apprentice in his godfather's printing factory. At eighteen he was hired as a foreman by a Kingston printing company, where he led a worker's strike in 1908 and was subsequently dismissed. In 1910, he left for Costa Rica, another big banana-producing nation. There he put out a news bulletin called *La Nacionale*, published specifically for plantation workers. In Panama he published another paper entitled *La Prensa*. Then in 1911 he went to England, where he worked several years for the Egyptian nationalist Duse Mohammed's *African Times and Orient Review*. Back in Jamaica in 1914, Garvey founded the Universal Negro Improvement Association (UNIA), which would in the following decade become the largest black movement in history. It claimed six million members under its red, green, and black banners and maintained several commercial enterprises in the United States, such as a chain of laundries, and the Black Star Line, a now-legendary shipping company.

Did Howell cross this great leader's path? When he first left the island in 1912, Howell was no more than a teenager, but there is proof that they met later, first in New York and then in Jamaica.

How did Howell travel from Jamaica to Panama and New York? He was not a professional man like Garvey, and his father was just a small planter at the time. But he had the wide shoulders of a docker, and he probably found work on the ships, as did many of his contemporaries. Even rich kids of the brown middle class had to work their way to America, like J. A. Somerville who, at the turn of the century, so described his passage to New York on a cargo ship:

> The name of the ship was the Tucapel. She carried a Chilean crew, hard-boiled men of the sea who spoke Spanish, wore earrings and carried bowie knives, with the hilts sticking out of their belt. . . . On the sixth day we were told to scrub the deck. We had to uncoil a heavy hose that almost threw us overboard when the pumps began to work. We did not remove our shoes while washing the deck. This enraged the boatswain, who swore at us and jabbered in Spanish. When we refused to comply with him he took us for stubborn and wouldn't obey any orders. He was a ferocious looking man, and we felt sure that he had designs on using his knife on us; instead he pulled out a pair of handcuffs and manacled Jim and I to a post at the stern of the ship in the blazing sun. We remained there chained, thirsty, hungry, until we could stand it no more. When no one was looking we bribed the colored sailor to take a note (written on my passport) to the captain and the doctor. I still have the old passport . . ."[4]

Traveling this way on boats was never easy. Black passengers, even when paying their fare, were limited to a section of the deck where they were unprotected from inclement weather. Thousands of youths stowed away on banana boats; when caught they were brutalized or jailed. In 1927, a twenty-one-year-old stowaway named Jonathan Gibson embarked on the Princess May in Kingston. He was caught and manacled like Somerville and his companion, but he had to stay there until their arrival in New York. By that time his feet were badly infected and had to be amputated.

But Howell was only fourteen in 1912, if his account is correct, and his planter father had connections on the banana ships; this may have ensured a safer trip for the teenager. Howell's father had also arranged a place for Howell to stay once he arrived in New York. However, exactly what happened when Leonard disembarked in the big city remains unclear. It appears that he may have stepped off the ship into a reality that was bigger than all his dreams combined.

In the first decades of the twentieth century, black New York was a cauldron of jazz, religion, and radical organizations headlined by powerful personalities. Many influential figureheads traversed the scene, especially among the West Indian population, who were less handicapped by feelings of inferiority due to their lack of contact with whites. Like J. A. Somerville, the young Howell probably exchanged the straw hat and red sash of Kingston dandies for a dark suit. His niece says that he stayed with a member of the family in New York—was it one of Charles Howell's brothers, or was it an elder half-brother? There were hundreds of Howells in New York. One of the most famous Harlem millionaires was Adolph Howell, entrepreneur of funeral parlors and black real estate. American archives carry no record of the teenager. His account to John Carradine states that he was studying medicine, but this story is a cover, probably borrowed from radical journalist W. A. Domingo, who came from Jamaica to Harlem in 1910, two years before him. Whatever the case, Howell admitted to Robert Hill that in 1916 he had gone back to Colón. England had just entered the war.

At that time, people were not calling it the First World War quite yet, as they hoped that it would be the last. How could Jamaica be linked to such a faraway conflict? For one who knows Jamaica only through reggae music, it would be hard to understand the powerful upsurge of pro-British enthusiasm that seized the island. Why die for the Empire? But when one considers the formation of Jamaican identity through colonial history, the reasons for this nationalism become clearer.

When Columbus arrived in Jamaica in 1494, the island was inhabited by the Arawak, a peaceful Indian population. After only thirty years of Spanish occupation, genocide was nearly complete. Jamaica retains very few Arawak traits (besides its name, "Land of the Waters," and Wareika, a Kingston district that became famous in Rasta history). In 1655, when the British conquered the island from the Spanish, they found that an important Sephardic community had already settled there after their flight from Spain a century before. In Port Royal, Kingston's old harbor, a big market had developed, where pirate ships exchanged loot until the destruction of the port in the 1692 earthquake. Then African slaves joined Spanish, Sephardic, and British settlers. After Emancipation came Indian indentured workers. At the turn of the last century, Chinese and Lebanese immigrants completed the mix.

Social coherence in a country of diverse cultures can sometimes evolve around nationality. Queen Victoria, "Missus Queen," had been credited by former slaves with their Emancipation and was cherished as a motherly figure. She was thought to protect the people from the arbitrariness of the Jamaican plantocracy, which led to bizarre consequences, such as the "Queen's Letter" affair in 1865, which eventually resulted in many deaths. During the American civil war, conditions on the island worsened due to the Northern blockade of Southern ports; crucial staple foods (salted cod, for example) became unavailable, and a petition was sent by Jamaican peasants to the Queen asking her to alleviate their plight. She answered eventually, advising them to work harder and take care of themselves.

This callous display of indifference was such a shock to the population that some chose to believe that the Governor had interfered, which was close to the truth. Others joined the protest movements of William Gordon and Paul Bogle, whose rebellion in 1865 brought an end to the plantocracy and the return of Jamaica (which had been a semi-independent territory) to the status of Crown Colony. This fondness for "Missus Queen" was die-hard. Even Howell would indulge in a prayer to her in the introduction of his Ethiopian Salvation Society's rules. This was probably meant to erase the memory of previous occasions when he had referred to her as a "harlot" and a "two-feet cat"!

But people were also enlisting in the war for economic reasons. In 1914 the Panama Canal was completed and emigration to the Canal Zone interrupted. On August 12–13, 1915, a hurricane swept through Jamaica, bringing a new contingent of distressed peasants out of the hills. On the limits of Kingston the fishing villages were swelling with country people looking for survival. Many of these people enlisted in the army in 1915, when Britain joined the Alliance. A draft was decreed in 1917 but never enforced—the colony had already provided eleven thousand volunteers.

Nineteen-sixteen found Percy Howell in Panama, where work was getting scarce. His father had raised him with a respect for uniforms—many in the family had joined the ranks, and the eighteen-year-old boy probably enjoyed the idea of going back to Jamaica in a starched uniform. According to Robert Hill, he claimed to have joined the British West Indian Regiment (BWIR) and to have served at Swallowfield Camp in Kingston. He is also said to have been stationed at Port Royal and at Bumperhall Hospital, then in the process of becoming an army air base. But he never went to the front. What prevented him from doing so? Did he take part in the Swallowfield mutiny on January 20, 1917, or in the Port Royal mutiny on May 16? It would appear that he had, but he claimed otherwise. He told Hill that in May or June of 1918 he boarded a United Fruit ship to Panama with his regiment. From Panama, he would go to Europe.[5]

He was supposed to go back to the front when he left Colón in 1918. There is little doubt as to why he changed his mind. Terrible stories spread about the war. There were the seven hundred volunteers whose ship was blown off its course into the Antarctic ices, and who came back with frozen fingers and ears. There were rumors of black soldiers being used as cannon fodder in the trenches, of soldiers sent to the front line without proper armament. Howell told Hill that he had found a job as a cook on an American army transport. He disembarked in New York from the S.S. *Metropan* on October 28, 1918, two weeks before the end of the war. For the next six years he went from country to country on five different ships, keeping New York as his home port. It was a fascinating period in the great city, and Howell probably shared the emotion of all of his contemporaries, from James Weldon Johnson to Claude McKay and Langston Hughes, every time he returned to New York, glittering symbol of the American Dream.

Harlem

"The age of Pericles and Socrates in ancient Athens had nothing on the present age of Harlem in New York," wrote the *New York News* on August 28, 1926.

> Coming out of the movies between 137th and 138th street on Seventh Avenue, we saw one of the biggest street corner audiences that we have ever met in this block, which is famous for street corner lectures, and the subject was "Evolution." This was not a selected audience but the "run of the street," and their faces were fixed on a black man who stood on a ladder platform, with his back to the avenue and the passing buses and his face to the audience who blocked the spacious sidewalk. . . . And what was he talking about? The theory of evolution, and its illustrations in different lines of material and biological development—the Darwinian science of the evolution of life, and the Marxian philosophy of the evolution of capitalism—and a possible development from capitalism to a state of communism.

Following Howell's footsteps, I dive into this incredible Harlem of the 1920s, where black porters and housemaids were exposed to the world's wisdom and got, as one put it, "their Ph.D. on the street corner." Day after day, browsing through the shelves of Liberation Bookstore on Malcolm X Avenue, scrutinizing the microfilms at the Schomburg Center, I explored Harlem in search of Leonard Percival Howell, but in vain. Radical historians have dismissed this particular Jamaican as one of those "quacks" or "crooks," as West Indian preachers were easily labeled. But it took little effort to imagine him standing on a ladder at a street corner, or in a bar among laborers and seamen, discussing the Russian Revolution or the coronation of an Abyssinian prince. Twenty years of Howell's life could occasionally be glimpsed in old newspapers and microfilms as I tried to track him through the glory days of Harlem.

A good beginning was Claude McKay, a Jamaican like Howell but a bit older, who also arrived in New York in 1912. His novels, or "new journalism" as one might say today, gave a voice to the emerging New Negro. He was an audacious writer, father to a new black literature and a precursor of the Harlem Renaissance. Although he was admired in white intellectual circles, McKay never deserted his people and the idea of an Afro-American nationalism: "Getting down to our native roots and building up from our own people is not savagery, it is culture."[6] Fascinated by the October Revolution and the ability of a people to change the course of history, McKay went to Moscow in 1921 to witness the fourth congress of the Communist International. In the same period he drifted away from the Harlem radicals who he suspected had no other ambitions than to be accepted in white radical circles. Traveling on ships, McKay ended up in Marseilles, where he enjoyed life in the company of exotic black expatriates—southern banjo players, Caribbean "monkey chasers" (as they were derisively called), New York adventurers, and African war veterans. In Marseilles, McKay chatted with Leopold Senghor and other African thinkers in the cafés, but he never identified with a formalist "Negritude" as defined by intellectuals; he already had a sense of "root and culture," one of Rasta's main tenets.

The Africans . . . were naturally defined by the richness of their fundamental racial values. . . . Only when he got down among the black and brown working boys and girls of the country did he find something of that raw unconscious and the devil-with-them pride in being a Negro that was his own natural birthright. . . . They possessed more potential power for racial salvation than the Negro literati, whose poverty of mind and purpose showed never any sign of enrichment, even though inflated above the common level and given the appearance of superiority.[7]

When McKay went back to New York, one year before Howell settled there, black Harlem was in the midst of its Jazz Age glory.

The Block Beautiful had gone black and brown. 125th Street was besieged and bravely holding out for businesses' sake, but the invaders, armed with nothing but loud laughter, had swept around it and beyond. And higher up, the line of racial demarcation, Eighth Avenue, had been pushed way back and Edgecombe, Jerome, Manhattan, St. Nicolas, and other pale avenues were vividly touched with color. The Negro realtors had done marvels.[8]

Through hard work, thrift, and shrewdness, the black community was taking over traditionally white immigrant neighborhoods in upper Manhattan. The district, once Irish, Italian, and Jewish, had tried to stop the "invasion," but once the United States joined the Great War, white men were sent to the front and southern blacks and Caribbeans filled the gap. Their wages were higher than ever before, and they began investing in brownstones. Maids bought houses, and Pigfoot Mary, who sold soul food on Lennox Avenue, became famous for buying a five-story building.[9]

In this new black metropolis, Caribbean immigrants had the impact of "leaven in the black dough." Marcus Garvey, the most famous among them, had crowds flocking to his Universal Negro

Improvement Association conventions at Liberty Place, and marching down Fifth Avenue in gorgeous parades. His Black Star Line
almost succeeded as a shipping company entirely owned by blacks.
Were the ships meant to carry the sons of slaves back to Africa? Garvey probably had no illusions of this, and his "Back to Africa" message was mostly metaphoric. But the Black Star Line surely
entertained one ambiguity—though it enhanced Garvey's image, the
idea of a possible return to Africa enabled Garvey's enemies to
accuse him of abandoning America's crucial black legacy of toil and
sweat.

> In Chicago, Felice had begun reading *The Negro World*, the organ
> of the Back-to-Africa movement, and when they came back she
> was as interested in Liberty Hall as she was in Sheba Place. She
> had even persuaded Jake to take a share in the Black Star Line.
> "Let's get on too, Dad," she said. "There can be some'n' in it.
> Times is changing, and niggers am changing too. That great big
> nigger man ain't no beauty, but oh lawdy! he sure is illiquint." [10]

After settling in Harlem in 1916, Garvey had modified his
agenda. From an endorsement of the Tuskeegee model—improvement of the Negro condition through educational and professional
integration—he turned to preaching political action, locally and
internationally, liberation of Africa from colonial powers, and a
campaign of economic independence. By 1921 he had enrolled several million black people (some say six million), and his parades
down Manhattan gathered crowds of two hundred thousand.
McKay did concede to the radicals that Garvey may be a charlatan
with "antiquated social notions," but the extent to which this charlatan had, in less than a decade, awoken the consciousness of the
dark-skinned masses, proved him the most influential black leader
to that point in history.

There's no doubt that Leonard Howell was deeply influenced
by Marcus Garvey, and that during his time at sea he'd become
familiar with Marxist doctrine. He had debated with the famous
tabaqueros, Cuban cigar workers who paid people to read to them—

newspapers, African history, novels, political essays—while they worked. They closely followed new trends in international opinion and were often thought to harbor "seditious" ideas.

In his *Autobiography of an Ex-Colored Man*, James Weldon Johnson tells the story of one such *tabaquero*, and Howell's path probably crossed many. He also crossed paths with a young Marxist writer from Trinidad named George Padmore, who joined the Comintern before becoming disillusioned with Stalin's African policies and joining ranks with Kwame Nkrumah's brand of Pan-Africanism. Padmore was still sending his publications to Howell in 1948.

But Howell was wary of politicians. In New York different parties competed for influence within the powerful Porter's Union— as a porter, he knew their strategies. This is probably where he understood that trade unions were preoccupied more with economic issues than with ideology. This knowledge helped when he was confronted with the same situation in Jamaica many years later.

In 1924, when he decided to settle in New York, he took a room on Horatio Street in the Lower East Side. His landlord was an Episcopal minister named Charles Clark, who at the time of the 1925 census housed two black janitors—the only black people in a neighborhood of Italians. Howell had naturally turned to the Protestant Episcopal church, the American counterpart of his childhood Anglican denomination. Like many West Indian immigrants, he probably didn't identify with the local black churches and their boisterous followings. In Jamaica you find them too, but Howell was not one for sentimental effusions. He barely shook hands with his own children. Later he is reported to have "spoken in tongues" and to have manipulated his followers' emotions, but in New York he was still the well-behaved immigrant whose only ambition was to find work. And it was not easy.

"Unless the job was definitely marked *COLORED* on the board outside, there was no use applying," discovered Langston Hughes when confronted with the problem. "And only one job in a thousand would be marked as such."[11] The only jobs available were those of porter, busboy, or janitor, but it is hard to see the proud Leonard

Howell cleaning floors or handling suitcases. His daughter Katherine protests when people suggest that her father may have worked such jobs, or worked as a cook on ships. "He couldn't even boil water!" However, in 1924 he wrote down "porter" as his occupation on his application for U.S. citizenship. He also worked in Hoboken, New Jersey, and then in Astoria, Queens, where he was a small construction contractor with his own team of workers.

In 1929 Howell was back in Harlem. A former Garveyite declared to Hill that Howell opened a "tea room" on 136th Street,[12] a famous haven for preachers and radicals and a stronghold of the UNIA. But the great association did not fancy what he was doing there, and "declared against Howell in New York."[13] What exactly was he doing that they disapproved of? Could the "tea room" have been one of the five hundred ganja dens that one particular police report of the day mentions?[14] Howell was indulging, the Garveyite said, in "a number of nefarious practices." He was even accused of being an obeahman.

Obeah is black magic, the Jamaican counterpart of voodoo. Leonard Howell was not a sorcerer. His magic potions were probably what Rastas of today would call "roots," vegetable tonics of rich nutritional value. Howell knew obeah, but he never indulged in its practice. One of his followers remembers that only one time did he witness a "sacrifice" performed by Howell. He reportedly threw a living lamb into a bonfire, but close enough to the edge to allow the lamb to escape—probably with the intent to create a new parable, that the lamb was ultimately to escape the fire and tribulation. But his followers misunderstood his gesture, and they caught the animal and threw it back in. Howell ran to the rescue of the lamb, but it was too late.

This explicit rejection of obeah is a characteristic of the early Rasta movement, and it ought to be considered by modern "sects" who sometimes endorse superstitious practices in the name of Ras Tafari. Balintine's "Royal Parchment Scroll of Black Supremecy" has a powerful declaration on this issue, later plagiarized by Howell in his *Promised Key*:

People that is guilty of Obeah must not visit the Balm Yard nor in the Assembly of Black Supremecy. NO admittance for Fortune Tellers and Witch and Old Hige. No admittance whatsoever for Ghost, Witch, Lizzards, Alligator, Snakes, Crabs, Flies, Ants, Rats, and Mice, and Lodestones, and Pins and Needles. Jan-Crows, the Ravens, and Candles, and Fast Cups, and Rum Bottles, and Graveyards are not required. . . . For this is the Ethopia Balm Yard, and we do not have leoprosy.[15]

Howell was not an obeahman, but he could have been a healer. "Balm yards" are traditional hospitals where sick and deranged people are brought to be healed by mystic men. Maybe he tried to adapt the concept of the balm yard to Harlem's cityscape. What else could he dispense in his tea room on 136th Street beside comfort to the disillusioned and lost?

Howell did not stay long in Harlem, if we rely on a Jamaican police report stating that he was arrested in New York in 1930 for grand larceny and then deported in 1932.[16]

But Howell can't be found in the police archives of New York. There is no criminal file on him whatsoever. If he had ever committed a criminal offense, it must not have been here. And the reason for his indictment is unclear. The colonial police report, which is usually quite accurate, does not state any source or detail. His children, his followers, and the people who knew him closely reject any idea of larceny or theft. Howell, the Anglican preacher's son, could be a rebel, but not a thief. Not one of the many indictments in his life ever got him convicted—except later for sedition and ganja.

In 1930 there was another reason why Howell may have had problems with the law—his healing practices. The year 1930 saw a full-fledged campaign against the illegal practice of medicine following the Jamaican Ginger affair. It all started on March 8 in Oklahoma, when eighty people were taken to the hospital with lower limb paralysis. Most confirmed drinking "Ginger Jake," a Jamaican tonic popular during Prohibition because it contained alcohol. In a few days the epidemic reached Tennessee (103 victims), and Cincinnati (fifty victims). By May 1, twelve people had died, and the police took serious action: fifty-one people were arrested, including the manufacturer in Brooklyn (who was, incidentally, not a Jamaican). Public opinion was stirred and a huge campaign launched against "quackery."

The leader of this crusade was Arthur J. Cramp, an officer of the Health Department of the state of New York, who had lost a ten-year-old daughter to quack medicine. He kept files on thousands of persons and products. His 1931 and 1936 reports, "Nostrums, Quackery and Pseudo-medicine," recount hundreds of cases he initiated against all kinds of nostrums: morphine baby syrup, electromagnetic belts, "magic" spring water (the famous California Water, still in use by African and Caribbean healers), and any number of opium and cannabis decoctions prescribed for cough and nerve disorders. The complete Cramp file is classified, but it seems likely that Howell was concocting ganja drinks in his "tea room" like those he had his adepts drink at Pinnacle. In those times of crisis and prohibition, ganja was balm to the aching soul. People were down, and ganja made them feel better and more positive. Half the Harlem population was out of work, blacks had little access to medical care, some suffered malnutrition. In despair they turned to tonics and the promises of their labels. Many of them contained coca leaf extract, which numbs hunger and provides a kick: Celery Cola, Rococola, Koka Nola, Kos-Kola, Coke Extract, Kola-Ade, Juni-Kola, Kola and Celery Bitters, Millburn's Kola, and finally the famous Coca Bola, a chewing gum containing 0.7 gram of cocaine labeled as a "remedy and substitute for tobacco, alcohol, and opium."

Could Leonard Howell have invented Ganja-Cola?

The sun is shining, weather is sweet. On Malcolm X Boulevard, once Lennox Avenue, elders slam down dominoes in the shade of shop awnings. Everything is cool. One Hundred Thirty-Sixth Street runs in back of the Schomberg Center. In Howell's time, Puerto Rican Arturo Schomburg was still gathering books for his great collection, his monument of African achievement, and the Center building was still a public library. The street was full of artists, associations (including the American West Indian Association), and storefront churches. One Hundred Thirty-Sixth Street is where Ethelred Brown, a famous preacher and journalist from Jamaica, delivered his first sermons at the Harlem Congregational Church. As for Howell, he settled at 113W, a three-story brick row house with a high stoop at the front door and a basement flat. Today it is painted dark red, the roof is crumbling, all the windows are blocked with tin. A young tree shoots out of the brickwork at the top. An old man came by while I was standing there and I stopped him to ask if he had ever heard of a tea room that used to be there. He shook his head. "Thirty years I have been living on the street, never heard of a tea room here. Always been flats. You want to buy it?"

"I am looking for a man who used to live here. A Jamaican healer."

The man looked suspicious. "What you want the man for?"

"He was a mystic man, the founder of the Rastas."

"Hey! That an important man then. Go to Schomburg Center, right here. They for sure have something on him." But I researched in vain in the Schomburg Center. No Leonard Howell is mentioned here, or any Harlem healers at all. It was surprising to see so many articles on Africa's healers and medicines and none on African healers in American black communities. It seems that intellectuals of the Harlem Renaissance did not want to be associated with those "ghosts of the past." In his search for the achievements of the race, Schomburg did not want to include those "backward" practices. His contemporaries saw healers and street preachers as "enemies of black liberation, as poor imitations of European religions, as static representations of the spiritual past of men, and so on."[17]

So apparently no one got on Doctor Howell's case. He managed to keep his practices secret. But Hope Howell, Leonard's brother, told Hill that he "had excellent hands with sickness and he helped many people, even well-to-do-people."[18] He probably knew of some plants—like any African grandmother—but he had a superior sense of human psychology. He didn't have to be a licensed physician to give his patients a strong sense of hope and a bit of confidence. Lately medicine has begun acknowledging its debts to tradition— eighty percent of all modern medicine comes from plants. People are realizing the interconnectedness of mental and physical health. But in Howell's times, science, rendered arrogant by its recent successes, rejected the mystical and holistic concepts that pervade traditional medicine, and discarded popular wisdom, especially when it came from blacks.

Nothing is yet certain concerning Howell's departure from New York. The recent opening of the Ellis Island files to the public might potentially give us a clue, but in the meantime we cannot know if he was deported, as Jamaican police claimed, or if he went back on his own. But that month, November 1932, was surely a dark one. In the depths of the Great Depression, immigration was at a standstill, shipyards were closing, and winter was coming. At Ellis Island, a record one thousand rejected immigrants were awaiting deportation. Among this thousand, three hundred people were voluntary deportees, turning their backs on the promises of the New World. Leonard Howell may very well have been among them.

5

Athlyi Rogers, Forerunner of the Rasta Movement

Nineteen thirty-two, the year of Leonard Howell's return to Jamaica and of his first circulation of Haile Selassie's portrait, is technically the start of the Rasta movement. But it would be unjust to assign all the credit to Howell alone. He was not the only ex-Garveyite to tackle the one question left unanswered by the UNIA—the question of religion. In his endorsement of modern practical thinking, Garvey had neglected the religious needs of millions of his followers. In 1921 he realized that he had to take a stand on the subject, and he allowed George Alexander McGuire, the UNIA chaplain, to create a new and independent Christian denomination—the African Orthodox Church. But this new denomination failed to satisfy the emotional and cultural needs of newly empowered African Americans, many of whom no longer wanted to worship a version of messianic Christ who was tortured to death on a cross, amid thieves.

What was needed was a new messiah, preferably black, and a king in *this* world. If Garvey wanted to succeed, blacks had to be able to identify with kings and princes, not with crucified slaves. As Garvey said, "Ambition . . . is a burning flame that lights up the life of the individual and makes him see himself in another state."[19] In order to rekindle this flame after four hundred years of racist brainwashing, his people had to find a more majestic model.

A new messiah was what millions of Garvey's followers sought in their leader, but he declined this grandiose opportunity. His integrity, and his formidable dignity, prevented him from playing God, and he was too astute to give black intellectuals and his many critics this stick to beat him with. It didn't matter. In New Jersey, another inspired black man heard the call to preach a new, black messiah. His name was Athlyi Rogers, and he could well be the missing link between Garveyism and Rastafari.

Back in 1924, the year Howell settled in New York, a flyer was posted on the streets of Newark, New Jersey:

> GREAT WORLD LEADER TO SPEAK
> Shepherd Athlyi Rogers: Make the Black Race an Economical Power to save it from Suffering, Best Service to God, saith the Gaathlyi Religion.[20]

The picture shows a young man standing, raised arms open wide, in a robe lined with three colors. He is dark like Howell, with strong regular features. Could Athlyi be one of the many avatars of the first Rasta? Those well-articulated brows, the strong jaw, the mustache split in the middle look like Leonard Howell. I show the picture to one of Howell's "babymothers" in Jamaica. "This is Mr. Howell!" she exclaims. But the old lady also has poor eyesight. Ras Miguel Lorne, a Kingston lawyer, writer, and champion of Rasta culture, insists that Athlyi Rogers and Howell are two different people despite the physical resemblance, similarities in their methods, and the fact that they both claimed addresses in Africa. Howell fancied himself in Accra (Ghana) while writing *The Promised Key* in jail in Jamaica. Rogers referred to a House of Gaathlyi, 252 Nyembane Street, Kimberley, South Africa, on a document printed in

Woodridge, New Jersey. Did the two meet in the States? Howell spent time in Hoboken, not far from Newark. He definitely read *The Black Bible* or *Holy Piby*, the founding document of Athlyi's religion, because he plagiarized some parts for his own *Promised Key*.

The Holy Piby is a slim tract of the kind missionary sects issued to their adherents. It is strongly influenced by Garvey, whom Athlyi declares "an apostle of the Lord God for the Redemption of Ethiopia." Garvey and Athlyi (Ga-Athlyi) are two angels, the double vision of the Gaathlyi religion, combining the mystical and the ecumenical. One depends on the other. The UNIA project of bringing social redemption to the black race is not possible unless each individual redeems himself first from mental slavery. This is the crux of the Rasta ideal. "What is the right wing of the house of Athlyi? The Afro Athlican Constructive Church. What is the left wing of the house of Athlyi? The Athlican green pasture."[21]

The "green pasture" is a social project, the UNIA program translated into Biblical terms. To stand up against oppression the black race must be economically strong. "I came not to baptize," Athlyi says, "but to concretize the rescue of suffering humanity. . . . A shepherd must seek his sheep and prepare a pasture for them to be fed." He then prays to the God of Ethiopia to "endow us with wisdom, and understanding to do thy will, that the hungry be fed, the naked clothed, the sick nourished, the aged protected, and the infant cared for. . . . The children of Ethiopia, God's favorite people of old, have drifted away from this divine majesty, neglecting economic life, believing that they on spiritual wings should fly to the kingdom of God." To get back in the favor of the creator, black people must "wash their hands against the slothful and fruitless life of the past . . . bringing themselves onward into a new and ever productive life. . . . Woe be unto the empty-handed, the slothful and the coward."

This was the social vision of the times recast in Biblical language. But Athlyi, unlike UNIA leaders, did not ignore the spiritual needs of the masses. He explored various levels of their class frustration, and even endorsed their petit-bourgeois aspirations.

Like the Bible, the *Piby* is a blend of burning prophecy, dietary rules, economic analyses, and soap opera:

> 18—Woe be unto a people, a race who seeks not their own foundations; their wives shall be servants for the wives of other men, and their daughters shall be wives of poor men and vagabonds, and there shall be tears of deprivation . . .

> 19—Woe be unto a race of people who forsake their own and adhere to the doctrine of another. They shall be slaves to the people thereof.

> 20—Verily I say unto you, O children of Ethiopia, boast not of the progress of other races, believing that thou are a part of the project, for at any time thou shall be cast over the bridge of death, both body and soul.

> 21—Forget not the assembly of thouselves and unite—working for the upbuilding of Ethiopia and he generations.

> 22—Then shall the nations of the earth respect thee and thy commodities shall be for their gold and their commodities for thy gold, but there shall be none to fool thee neither shall ye be their slaves.

> 23—For thy emblems shall rank among their emblems, thy ships among their ships and thy men of war among their men of war; great shall be thy name amongst the nations.

> 24—The Lord God, father of Ethiopia, shall glory in thee, with thee shall the angels rejoice, great is thy reward in the Kingdon of Heaven.

> 25—Thy daughters shall work with clean hands and soft clothing, thy sons shall enjoy the fruits of their colleges.

This Sunday school version of Marcus Garvey's program is one of the most interesting proto-Rasta documents; it shows the clear linkage between the first Rastas and the Garveyites.

What do we know about Athlyi himself? In his introduction to the new edition of the *Holy Piby*, Ras Miguel Lorne says that Athlyi was born in Anguilla, and "migrated to the U.S. at an early age, consolidating his activities at Newark, New Jersey." The *Piby* pictures him in 1917 preaching in Newark; it lists the names of his first followers. Then he went to Springfield, Massachusetts, from where he embarked on a tour of "South America and the West Indies." In 1919 he was back in Newark "parading the streets of Newark with a host of Negroes, protected by riding officers of the city and accompanied by members of the Salvation Army carrying banners, proclaiming a universal holiday for Negroes and foretelling of their industrial and national independence." On July 13, the followers gather at Israel Memorial AME Church in Newark, where Reverend Bonfield reads a text about Marcus Garvey. This brings shepherd Athlyi to question himself. Is the UNIA leader on a divine mission? "I almost believe this is one of the apostles of the twentieth century, but where is the other? For I look for two, however by the map of life I shall know the one." Then in 1921 he says, "Marcus Garvey spake, saying: I have no time to teach religion," and Athlyi "took up his pen and was about to declare him not an apostle of the twentieth century" when Garvey changed his mind and "issued a religious call throughout the world which fulfilled the last item upon the map of life" (probably the creation of the African Orthodox Church in 1921, not 1922 as Athlyi states).

According to the *Piby*, Garvey and Athlyi met in Detroit, Michigan, and acknowledged a common vision. From New York Athlyi left on an African mission. He gives no details of his round-the-world trip except for his mystical experiences. "Go the way of the Atlantic and return by way of the Pacific," the Lord has said, and in the Straits of Magellen he reappeared to teach Athlyi the message of the two "wings," the church to teach, and the green pastures to provide.

Athlyi went all the way to Kimberley, South Africa, where he founded a church called the Afro Athlican Constructive Gaathly. B. G. M. Sundkler, in his 1948 study of the Bantu prophets of South Africa, quotes it as an example of a Negro church that "sometimes introduces a decidedly anti-white note into this Ethiopian ideology." He goes on to quote the *Holy Piby*, noting that "the influence of Marcus Garvey—the negro prophet, visionary and agitator—is strong in the Afro Athlyican Constructive Gaathlyi, centered in Kimberley, but with few contacts with Zulus."[22]

Athlyi had the revelation of his mission in 1922, and was back in Newark by 1924, which illuminates the forceful aspect of his personality. In less than two years he managed to travel from New York to the gold mines of Kimberley, on the other side of the world, to establish a church that still remained active there twenty-five years later. He still went home "by way of the Pacific"! This ancestor of the Rasta movement must have been a tough one.

As early as 1924, Charles Goodridge, whom Lorne identifies as a "strong leader within the UNIA," began disseminating the *Piby* in Kingston. In November 1925, the cornerstone of the Afro Athlican Constructive Gaathly, or Hamitic Church, was laid in Kingston at 7 Elgin Street, Smith Village. The UNIA was present. There is no mention of Athlyi being there; the leader of the project was a woman called Grace Jenkins Garrison, known as "the Comet." Where did she meet Athlyi? In 1924, when Athlyi was returning from Kimberley "by way of the Pacific," he must have come through Panama, where she was living at the time. However, the Elgin Street church was never completed, and the Athlican church remained unknown until Leonard Howell arrived to pick up the pieces.

The Athlyi connection with South Africa is interesting. There, as in America, black churches are classified in two denominations,

Millenarist and Ethiopianist. But the Gaathlyi religion borrows from both. Millenarists (or Zionists) believe in heaven on earth. A prophet will lead them there at the end of Time. They believe in self-sufficiency; they build towns, schools, factories; they use plants as medicine. The other current, the Ethiopianist, is more concerned with the redemption of the black self-image, and they color their Christian faith with African practices. In South Africa, the dissident "Ethiopian" churches are often linked to a particular traditional chief, who rearranges Christian doctrine to legitimize polygamy and other local practices.

Athlyi reconstructs these two messages into the two "wings" of his religion. Sundkler writes that the cult has "but few connections with Zulus," which is really no surprise. No doubt his church attracted a majority of lost individuals: despised minorities, drifters from the mines, children of multiethnic origin who had had the same acculturation problem as Jamaicans. The proud Zulus do not have this problem. Memories of Shaka, fierce conquerer of a vast empire, still lingered, and they had no interest in the son of slaves from the West Indies. Athlyi's identity message is not for them. Now, many years later, after decades of apartheid, young South Africans are attracted to the Rasta message. But in 1923 Athlyi probably met with a discrimination he was unaccustomed to from black people. This could explain his departure from Kimberley, leaving behind a church that survived more than twenty years before disappearing in the maze of South African denominations.

What happened to Athlyi Rogers? Ras Miguel Lorne says that he died in Jamaica. In despair at being ignored, he cut his veins and spilled his blood as a sacrifice. Sometime later he swam out to sea and drowned himself, offering his life to martyrdom. (Were not the martyrs of old called "athletes of faith"?) Through his sacrifice he was probably trying to redeem the prediction of the *Holy Piby*: "The blood of a prophet within the law shall break to pieces the oppressors of Ethiopia." Did Athlyi's sacrifice open the floodgates to the glory days of Rastafari?

6

Early Companions

Red Lands, 1932. Leonard Howell is back home on the edge of the plateau, resting his eyes on the distant hills and the blue-green expanse of cane fields below. Was this a relief after the chaos of New York? After twenty years on the road, Howell had not found paradise on earth. One day he explained to his son Blade that Jamaica and the United States were the same, that the world was one. Oppression was the same everywhere. Running away to chase a dream was not the solution. A man had to build right where he stood.

Howell had no intention of assuming his place in the family when he arrived back in Clarendon. Was it even his family? He had never met his youngest brothers and sister, and the eldest had emigrated. His mother had died in 1919, his sister Morrios in 1931. He had never met his father's second wife, the one who who raised the children. As for his Anglican father, he was tougher than ever. Having become a justice of the peace, he was now the most influential man in their rural district. When Percy came back, Charles was on the verge of taking a third wife. Charles would have liked to keep his firstborn with him, but Percy wouldn't have been satisfied planting bananas, even if their strong personalities hadn't perpetually clashed. Percy had a plan. Of this plan we do not know much. The innumerable notebooks he spent his life writing were destroyed in the police raids, but we can try to follow him as he goes into action.

Howell often told his family and his followers that when he returned to Jamaica the police seized all his belongings. If he had really been deported from the United States, he might have concocted this excuse for not bringing the presents and riches expected from a successfully repatriated emigrant. Maybe the police did seize everything when they found "seditious" literature in his luggage. In any event, the story told by his followers was that the authorities at first refused him entry to the island because he didn't have a Jamaican accent. He had to send to Clarendon for a birth certificate before they let him in. With a bizarre logic, his followers say, "God had made him be born in Jamaica so that he could come back and save us, otherwise they would have not let him in."

So Howell was back in Redlands, the prodigal son in fashionable New York clothes. At thirty-four, he glowed with an aura of physical and spiritual strength. "I never met anyone like my father," says his son Blade. His penetrating eyes, his bold attitude revealed a man who was secure in his beliefs and supremely confident. His 172 pounds of muscle and his large shoulders made him look taller than he actually was. His female relations competed to catch his eye. A learned, well-traveled man, and so handsome! One of the ladies—a cousin on his mother's side—had a sixteen-year-old daughter. Did he need someone to take care of his house? No. Percy was not ready yet.

His father gave him a cow, which he sold—half the proceeds he distributed to the old and needy of the village, with the other half he began his crusade.

There were many people Howell wanted to see in Kingston. As soon as he got there, he visited with Marcus Garvey. Framed on a tax charge and deported from the United States five years earlier, the UNIA leader could not afford to alienate any ally in the struggle against the hostile Jamaican establishment. In Harlem, Howell's mystical tone and Biblical references had not had the same mesmeric power as it did over the people of Kingston; he was now no longer worried about being taken for a charlatan or a sorcerer. Garvey came to lunch at Howell's house in Kingston. Howell's young (and pretty) cousin from Red Lands was now his live-in helper. "I served Mr. Garvey with these very hands," the old lady still marvels. "He was Mr. Howell's best friend. So nice and so charming, and such a gentleman!"

The friendship wouldn't last long. By August 1934, the Kingston UNIA Convention denounced all "new cults [that were] entirely contradictory to the set principles of true religion," and a delegate from Indiana ventured that Emancipation cults and religious fanaticism still maintained a grip on Jamaica a hundred years after slavery was abolished; he expressed astonishment that such beliefs could still be entertained in the civilized world.[23]

Yes, these Jamaican intellectuals of the UNIA were perhaps over-civilized. And they were concerned primarily with integration and economic issues. Since they chose to ignore the masses and their "savage" cults, it was left to Howell to cater to those masses. He didn't approve of "those religions that howl" any more than Garvey did, but he recognized his people—the old, the sick, the downtrodden, women, the illiterate—those for whom the Bible had been their only solace in four hundred years of slavery. This is whom he was going to preach to.

Among possible allies was the Athlican group, or what remained of it. Among them he met another strange character, Balintine, whom the Rastas remember as "Valentine."

Reverend Fitz Balintine Pettersburgh had also lived in New York. He returned in 1924, the same year as Athlyi's "Comet," Grace Jenkins Garrison. In 1926—one year before the young Ethiopian prince Tafari became *ras* (chief), and four years before he was crowned King of Kings under the name of Haile Selassie I—Balintine issued an esoteric pamphlet, *The Royal Parchment of Black Supremacy*, filled with references to the "King of Kings of Ethiopia." The *Daily Gleaner* (June 6, 1927) dismissed it: "the grammar is like the sense, which seems to us to be indistinguishable from nonsense, and the whole concoction is so putrid that we must wonder what class of people could ever take such rubbish seriously."[24]

The truth is that *The Royal Parchment* is indeed hard to read. The text is a long poem, jumping from bold political assumptions— "Ethiopia is the Succeeding Kingdom to the Anglo-Saxon Kingdom"—to pure surrealist poetry: "I am the copyright of this world" ... "The BARBWIRE eternity is Mine" ... "I am going to teach the princess to fly around the poles." Numerous repetitions suggest that the possibly illiterate Balintine could not reread what he dictated. The transcription sometimes sounds awkward; it is even possible that the printers deliberately cut up Balintine and turned his poetry into gibberish. But the preacher's language seems designed to trick the establishment. Under the Biblical jargon, esoteric wordplay, and arcane Masonic symbolism there is clearly a "seditious" message, and sometimes the language is openly raw ("I poled White Supremacy") and modern ("God almighty is INSULTED by astrologers" ... "The root and foundation of World's buildings is by Communication; the wisdom of GOD DEPENDS on Communication").

Nevertheless, from the inchoate ramblings and erotico-mystical poems one can extract clear political implications. Unlike Athlyi, who refers to a symbolic Ethiopia, Balintine appeals to a very practical racial supremacy:

"We are the foundation stones of the resurrection of the Kingdom of Ethiopia."

"Ethiopia is the Succeeding Kingdom to the Anglo Saxon Kingdom."

"We are not business with Anglo Militant Nakedness."

"BLACK MUST NOT MARRY WHITE NOT WHITE BLACK: RACE ENMITY."

"Adam-Abraham-Anglo-Saxon, the LEPROUS-TEACHER."

"Before I trust a White person, I trust a snake."

Balintine also ran a "balm yard," a gathering place for spirituality and folk healing and a precursor of later "Rasta yards." "We pick you up from out of the midst of the raging misery of the land and HIDE you from the raging Wolves of the land into our Balm Yard." There Balintine cleanses his followers of "White bondage and filth." "Baptism is a very important subject to Black supremacy. . . . All must wash their Hands and Souls, Minds and Hearts from Adam-Abraham-Anglo-Saxon, the leprous teacher. . . . Follow me with your cup of Troubles to the Burying Place of sin and shame."

Slavery is not just history, it is a stain that keeps the black man away from his creator; he has to "wash" his soul to be reunited with Him. Then man can reclaim his divine nature: "I and my creator are one in purpose . . ."; "I, personally, am his Majesty King Alpha, the King of Kings . . ."; "Millions living now will never die . . ."

But "first and last every soul for admission must believe in the Power of the Living God."

The King of Kings, the living God redeeming the black race and saving it from death—is this not the Rasta concept? Balintine could also have been the "first" Rasta—except that his era was as yet unaware of Ras (king) Tafari of Ethiopia.

Balintine was linked with the Athlicans. He knew Athlyi Rogers, the "good little messenger" who let himself be fooled by "one fallen angel called Douglas." "Pilot Marcus Garvey" was also fooled by a fallen angel, "Lady Astonishment, the Anglo-Militant Upside Down Queen." Balintine also cited other members of the little group: Grace Jenkins and Professor W. D. Davis, who met with him "at the World's Capital [Kingston] with the little Piby," Reverend and Mrs. Charles Goodridge, who were also "gone with the message," as well as Reverend W. R. Carter and his sister Adde, who were without a doubt Athlicans.

Grace Jenkins "the Comet" Garrison left Panama for Jamaica in 1924. In 1925, while Balintine was writing his book, Grace was struggling with her own small group and trying to build the Hamitic church in Kingston. Meetings were organized in other towns, and branches opened in Falmouth, Morant Bay, Bath, Mount Charles, and Spanish Town. On November 20, plans were made to build the first stone church at 7 Elgin Street, Smith Village (next to Trench Town), with the backing of the UNIA and in the presence of its president. But the church was never built, and by 1927 the Garveyites had totally rejected this mystical bunch. The sect's impact had not been strong enough. Its new leader, "Arch-Comet Charles Goodridge," lived in one room with his wife and several children. Their survival depended on the meager donations of their forty congregants, according to police reports. They were ready for a new leader.

Howell found another ally in Robert Hinds, an old Bedwardite. Bedward was a Baptist preacher who ended up in a psychiatric hospital because of "seditious" conduct; his story prefigures that of Leonard Howell.

Bedwardism sprang up in Spanish Town at the end of the nineteenth century with a barefoot prophet called Shakespeare. "H. E. S. Woods, more commonly known by the name of Shakespeare, came from America at an early date not exactly known, and lived in Spanish Town. . . . He was very peculiar, and lived in a stone hole or cave in the wilderness; whence he habitually came on missions of love, preaching the word of God and prophesizing: for prophet indeed he was."[25] In 1876, Shakespeare left his cave in Spanish Town (could it have been Pinnacle?) for August Town, a village along the Hope River bordering eastern Kingston. One of his followers was a young man named Bedward who had also worked in Colón until a religious vision called him back to Jamaica. When Shakespeare died in 1901, Bedward replaced him at the head of the congregation, which was to become the powerful Jamaica Native Baptist Free Church.

As in Balintine's *Black Supremacy*, the center of Bedwardist religious life is baptism, a ceremony held not in the "leper's churches," but in rivers, lakes, or the sea. Fasting is part of the purification ritual. But the balm yards and offerings to the dead are not proscribed.

> The Society strictly prohibits what is commonly called Revival or shaking the head and tramping the ground and wallowing on the earth and saying "It is the spirit." These are not the spirits that the Lord teaches us to pray for, those are the spirits that work in disobedient children. God's wish is for the revival of the heart, the revival from sin to grace. . . . (from the "Rules and Regulations" of the Bedwardite Baptist Society)

Bedward appears to have been an intelligent and kind leader. Thousands of poor and illiterate people came to him to be "washed" from degradation and servitude. His famous healings in Mona River seem to be of a psychological nature, but to the sufferers they were real. His adepts suffered from depression, and Bedward restored their sense of dignity. Rastafari owes a lot to Bedward, whose speeches have the same arrogance as Howell's. He was persecuted like Howell as well—his first indictment for sedition dates back to 1895, and he suffered all his life at the hands of the establishment. He was finally arrested in 1920. It seems that, secretly informed of the impending arrest, he went home and informed his followers that "they were coming to remove him." They interpreted this as "he was going to fly away to Africa," which allowed the authorities to pronounce him a lunatic and lock him up in Bellevue psychiatric hospital. He died there in 1930. In 1932 one of his disciples named Hind found a new leader in Leonard Howell.

There was one last group that Howell was associated with in those early days—the Ethiopianists. Their history went back as far as the eighteenth century, and since then they had spread out all over the black world. But in Jamaica, magnified by the Rasta movement, they took a new direction.

7

The Ethiopianists

In 1935, just before the Italian invasion of Ethiopia, an American ethnologist visiting Addis Ababa chanced upon two African Americans playing banjo at the chic Tambourine Club. He was astonished to learn that one was a black rabbi well known in Garveyite circles. This was Arnold J. Ford, a professional musician born in Barbados. He had come to New York in 1918 and had been the official composer for the UNIA for several years, writing many anthems, including the famous "Ethiopia, Land of our Fathers." Several of his hymns are still remembered by Pinnacle survivors and Rasta elders. He wrote lyrics that resounded with the high hopes of the times:

> O Africa awaken!
> The morning is at hand.
> No more are thou forsaken,
> O bounteous motherland.
> From far thy sons and daughters
> Are hast'ning back to thee;
> Their cry rings o'er the waters
> That Afric' shall be free!
>
> (PUBLISHED BY THE UNIA FOR THE 1922 CONVENTION)

Ford was, like many West Indians, a dedicated Bible reader, and he was impressed by the similarity between the Jewish bondage in Egypt and the enslavement of Africans in America. Jumping the gap between "similarity" and "identity," he decided that black people *were* the original Jews. The Ashkenazim of Eastern Europe he had met in New York, Ford reasoned, were only a discolored offshoot of Solomon's seed. Ford learned Hebrew, joined the Beth B'nai Abraham congregation known as the Black Jews, and later became a rabbi.

Harlem had been a Jewish and Italian neighborhood before it became black. The Jews and African Americans of the area maintained crucial financial contacts. Jewish nightclub owners, talent agents, publishers, and journalists were instrumental in bringing jazz musicians and Harlem Renaissance literature to public acceptance. The 1920s were also a time when European Jews discovered the existence of the Fallashas, the Ethiopian Jews whose tradition dates back to the union of King Solomon and the Queen of Sheba. In 1924 one Jacques Faitlovitch opened a school for them in Addis Ababa, and he came to New York several times to raise funds. In 1930, accompanied by the Fallasha rabbi Tamrat Emmanuel, Faitlovitch arrived in Harlem to meet with the Black Jews. In this gloomy dawn of the Great Depression, with Marcus Garvey in exile and the UNIA falling apart, it comes as no surprise that Arnold Ford decided to go to Addis.[26]

In Addis, Ford joined the small Afro-American colony (mostly West Indians), which was said to include about 150 individuals but easily could have been larger. Blacks from the New World had been going to Ethiopia since the Abyssinian Emperor Menelek's reign in the nineteenth century; his private surgeon (and a tutor of Prince Tafari), Dr. Joseph Vitalien of Guadaloupe, had been the first foreign black resident. Businessmen, adventurers, and African Americans in search of a spiritual home followed. At its 1922 convention, UNIA deputized a mission of skilled workers to go to Ethiopia, but the plan died from lack of funds. It was for the same reason that Dr. Charles Martin, an envoy from King Ras Tafari in 1927, failed to find suitable black candidates for fifty-three technical jobs; Indians were hired instead. But Selassie did hire black American war veterans to train his personal guard, and he managed to secure the valuable help of John Robinson, a black pilot from Chicago, who became his personal aviator. David Talbot, from British Guyana, was to become his minister of information. West Indian war veterans of the BWIR were hired into the army, and a Trinidadian pilot named Hubert Julien served in the Ethiopian war. Julien was a flamboyant character who had become famous in New York for "doing the parachute jump clad in the red tights of Mephistopheles and tooting a saxophone during his descent."[27] But the most common black American immigrant types in Ethiopia were missionaries like Ford, or Daniel R. Alexander, who, in following the dream of Ethiopia, came in search of the Promised Land.

Ethiopianism had been an important tenet of black Baptist churches since at least the late eighteenth century. It sprang from the fact that in the Bible, the Greek word *Ethiopia* (from the Greek *Aethiops*, "land of burned faces") denotes the whole of Africa. The temporal kingdom of Ethiopia was known as Abyssinia. When black slaves in the West gained access to the Book, they saw their ancestral continent's spiritual power revealed in scripture, and began to wait for the fulfillment of the prophecy of Psalm 38: "Princes shall come out of Egypt, and Ethiopia shall stretch her hands unto God." By the 1920s, Psalm 38 had become a key text for the Garveyites, the barefoot prophets, and other divines.

But Ethiopianism took root in Jamaica in 1784, long before the rise of King Ras Tafari. This was the year that George Liele founded the Ethiopian Baptist Church, which would become the first truly popular Christian organization serving the black community. An American slave, Liele had followed his master, a loyalist opposed to the American Revolution, into Jamaican exile. Ordained by the Baptist Church of America, he structured his church in Jamaica on the same model. The church did so well that Liele employed new converts as preachers. Before he could do anything about it, these new preachers were introducing different elements of African religious ritual—drumming, dancing, and chanting—into their worship services. The Ethiopian Baptist Church soon became the most culturally sound, deeply Jamaican branch of Christianity. The Baptists practiced what they preached, and they backed every step of the Jamaican struggle for freedom. They joined forces with the abolitionists, and after the Emancipation in 1835 they became the organizing force behind buying land and establishing free towns for manumitted slaves. The 1865 Morant Bay rebellion, which signaled the end of the planters' political monopoly, was led by a Baptist preacher named Paul Bogle. The Native Baptist Free Church of Bedward belongs to the same family.

And for good reason—does Baptism not stand for purging yourself of a haunting sin that you have yet to commit? At all times the redemption of black identity was at the forefront of Baptist efforts. In 1924, an important year for the little band of proto-Rastas in Kingston, a white Baptist preacher named Lloyd Cowell delivered a daring sermon in a church on East Queen Street. He told his believers that the Bible should be reinterpreted in order for readers to see the light. "The New Testament version of [the Song of Solomon] reads: 'I am black but charming.' It is not enough for a Christian to say: 'I am content to be black if the Lord will.' We must say: 'I am glad to be black. . . . I have a Divine Lover, and he loves me all the more because I am black.'"[28]

Three years later, Ethiopianism was revived by a portentous international news event. A new king, Ras Tafari, had been crowned in Ethiopia, and every newspaper published his picture. In August 1928, *National Geographic* published an entire issue about Ethiopia. When copies arrived in black neighborhoods, people were enthralled by the rich images of African splendor. Why dream if the Promised Land already exists? What are we waiting for?

Annie Harvey belonged to this current. She must have been of Howell's generation. Professor Hill says that Annie met David Har-

vey in Port Limon, where they got married. At the beginning of the
1920s they left Costa Rica for Panama, Cuba, and finally the United
States, where they became connected with the Black Jews and
adopted their views. Now they were "Israelites," which seemed to
be a way to escape the word *negro*, which was hard for Annie Harvey to swallow.

> This race of ours which was so blessed by God has become tired
> of being called by the accursed name of Negro, which continually
> brings down the integrity of a race of people. Our ancestors were
> given that name when they were made prey; becoming slaves.
> Those dark days have passed. . . . Sir, I earnestly beg for a remem-
> brance of God's promise towards the seed of Abraham, and David
> who was king of Israel. As the Holy Bible tells us that his seed
> would be remembered and in due time would be restored back
> out of the Isles from whence they were carried to in captivity back
> to their father's land Canaan, and find rest once more from their
> wants and oppressions. . . . Africa (Ethiopia) is still filled with rich
> treasures. A land that can prevent wants and poverty, and will lift
> the burden of terror from our race.[29]

This kind of thinking and feeling became the basis of the Back-
to-Africa movement, the final incarnation of Ethiopianism, and an
important component of the Rasta movement.

Back in Kingston in 1924, Annie Harvey was called to Ethiopia
"by vision." She went to Addis Ababa with her husband and stayed
for five and a half years. Ford stayed longer, and died during the
Italian invasion. The Harveys went back to Jamaica in 1931, heralds
bringing crucial information from Ethiopia.

In 1930, Ras Tafari had been crowned emperor under the name
of Haile Selassie I ("Power of the Trinity"), and given the extraordinary titles of King of Kings, Lord of Lords, Light of Saba, the
Conquering Lion of the Tribe of Judah. The coronation ceremonies
lasted ten days and were heavily publicized around the world in a
politically astute display of the Ethiopian nationality. Seventy-two
nations were officially represented. As a gift, England's King

George V returned a royal scepter to Ethiopia that had been dis-
played in English museums. It was returned by George's son, the
Duke of Gloucester, who later became George VI. In June 1931,
National Geographic published another special issue on Ethiopia, the
second in two years, featuring the coronation of young Tafari in his
gold embroidered robes. Even the *Daily Gleaner* published his picture on its front page. To the Ethiopians of Jamaica, the whole affair
had evident messianic and Biblical dimensions. The following
account would be given by Howell in *The Promised Key* in 1935:

> In 1930, the Duke of Gloucester undertook one of the most inter-
> esting duties he had ever been called upon to execute. The occa-
> sion was the coronation of his Majesty Ras Tafari, King of Kings
> and the Lord of Lords, the Conquering Lion of Judah, the Elect
> of God and the Light of the World.
>
> The Duke was to represent his father the Anglo Saxon King.
> The Duke handed to his Majesty the King of Kings and Lord of
> Lords a scepter of solid gold twenty seven inches long that had
> been taken from the hands of Ethiopia some thousand years
> before.
>
> The Duke bent down on his knees before his majesty Ras
> Tafari the King of Kings and Lord of Lords and spoke with a
> loud tone, "Master, Master, my father has sent me to represent
> him, Sir. He is unable to come, but said that he will serve you until
> the end, Master" (Psalms 72:9–11, Genesis 42:10). . . .
>
> It was an extraordinary ceremony. The church filled with
> brilliant Ethiopians in special robes; they had discarded their pre-
> cious white robes and wore jewels of great value. The men held
> heavily ornamented swords. On their heads they wore gold
> braided hats under which you could see lion's manes. The women
> on the other hand were heavily veiled and cloaked. His and Her
> Majesty King Alpha and Queen Omega came to the cathedral in
> a carriage drawn by six white Arabian horses. Queen Omega

wore a robe of Silver. The escorts on mules formed a procession outside the cathedral and wore lion's skin over their shoulders. . . .

King Alpha was presented with the orb, scepter, many swords, and other mighty emblems of his high office. Dignitaries and grand powers of the world presented King Alpha with the treasures of the oceans.

The Emperor attended to the preparations for the reception of His thousands of guests alone, and day after day could be seen rushing about in his scarlet car seeing to how his white laborers were getting on with the new road and lawns, and the extension of electric lights throughout the city that he had ordered.

This description might appear overly embellished, especially the image of a hyperactive Haile Selassie I personally overseeing the "white laborers" (although throughout his reign he preferred European technicians and engineers, which so offended Marcus Garvey). One also notices the image of "King Alpha and Queen Omega," taken from Balintine. Was it Annie Harvey, the "missionary," who recounted the event to Howell? No one else in the small group other than Annie and her husband had been there. Henry Dunkley, one of Howell's first followers, told Professor Hill that it was from Harvey's sect—known as "the Israelites"—that Howell obtained a copy of what he described as "the Prince of Peace photograph" of Selassie. Dunkley said, "After he came back from New York, Mr. Howell went round their headquarters on Paradise Street and got hold of one of the photographs. He was the one who brought the photo forward to the public and told them that the eternal messiah had come back."[30] Annie Harvey might have brought the picture to Jamaica, but she didn't know what to do with it. Howell had the vision. An *image*! This is what the people needed—a kingly image with which to identify. He reprinted the photo of Selassie and it became his emblem as he distributed copies to the faithful. When he died, there were a bunch of them—all blurred and cracked from many reprint-

Ras Tafari: an original picture sold by Howell. COURTESY OF THE SPANISH TOWN ARCHIVES.

ings—in the small cardboard suitcase that was his only material legacy.

The man with broad shoulders stood by the shore, the little picture in his hand, ready for the Divine Leap. He never looked for any other kind of work. He never looked back to his free wandering life. "He reflected that he was no longer a wild stallion, but a draft horse in harness with the bit in his mouth and a crupper under his tail, and—he liked it."[31] Howell was under the harness of the Living God.

8

First Sermons in St. Thomas

Those who remember Leonard Howell from the early days, like Canute Kelly from the parish of St. Thomas, remember their prophet with awe. There was definitely a mystical element about him. One minute he was at the door of your house, a minute later you turned your head and there he was again up on a platform, preaching the divinity of Ras Tafari. He could shift locations in the blink of an eye. When he spoke he carried you up to lofty heights, or struck you down as if you had been hit by lightning. You could get so easily entangled in his visions that you would no longer see his face. Try to conjure him in your memory? Pffft. Gone. His image was ephemeral. He seemed to leave barely a trace on your visual memory. But regardless of the length or quality of a meeting with him, Howell always left you with an intense sensation of presence. He was a powerhouse of spiritual energy.[32]

This is the man the Garveyites chased from the Coke Chapel steps, the man Kingston police deemed dangerous and told to get out of town. But Howell found fertile ground for his new ideas in St. Thomas Parish in southeastern Jamaica. This remote agricultural parish was notoriously the most backward on the island, and its mentality was deeply colonial. Working people, be they African or Indian indentured laborers, lived in near peonage. Grievances had been piling up in St. Thomas that would eventually erupt into the violent 1938 Serge Island strike. It's no wonder that Howell's theories captured hearts and minds there. Abandoned mothers, redundant cane cutters, war veterans, and uprooted East Indians all found solace in his sermons, and his nighttime Ras Tafari meetings drew crowds of hundreds.

The evening meeting on Tuesday, April 18, 1933, in Trinity Ville was not the first Howell had held in St. Thomas, but he had an unusual onlooker that day in John Ross, a combative local planter. It was around nine o'clock, the hour when Jamaicans, freshly bathed and dressed, usually go out to enjoy the cool of the evening. Howell had set up his speaking platform, a barrel with a board across it, at the marketplace. There were two or three hundred people in attendance, a police officer named Leonard Thomas later testified. He reported on the preacher's sermon: "'The Lion of Judah has broken the chain,' said Howell, 'and we the black race are finally free. George the Fifth is no longer our king. George the Fifth sent his third son down to Africa in 1928 to bow down to our new king Ras Tafari [sic]. Ras Tafari is King of Kings and Lord of Lords. The black people will no longer look to George the Fifth—Ras Tafari is their King!'"

"What year did you say this took place?" interrupted John Ross, the planter.

"1928," answered Howell.

"You're a bloody liar!" Ross shouted.

Howell came down from his platform and walked straight up to Ross. He said, "Sir, you should be arrested for disorderly conduct!"

"If I am charged and found guilty, then I will pay." The crowd started to gather angrily around Ross, and the officer, who knew him, tried to disperse it. Howell resumed his speech.

"The Negro is now free, and the white people will have to bow to the negro race. . . ." The district constable, one Thomas Kelly, arrived and began to argue with Howell. "This is the greatest ignorance that I have ever heard," he told Howell.

"If you do not believe me you can write to the governor or the inspector of police!" retorted Howell, adding that no police officer should lay a finger on him. He proceeded to speak about the BWIR (to which he belonged during his short stint in the army) and about the tribulations of war veterans who were left to starve when the regiment was disbanded in 1926. He passed around a photograph of Haile Selassie and the Duke of Gloucester. The picture cards of Ras Tafari, on sale for a shilling apiece, were to be sent to Selassie directly: "If anyone has any grievance, he must write to Ras Tafari, the King of Kings and Lord of Lords."

Howell ended by asking the crowd to sing the national anthem, "God Save the King." "But before you start," he added, "you must remember that you are not singing it for King George, but for Ras Tafari, our new king."

After the meeting, "there was much hostility directed at John Ross from the crowd," Constable Thomas concluded. "He could not get too far from me on his way home."

Ross was outraged by the public preaching of treason. What if his cane cutters actually believed this wild man? Howell must be silenced, and quickly. But at this point he met with indifference from the establishment. "It seems from his appearance and his speech, that Howell is suffering from an obsession which may eventually land him in the Lunatic Asylum; he would revel in the advertisement of a prosecution," stated one police report. "The man is a stupid ranter who puts forward an imaginary being or person whom he calls 'Ras Tafari' and whom he describes as Christ as well as King of Ethiopians," the Crown Solicitor concluded. "I think we can leave Howell unadvertised so far as the annex statements are concerned." The Attorney General was of the same opinion. "I should treat those statements as his ravings go unnoticed."[33]

But Howell was soon rabble-rousing in Kingston, supported by Joseph Nathaniel Hibbert (the mason from Panama) and two others.

At eight o'clock in the evening on June 14, 1933, he was selling pictures of Ras Tafari on the steps of Coke Chapel, Marcus Garvey's favorite speaking spot, which threw the Garveyites into a rage when they concluded that Howell was speaking "seditiously." "I am here to inform you that King George's flag is no flag for you. Yours is the Ethiopian flag—the green, yellow, and red flag, the robe of the Virgin Mary. This is the Ethiopian Flag!"

He spoke against the churches—they did no good, they were corrupt, the priests were thieves. He read aloud newspaper articles about the race problem in the United States. He also taunted the authorities. "Go down and get the police to lock me up. I am telling you at this moment that the Governor of Jamaica cannot lay a hand on me, much less an insignificant jackass!"

Howell was not impressed by "jackasses" in uniforms. He had worn many in his two decades of traveling. He used Garvey's technique to combat fear. "When you are afraid of something, walk straight towards it!" he advised. A few days later he went to the police station and complained that undercover policemen were attending his meetings and taking notes. The police officer explained to him that they were just doing their job, and took his visit as an opportunity to tell him that "his foolish talk was misleading, and that Ras Tafari, King of Abyssinia, came from a very ancient family that would never acknowledge him as their representative, and that selling picture postcards of Selassie for a shilling comes very close to a criminal act." "He took my warning in good spirit," noted the officer, "but I doubt if it will have any effect."[34]

He was wrong. Howell already had another tactic. On September 13, 1933, before a Ras Tafari meeting at Crossroads, Port Morant, he went to the police station and invited the police officers to attend. Inspector B. Smith, of the Port Morant station, arrived with two constables.

"The meeting was opened with the singing of hymns. He amused himself by taunting the clergymen of different denominations and told people not to go to church because the ministers were liars." He then talked about slavery, and how "the White Man stole Africa from the Africans, and that the Black people should think that Africa is their home, not Jamaica. . . . In 1934 there will be a convention in Jamaica, such as was never been seen before, and there will be ships here waiting to take Black people back to Africa, those who want to go. . . ."

The report noted that the respectable people took no note of Howell. The other classes were divided. Some thought that if Mr. Garvey could not bring about what he spoke of, Howell didn't have a chance. The next day Howell went back to Kingston on a bus, and Inspector B. Smith concluded that "there was no cause for alarm." But a Corporal Coombs advised that Howell and his cohorts "should be warned against stirring up ill feelings."[35]

On Sunday, October 8, in Port Morant, Howell again preached against the clergy.

> He chiefly in his speeches abuses the Parsons by calling them thieves and robbers and that they should be driven out of the Churches and the Churches locked up. He also abuses the white men by calling them white rascals and scoundrels and that they are robbing the people and keeping them down, but their eyes are now opened to everything and that they can live independently without the white men. He urges to support his movement for the Negro King Ras ta Fari is doing great things for them and they will be taken to Africa next year August by ships provided for the purpose.

He again promised the faithful that in August 1934 a ship would arrive to carry them home to Ethiopia.

Howell continued to hold meetings within a twenty-mile radius from Port Morant. In Airy Castle he was the target of jeering, but in Pear Tree River the population was enthusiastic. Although he was at first "very cautious of his remarks" and limited himself to the religious, he quickly made enemies with his verbal abuse of the clergy. On October 31, 1933, Inspector Adams of Morant Bay received the following letter from one Elder W. E. Barclay of the Church of God, a protestant denomination active in Jamaica and based in Nashville, Tennessee.

> The Ras Tafari gang are defying British law by proclaiming that their kingdom is Africa. . . . Two men, L. Howell and Valentine [sic], are holding meetings and teaching several practices contradictory to the laws of our country. . . . They are acquiring money on false pretenses, claiming themselves ambassadors of this African king, by collecting funds from the people and promising them free transportation to Africa if they pay a certain sum. This man denounces ministers, myself included, and has the audacity to call us thieves and vagabonds at his open air meetings. . . . They make ignorant people believe that this man [Selassie] now crowned is Christ, and that he has come to redeem the negro race. . . . Enclosed you will find one of their tracts.

This is the first documented link between Howell and the Ethiopianist preacher Balintine. The "tract" is a digest of Athlican theory. Three of ten verses are extracted from the *Holy Piby*:

> Woe be unto a race of people who seek not their own foundation. Their wives shall be servants to the wives of other men, and their daughters shall be the wives of poor men and vagabonds—and there shall be tears of deprivation.

> I strongly appeal to you to seek and learn of your own foundation. Woe be unto a race of people who forsake their own doctrine for another. They shall be slaves of the people thereof.

> O people of Ethiopia boast not the progress of the white race, believing that you are part of the project. You shall be cast over the bridge of death both body and soul.[36]

Of interest here is the overwhelmingly social and political tone, without mystical stylings. One might infer that the basis of Howell's project is economic independence, the "green pasture" of the Athlicans.

"The white men gave the black men the wrong doctrine. They told them to condemn silver and gold, and seek heaven after death. . . . Under the doctrine of the white man, the black man slights the things of life and seeketh Heaven after death; this manner of thought hath brought us nothing but hunger and deprivation: life in disgrace and death in dishonor." There is no mention here of Africa. This is a call to action for black men to establish an economic foundation independent of whites. Selassie is not mentioned as a messiah, but as the "living Lord God of Ethiopia," with Howell as his local representative—"in his hands the law is given." The tract begins with the heading "On H.M.S." (On His Majesty's Service), familiar to soldiers and sailors. Technically it proclaims allegiance to a foreign sovereign—a crime then punishable by death in the British Empire.

On November 13 in Stokes Hall, at a Ras Tafari meeting in the very heart of the canefields, with Howell not present, ex-Bedwardite Robert Hinds and three others were arrested for sedition and then freed on bail. Nearly a month later, on December 10, Howell and Hinds preached Ras Tafari in Seaforth, up in the mountains near Stony Gut, Paul Bogle's home town. When they arrived a revivalist preacher was working the crowd, and Howell followed. He started by singing the newly composed Howellite hymn. An audience of three hundred all followed in unison.

Lennard seeks me, Lennard finds me,
He fills my heart with glee.
Glory to Lennard, I am free!
For I know what Lennard Howell is doing for me,
And he keeps me happy all day.

This meeting, although quiet and orderly, was the pretext for arresting Howell a month later. At the end of the meeting, plainclothes officers tried to buy photographs of Ras Tafari, but when the two cops refused to give their names, Howell took back the photos. "Some might have the same names, but not the same nature," he said, "and you, sir, look like a police informer."

On December 16, Hinds and Hibbert, Howell's lieutenants, were back in Trinity Ville, the hometown of John Ross. Again their charismatic leader was not with them to keep the police at bay, and the rabid Ross was on the warpath. He had rallied pillars of the local establishment—the Methodist minister of Morant Bay and Seaforth, Reverend M. C. Surgeon; a justice of the peace from Port Morant, Ronald Robinson; and the august Thomas Warfinger of the Port Morant branch of the Jamaica Producers Association. As soon as Hinds opened his mouth he was arrested for disorderly conduct, but the crowd came to his rescue and the physical confrontation Howell wanted to avoid took place. Hibbert, with the help of the onlookers, attacked the constables and managed to free Hinds. But John Ross and his men joined the police and managed to arrest Hinds, Hibbert, and six of their followers.

The next day John Ross and his gang, armed with cudgels and cutlasses, tried to ambush Howell at a Ras Tafarian meeting, but Howell didn't happen to show up that evening. On the 19th he was in Morant Bay to support his friends who were being tried the next day. An order had come from Kingston to postpone the trial, but the police—under pressure of Ross and his thugs—later claimed that this telegram had arrived too late.

Meanwhile in Kingston the authorities were perplexed. In St. Thomas the local planters, clergymen, and businessmen were pushing for repressive action. But the attorney general and the governor concluded that legal action would transform Howell into a martyr. In June, the Crown had "instructed against laying charges of sedition without the Governor's approval." But Ras Tafarians had been arrested anyway, and the trial held against orders. Ross and his downpressors were out for blood.

Nineteen thirty-four arrived in a mood of expectancy. Howell did not go back to Kingston, but remained in his "tabernacle" hideout in Port Morant. He resumed his meetings in nearby Chapel Hill, refraining from direct attacks on the colonial government, muting his "sedition" with mystical language. Ross and his accomplices kept up the pressure, sending a letter to the chief of police, in which they denounced Ras Tafarianism as "rank atheism that breaks down people's morality . . . very direct teachings against Ministers and established religion . . . extremists who provoke rebellion and bloodshed . . . a movement spreading and growing . . . despicable effort to undermine the authority of Church and State."[37] Urgent measures need to be taken, the government was advised, before this movement got out of hand. In the end the judicial apparatus gave up and indicted Howell, Hinds, and two of their followers, Theophilus Jackson and Osmund Shaw, on several counts of sedition. They were arrested, then freed without bail.

This trial began on March 13 at Morant Bay Court House, where Paul Bogle had been tried and executed in 1865. His body still lies in an unmarked grave behind the building. Hinds got one year. Howell got two. What the governor had tried so hard to avoid—Howell as martyr—now took place. Even the *Daily Gleaner* made Howell into a cause célèbre. In three detailed and dramatic reports published on March 14–16, 1934, literate Jamaica was first exposed to the theories of Ras Tafari. These unsigned articles are among the unsung but defining documents on the beginning of the movement. They carefully described the atmosphere in the crowded courtroom, the tension among the spectators, the explosive hymn singing in stressful moments, and the nervous sniggers from the jury benches.

"Howell, an athletic figure in black with a beard not dissimilar to that worn by the king of Abyssinia, whose photograph and name figured largely in the evidence, was undefended by counsel. With him he brought sheaths of documents and a few books of unusual proportions. In his buttonhole, he wore a yellow, green and black rosette similar to that worn by a large number of men who accompanied him to court."[38]

H. M. Radcliffe, the assistant attorney general representing the Crown, opened the case by reminding the jury that "the law in a

British colony was not against the free speech and liberty of a subject. A subject was at liberty to criticise the Government, once he did so constitutionally. When one however went beyond that limit, and uttered language liable to stir up hatred between classes, and bring the Sovereign into contempt, and government and those administrating it into hatred, it amounted to sedition." The jury, Radcliffe went on, "might very well think that a great deal of what the accused was reported to have said was nonsense, bosh, and twaddle, but not because it was nonsense to them, as intelligent men, why they should not judge what might be the effect of it on the mind of those members of the community whose intelligence was not high and who were ignorant and might therefore be easily misled." He therefore advised the jury to "find the accused man guilty of the charge of sedition."

Howell objected to five jurors from Seaforth and Morant Bay, as "it was rumored that the jurors from both places were too eager for the chance to sit on this case." But the chief justice overruled Howell's objection. Howell also refused to swear on a Bible, claiming he was a Muslim.

The prosecution witnesses, constables Brooks and Gayle, then proceeded to read from longhand notes, allegedly taken by them at the meeting. Howell noticed that their handwriting was suspiciously regular despite the fact that they had supposedly been writing in the dark. He proceeded to dictate something to them so the jury could compare their note-taking skills. This was planned as a way to indicate that "the charge was trumped up against him." The dictation is worth recording: "What we need today is an international salvation, not individual salvation. God never intended individual salvation." But although the handwriting in the dictation was not as clear as that in one of the "notes," the constables' testimony was too similar to what we know of Howell to be seriously questioned.

The Crown's accusations rested on two main points: Howell had called Queen Victoria "the Harlot Queen," and told British subjects that they were, in fact, Ethiopians.

And this the defendant never denied.

Leonard Howell's long defense in the shape of a sermon amounts to a declaration of the Rasta doctrine, and deserves to be reproduced here. It's clear that the journalist reporting it was fascinated by this character. Howell got exactly what he had always wanted on that day, a crowded courthouse and a pack of journalists to listen to him. So he took his time. For one whole day, under the pretense of explaining his speech at Trinity Ville, he publicized his doctrine to a national audience.

His first aim was to convince the establishment that his intention was not to violently transform society. Holding up a picture of Ras Tafari, he said, "I told the people that he was a descendent of the same man who told Peter to 'put up [his] sword, he who lives by the sword shall perish by the sword.' I spoke to them of His crucifixion and of His ascension, and that the Ethiopian [sic] sons and daughters would soon enjoy His kingdom, that he had gone before to prepare a place of rest." He then proceeded to position himself, not in terms of color, but in terms of religion:

> We were told that we were Gentiles, but thanks be to God we
> have been awakened from our sleep by the coming of the Messiah
> to a fuller understanding that we are the Jews, and the reason we
> were sleeping was because our last king of Israel, Hezekiah, had
> his eyes plucked out by Nebuchadnezzar and the head of his two
> son lopped off. From then on we were blind, and could not see
> the light of the Lord God of Israel, until the messiah came back
> to this world in the form of Ras Tafari (2 Kings 24:7).

Then came Howell's standard recounting of the King of King's coronation:

> His Kingdom shall have no end—a kingdom that all kings of the
> earth had to bow down to as he was the only king in the world
> today as an ancient king. . . . At his coronation all the powers of
> earth sent down diplomatical presentations, namely Gold, Frank-
> incense and Myrrh, to denote Marriage, Death and Birth. The
> King of England sent down his third son with great gifts . . . they

weighed a ton in gold. The Duke of Gloucester represented King George the Fifth of England at Abyssinia at King Ras Tafari's coronation, and representatives all over the world went to pay tribute to the greatest King. . . . As Ethiopians, we were worshipping the god of idolatry—the king which Nebuchadnezzar set up in Babylon for the people to worship after he overthrew King Zedekiah. Nebuchadnezzar placed an image in Babylon and called the governors and chiefs of far and near to come to Babylon and worship the image he had set up. But there were three Jews who refused to worship the god which Nebuchadnezzar set up, and they said to Nebuchadnezzar: "We shall not worship that god you set up." And Nebuchadnezzar said: "Then I will place you in a furnace of fire." And they accepted, saying that they knew their God. They were put in a fiery furnace—made seven times hotter—and the God of Israel saved them.

The parable of Shedrok, Mished, and Abendigo would later become a staple of reggae lyrics. Was not this "other man" in the furnace a reminder of Athlyi's Messiah and his two angels?

"I told the people," Howell continued, "that the same God had come back to earth to lead mankind toward the path of righteousness. He was thirty-three years and six months when he was crucified. He must come back to earth and take up his full power when the same thirty-three year and six months has expired. We are now in the year 1933—in April of 1934, thirty-three years and six months will be accomplished."

Since the birth of Christ was counted as year one and not zero, Howell was preaching that April 1934 was exactly two thousand years from his death. "He promised, he said, to return the same way that he left," surrounded by "two men in white apparel," and that His return must be "identical to the descendents of David."

One of the most important messages of this millenarian formula was that heaven belonged to *this* world and not any other; but the prophecy that followed was a bit obscure. Howell may have been manipulating numbers to his liking, or adapting ancient folk beliefs—like considering creation to have begun in 606 B.C.—to suit his needs. He went on in the same Nostradamus mode:

> The world would last 2520 years. It began in 606 and should end in 1914. In 1914 there was a war in "Jugo" (the Great War) which proved the coming of Jesus Christ on earth to reign as righteous king and set up his righteous law. The war lasted from 1914 to 1918. Every nation was present at the "funeral procession," the likes of which had never been seen before. . . . On November 9, 1918 a man was seen at the River Jordan, and some say he was Christ himself. Two days later an Eagle was seen. That same day the war ended and the Armistice signed. Fifty days after the Lord God of Israel started his reign. That was 1919—the first day of the first month of the first year. Christ returned to kill the Nebuchadnezzar image.

Howell then went to Revelation's prophecies concerning the end of the world at Armageddon.

> In 1120 Whitecliffe and Bishop Jewel proclaimed the anti-Christ in England and the same as such on all of earth. England, mother of all nations, promulgates one religion all over earth, but a meteorite of epic proportions shall come and smash it all to bits. . . . After 1934 every church must close its doors, for the spirit of God has deserted them. The clergy does not tell the truth, and great shame will come to them. Twenty thousand churches in America will soon be little more than empty shells.

He then proceeded to read from 1 Thessalonians 4:11 (". . . you have learned from God to love one and all equally, and to work with your own hands as we commanded you"). He then denied having called Queen Victoria a "Harlot Queen"; it was Babylon, he said, that this Biblical verse referred to.

> And the Woman was clad in purple and scarlet and decked in gold and precious stones and pearls, having a golden cup in her hand full of the abominations and guiltiness of her fornication.

And upon her forehead was written MYSTERY, BABYLON THE GREAT, THE MOTHER OF HARLOTS AND ABOMINATIONS OF THE EARTH. I saw the woman drunk on the blood of saints, and on the blood of Jesus' martyrs . . . (Revelation 17:4).

At no time, Howell said, had it to come to his mind to speak disrespectful words to anyone at Seaforth. "I said: people, you are poor, but you are rich because God planted mines of diamonds and gold for you in Africa, your home." He told them that 700 billion pounds had been sent from Africa to England, and urged them to go back to Africa, home of their forefathers. "I told them that our king had come to bring them home to Africa, their motherland, that though there was an enormous amount of people identifying themselves as British subjects, the British Government only protected them until their king came, and when he came, the Crowned Head of England would turn them over to their King. 1934 was the beginning of a successful change." He had counseled them to be content with their present conditions, as happiness and prosperity were near.

"But they should have L-O-V-E—L for Long love, O for Overflowing love, V for Virtuous love, E for Eternal love. Love and equality would reign on earth. Their King was Ras Tafari who was the King of Kings, Lord of Lords, Elect of God, Conquering Lion of Judah, and father of the world to come. The English Government accepted their king as they sent diplomatic presentations and promised to serve Ras Tafari, who was the true Messiah. . . . He had not prepared a mansion for them, but they had not lived in a mansion in Jamaica. They lived in small huts for which they were compelled to pay taxes. . . . He told the people that when they sang the national anthem ["God Save the King"] they should think of Ras Tafari as he was their king. King George had told them as well with his representative.[39]

Under all this prophetical mumbo-jumbo—the African Jews, the apocalypse, the two angels—Howell was outlining an idealistic political program. There were the social ideas of the *Holy Piby*, and the notion of the Promised Land where Africans would live independently from whites. The story of the recent apparition of Christ on the Jordan River came from BWIR war veterans stationed in Palestine at the time of the Armistice. Babylon was now a symbol of the corrupted world. Who were those "gigantic men" whom Howell met in Europe, speaking so clearly about Ethiopia? Maybe the modern historians and ethnologists, who in the 1930s started to give Africa its due, like Duse Mohammed Ali, friend of Marcus Garvey in London, or George Padmore and other anti-colonialist Marxists.

Radcliffe's cross-examination allows us to check Howell's version of his biography:

"Ras Tafari is the Messiah come back to earth?"

"Yes, your Lordship."

"Have you had any communication with Ras Tafari?"

"No."

"Did you advise that your people to go to Abyssinia?"

"No, sir."

"What is the good of the picture?"

"To know that Ras Tafari is their king."

"Not as a passport?"

"No, sir."

"When did you first conceive that idea that Ras Tafari was the Messiah?"

"Through a prophecy."

"When was it that you made this discovery?"

"In 1930, when Ras Tafari was crowned."

"Where were you at this time?"

"In Africa."

"Have you been to Africa?"

"Yes. All over Africa."

"Were you born in Jamaica?"

"Yes."

"When did you come back?"

"December 1932."

"Have you been preaching ever since?"

"Yes, I started in January 1933."

"Where did you get your start?"

"Kingston, Jamaica."

"Have you always preached about Ras Tafari as the Messiah?"

"Yes."

"Is this your chief subject?"

"No. I wanted to show people the wealth of Africa. . . ."

When asked about the indictment, Howell "spent some time reading the contents of the document and then said: 'This is contrary to my lecture.'" Radcliffe also asked what he was doing with the collections he took up.

"Did you send them to Abyssinia?"

"No sir. I help a lot of poor people. Or buy oil for the lamp. If a man is in need I help him."

"Does any part of it go to you personally?"

"No, not unless any is left over. When I go out with Mr. Hinds, I let him hold it."

The reporter from the *Daily Gleaner* emphasized the polite deportment of the accused before his judges, and the laughter when Howell declared that Ethiopia would reign over the world. Testimony from a witness tells us that powerful Howell preached "in a stone of a voice." At one point a rooster, probably inspired by one of Howell's passionate speeches, hopped up the steps of the court house and loudly crowed after each of his sentences. The police chased it away, but it came back several times. Some thought this was perhaps Paul Bogle's "duppy" coming to pay homage from behind the court house.

Just before the verdict was read, Howell warned the jurors

> to tell the truth and nothing else. Of course he was not asking for sympathy. He knew he was innocent. He was born a hero, and beyond any shadow of a doubt he would die a hero defending his race. If they thought honestly that he was guilty, let them pronounce him guilty without hesitation. It would only be a matter of time. For how better could a man die than in the face of an immense obstacle, for the ashes of his fathers and the temple of his Gods?

It took the jury a mere fifteen minutes to find Howell and Hinds guilty as charged. Howell got two years in prison, while Hinds got one. Howell declared that he would appeal. The Chief Justice said there was no appeal. Howell paused for a little while, and then spoke for the last time. The future lay before him. And as a brave hero, he would bear the consequences and come back more gigantic than ever. He had no knowledge of this at present; all he knew was that he would have to acquire a new wealth of knowledge for his return. His King Ras Tafari would deliver him soon, perhaps not in Jamaica. But he would meet the jurors in his case when the kingdom of Ethiopia called home its scattered sons and daughters. He would be a lord in that kingdom. He would have his crown at last.

Jail House

We don't know what Leonard Howell felt on his way to jail in 1934. Was he exalted, sanctified? Did he feel the sting of martyrdom? We do know that his great spirit was unbroken. Now his cell was his pulpit. As soon as Howell arrived at Saint Catherine's Prison, his voice resounded through cell block and mess hall, and his captive audience listened carefully. "You all!" he would say, "Transgressors of a lawless regime, you are no longer the subjects of this kingdom of inequity. You are *Ethiopians*! The Lion of Judah has broken every chain!" In jail he found more than a captive audience—he found devoted followers of his new faith. The inmates called him "Gong," which means "tough guy." (Some also say it means "gun" in ghetto slang.) We can imagine Leonard Howell's life in jail through comparison with that of another kingly rebel, Nigerian saxophonist Fela Anikulapo Kuti. Whenever Fela was imprisoned, the other prisoners saw to his every need. They washed his clothes, gave him food, found herbs for him. Howell, like Fela Kuti and Bob Marley, gave a sense of dignity to criminals and outcasts. Proud and powerful, Howell imbued the prison with the aura of Ras Tafari, a new christ-force for the sufferers. He did not need to be "related" to Selassie (as the judge had suggested) to be his ambassador—day and night he radiated his divinity. In dank cells, in the dark of the tropic night, hushed voices recounted the coronation of the King of Kings.

Meanwhile in St. Thomas, where most of Howell's followers remained, the witch hunt had begun. Officials were using any pretext to force the peaceful Rastas to "drop their pernicious doctrine like a hot potato!"[40] The attitude toward this new idea was "Kill it before it grows." But since Ras Tafarites were orderly, nonviolent "decent citizens," the only way to arrest them was by provoking and harassing them. One farcical example of this was well documented by police.

The day is Saturday, August 4, 1934. An evangelist is preaching at Seaforth market. District Constable Robert Powers swaggers through the crowd and enters Chung's grocery. He is in high spirits and buys a round of drinks. Tonight, he says, he is "out for every damn Rasta people." Who wants to join him? He asks some youths—mento musicians—to make up lewd songs ridiculing the Ras Tafarites, just to warm up the audience. "And they must not be afraid to disturb the peace, because he will back them up in anything which they may like to do."[41] He gives them the names of six Rastafari brethren to put into their songs.

The youths work up some dirty little lyrics, the type that mento minstrels improvise, and they go out into the marketplace and sing them. Their loud, unpleasant voices disturb the crowd listening to the female evangelist preacher. One Melrosa Francis loudly complains to her neighbor on "the ill behavior of young people . . . if the older people will show better example to the younger ones, they could not be so rude and uncontrollable." Constable Powers "abruptly entered the conversation and said, 'I have a wife and children that cannot misbehave themselves.' [Melrosa] asked him if he marry a wife, he said no. [She] said since you haven't a wife I am not speaking to you, the statement cannot be applied to you.'" Pointing his finger in her face, the constable shouted at the top of his lungs,

"'Who are you talking to? If you speak so hard I will arrest you because I am out for every damn Rasta tonight.'" Now Melrosa's boyfriend hurried over and told her to leave. In front of Gordon's jewelry shop, Powers grabs her and shouts, "'I come to show you that my backside is not weak.'" Melrosa whips her hand away from him, and her friend accuses the constable of harassment. But Powers now has a posse with him; one of them, his son-in-law Cyril Grant, jumps onto Melrosa, lifts her up and throws her "flat on the ground," calling Powers to come and arrest her. Powers, now stone drunk, stumbles over the two of them struggling on the ground and bashes his head hard on the jeweler's door, enraging him even more. Onlookers disentangle the three of them and the stunned Melrosa escapes into the shop. Powers follows her, picking up a bottle, claiming she smashed him with it. "You must pay for anything you break," the jeweler cries. A brawl ensues, "causing the destruction of many valuable articles." A policeman on duty appears to tell Powers to leave the matter to him. Melrosa, sure of her rights, quietly follows the policeman down to the station, where witnesses are summoned. Powers takes one witness to the side and offers her money to be a witness for him, but she refuses. The case is ordered to be tried by a local magistrate who "would allow neither statement nor evidence" from Melrosa's witnesses; they are instead all fined forty pounds, or thirty days in jail, along with other local Rastas who were not even present that day. The jeweler's losses were not covered.[42]

This unfortunate but slapstick scene is drawn from police records filed in the Spanish Town Archives under "Pinnacle Papers." It says a lot about British ambivalence in legal matters. On one side there is a sense of legality, with every witness statement carefully annotated and filed. On the other hand, crucial decisions are informed by the most arrogant class prejudices. It reflects the tragic ambivalence of colonial administration. Bureaucrats and clerks mainly spring from the middle class of blacks educated with Christian and humanist ideals, resigned to a system in which color overrules merit. They were sometimes of Garveyite leanings, concerned for human rights, but they were blinded by their repulsion for African cultural nationalism. White officials on the other hand were caught between the plantocracy's class arrogance and the official "legalist" position. The "Pinnacle Papers" display correspondence recommending that the police not go beyond their prerogatives. But in the colonial mind, everything black is inferior and should not be allowed to challenge the status quo. In both cases, Ras Tafari represents everything that Jamaican society abhors. The brown elite, in "heightening" its color by appropriate marriage, despises everything that enhances its "blackness," especially African cults with their "pagan" dance and "savage" rhythms.

But in the mid-1930s those cults were thriving. The worldwide financial depression had revived the Great Revival, the movement of spiritual rebirth that had swept America and the West Indies seventy years earlier. Revivalist churches flourished in every ghetto. Baptized in God's natural fonts—the rivers and the sea—the sons of slaves were cleansing themselves of the sin of slavery, free again to live in accord with their culture and their conscience. The Revival invoked Christ but, as Garvey put it, "We shall worship him through the spectacles of Ethiopia."[43]

In Jamaica, cults like the Pocomaniacs went further. Their dances of possession called to the Spirit; they lent their bodies to its embrace as in a voodoo ceremony. And Kumina revivalism was even more African. Based in St. Thomas, where African indentured workers kept arriving long after slavery, Kumina mysticism progressively drifted to the West Kingston ghettos, where their "yards" were to mingle with the Rastas'.

These stark survivals of African religion revolted the brown middle class, picking at the scab of their "darkness," their secret wound. Bishop E. J. Robertson described for the *Daily Gleaner* this "ugly canker" eating away at the country:

These soulless atheistic performers . . . sow the seeds of unrest . . . resuscitating the superstitions of a revolutionized world and the sexual licence of the cult of Baal. Heathen practices from the darkest recesses of the Dark Continent are given new life. They live loosely and keep the ganja trade flourishing. They paint the white man with colors of hate and teach that God and Christ are black. . . . The Pocomaniacs are the most tenacious parasites known to the animal world and some of them are a most severe curse to a gentlemen's poultry yard or goat pen. I often pass them in the height of the day—ten or more of each sex together— drunk on the orgies of the past night, or fast asleep on the low banks of a country roadside. . . . These hundreds of religious beggars keep respectable and hard-working citizens awake night after night, and sleep when they should be doing some sort of productive work. The pittance they beg can't support them, hence they prey on the substance of industrious people and eventually become liabilities to the state, to be supported in the Alms House by your taxes and mine.[44]

But if some were horrified by the Africanist sects, the real danger came from Ras Tafarians who were "playing with fire," as the *Gleaner*'s editor stressed.

Those silly people of the laboring and small producing classes in Eastern St. Thomas who have allowed themselves to be saturated with a dangerous cult that has been labeled "Ras Tafari" . . . have become passive resisters. They have been informed by someone, a trickster no doubt, that the Emperor Ras Tafari of Abyssinia prescribes all those who own holdings in this parish to not pay taxes to the government. Neither must all others who pay rent for plots owned by the government on which they squat and cultivate. What will occur when either the Crown Lands Department or individual property owners decide that passive resistance will not suffice? It is up to the high officers of the government to draw their own conclusions on this phase of the question. It demands early attention and action in at least one direction—to destroy a dangerous cult which has taken root in several districts of St. Thomas. . . . But we are not without hope that the attention they are receiving form the police department will cause them to drop their pernicious doctrines as each would a hot potato.[45]

What was the UNIA doing? The organization that should have been supporting the Rastas sided with the establishment. The thirteenth convention of UNIA at Eidelweiss Park opened on August 14, 1934, with a debate on religion that continued through the day. The "prevailing religious fanaticism existing among certain classes of negroes" stemmed, the chairmen said, from the fact that "the race had not properly settled upon a sound religious policy, but rather that every day, very simple and ignorant people were founding and organizing new cults which were entirely contradictory to the set principles of true religion, and that it was to the race's benefit to use its intelligence to curb this spreading fanaticism." Mr. Johnson, a Kingston delegate, described "Negroes claiming to be Abyssinians, who were beginning to grow beards as an indication of their religion, and had announced that on a certain day they would walk the sea from Jamaica to Abyssinia, and that their beards were to part the sea, so as to give them an easy passage." Delegate Forrest of Kingston

> blamed Kingston and the Saint Andrew Corporation [the governing body for the area around the capitol] for allowing Trench Pen to be used as a center of these local religious demonstrations, and stated that all night the tom-tom drum could be heard beating, and that parents would take their little children to these weird night practices where they would sit up all night long. In the early morning, he would see these children returning with their parents showing signs of exhaustion from the night's ordeals.[46]

An American delegate spoke of the "sweeping growth of a similar fanaticism among the ignorant negroes of America, especially in light of the growing depression, which seems an opportunity for those unable to find employment to live off of their ignorance. . . ." Delegate Charles James of Gary, Indiana, said that simple-minded negroes were turning into

> Moors, Arabs, Abyssinians, and even claiming to be followers of Zoorastre [sic]; even though they have never changed their residences from the time that they were born, they were still growing beards and refusing to cut their hair. All this to prove that they were indeed Moors and had even gone so far as to change their Christian names to be known as Mohammed Ali or Mohammed Bey or some peculiar Moorish or Mohommedian religious mystical names.

Garvey's position may have been a bit different, and Balintine disassociated himself from the "upside down anglo-militant" UNIA. Garvey, who never lost an opportunity to express his opinion, is not known to have personally denounced his "friend" Leonard Howell. Garvey's acute sense of human psychology probably enabled him to understand the mystical background of millenarian ideas that, deep down, were similar in spirit to his own. But Garvey also wanted to penetrate Jamaica's civil politics, and the last thing he needed was an association with a radical fanatic who preached actual African repatriation and passive resistance to authority. In Jamaica in 1934, voting was limited to landowners, or about twenty thousand people—less than two percent of the population. Garvey was depending on this tiny minority in order to be elected to office, and it was not by an alliance with the Rastas that he would gain their support.

Only a year later, faced with disrespect, indignities, and harassment, Marcus Garvey gave up and sailed for England. But if Jamaica's colonial mentality was responsible for his departure, perhaps the future national hero was also escaping the provincial outlook of the local branch of the UNIA. Marcus never returned to Jamaica, and never set foot in Africa either. He died in London in 1940.

10

The Nya-Binghis

Nineteen thirty-five was a critical year for the growing Rasta movement. In his cell in St. Catherine's prison, Leonard Howell heard the distressing news that Italy, under the fascist dictator Benito Mussolini, had invaded Ethiopia on December 5, 1934. The Italians were eager for a strategic presence in Africa, and, in the wake of the invasion, looted religious artifacts and treasures were shipped back to Rome. Europe was now faced with a dilemma that would sear the consciousness of the West. Ethiopia was a member of the League of Nations, the predecessor of the United Nations, and had the nominal protection of other League members in case of military aggression. But the European powers were in a bind. If they took action against Mussolini in Ethiopia, Italy would formally ally itself with Adolf Hitler's Germany.

Until August 1935 the Ethiopian situation remained uncertain. Haile Selassie made his legendary stirring appeal before the League in Geneva to help him repel the Italians. There existed an overpowering temptation to abandon faraway Abyssinia to Mussolini's clutches in order to avoid another war in Europe. Selassie was advised to put himself under British protectorate, but this was not in Negus's nature. "I would be unworthy of my great ancestors, beginning with Solomon, if I submitted to Italian vassalage," he told George Bernard Shaw. "Nor can I, as sovereign of the oldest empire in the world, accept a British protectorate or an Anglo-French regime. We cannot cut Ethiopia like a cake, handing the frosted parts to this country and that just to win their smiles and satisfy their sweet tooth."[47]

That August, Ethiopia readied for war. The *Gleaner* reported Ethiopian women wanting to take up arms with their husbands. In jail Howell might have seen the *Gleaner* headline "The Emperor of Ethiopia, A Humble Monarch" over an article about Negus: "Haile Selassie's philosophy is that majesty and humility are linked, so he often travels miles on mule's back, visiting his subjects in their humble homes."

On August 5, the Rastas were delighted to see a prominent photograph of the Emperor in the *Gleaner,* but the news was bad and war now seemed unavoidable. Letters from BWIR war veterans asking to be sent to Ethiopia started to pour into the governor's office. Some came from as far as Honduras. "Owing to the fact that war is afoot between Italy and Ethiopia our mother country, we as negroes in Honduras think it is our duty to go there and die. Therefore we would like to know if there is any chance of us siding with those from Jamaica and other West Indian islands. Be quick with reply, for we are ready to jump. We don't want the last Italian to die before we get there."[48]

It would take six years and untold thousands of civilian victims before the aforementioned last Italian was finally expelled from Ethiopia, but Howell and his followers never doubted the issue. The Book of Revelation, after all, had already promised "these [the ten kings allied with The Beast] shall battle with the Lamb, and the Lamb shall overcome them: for he is the Lord of Lords, King of Kings. And they that are with him are called, and chosen, and faithful" (Revelation 17:14). And if their spirits did falter, the crucial article about the so-called Nya-Binghis came just in time to bolster and strengthen their faith.

On December 7, 1935, the *Jamaica Times* published the strangest of all of the founding Rasta documents. It had first appeared in a Vienna newspaper on August 17 and 24, 1934, under the byline of Italian journalist Frederico Philos, and was then reprinted in English by a Canadian journal, *Magazine Digest*. It was in fact crude Italian propaganda, supposedly revealing that an African secret society, the Nya-Binghis, had gathered an army of twenty million men under the high command of Haile Selassie with the goal of ridding the world of the white race.

> Up from the depths of the jungle and out of the heart of modern cities, from all parts of the African continent and from countries where colored people live, the blacks are flocking to a new organization which dwarfs all similar federations. . . . Its name, Nya-Binghi, means "Death to the Whites" or "Death to the Europeans." It sprang to life in the Belgian Congo. Angered by the penetration of white people into their territory, King Mocambo the Second and his nephew formed a dual alliance and swore bloody revenge on the intruders. At the time of its inauguration in 1923 it was insignificant, but since then it has become a menace to Europe.[49]

According to Philos, in 1930 a congress was organized in Moscow with eighty-two representatives. At the close of this conference,

> the negro Haile Selassie was unanimously given supreme powers in the Nya-Binghi. He accepted the position and swore to make war with the Europeans. . . . Haile Selassie is regarded as a veritable messiah, a savior to colored people everywhere, the Emperor of the Negro Kingdom. Whenever one mentions the word "Negus," the eyes of blacks gleam with mad fanaticism. They worship him as an idol. He is their god.

Who was this Philos? His name and preoccupation with Europeans in Egypt and Africa might be an indication of Alexandrian birth, or of Greek merchant origin. He was familiar with Selassie's regime, whose international politics, adoption of European customs, and use of foreign technicians he described with accuracy. But he also was aware of black nationalism in the West. He alluded to the "Ginger Jake" incident of 1930, reporting the following rumor: "Ku Klux Klan leaders in numerous American cities such as New York and Washington have been smitten with a strange disease. The illness is fatal. They could not determine its mysterious nature. Sam O. Wiking, the assistant chief of the Ku Klux Klan, was found dead in room 720 on the 26th floor of the Birmingham Hotel. Members of the Klan fled the country. Black hands had poisoned its members!"

Was there any unnatural number of Klan members among the victims of Jamaican Ginger? It is possible, since Ku Klux Klan recruits mostly came from the poorest section of the white population, people who tended to drown their frustrations in cheap alcohol. By presenting the poisoning as deliberate, the Klan offered itself as a victim and fed its core of festering paranoia. With the Nya-Binghis, racists had conjured the ideal suspect, mysterious and terrifying—a black secret society! Philos, who was apparently in contact with white racist circles in the United States, picked up the scaly rumor and waved it in the white world's face.

According to a modern writer in the American music magazine *The Beat*, the Nya-Binghi sect did once exist. It was a female secret society based in Rwanda-Urundi (today Uganda and northern Rwanda), a territory placed under the Belgian protectorate in 1923. The name was inspired by a legendary queen named Nayingi, "the queen with full hands."[50] But like many secret societies in modern Africa (such as the Mau Mau, or the mysterious group to which Fela Kuti's mother was rumored to belong), the Nya-Binghis supported the anticolonial struggle with traditional magic and potions. Poison was their weapon of choice, as it was the easiest and best way to terrify the whites. In 1928, the Belgians outlawed the Nya-Binghis;

after that, the organization remained underground until stories about it surfaced during the invasion of Ethiopia.

For the veteran Jamaican journalist Harley Neita, there appeared to be some linkage between Leonard Howell, Ginger Jake, and the Nya-Binghis. But there's little evidence to support this idea. Even if Howell and his friends had heard of this obscure secret society, they probably didn't have contact with it when visiting Matadi or other Congolese ports. They would have had to travel deep in the bush country, which seems unlikely. And if Howell did make "magic" potions in the States, there is no record of an arrest in connection with Ginger Jake. When the Nya-Binghis came to prominence in Jamaica, the only information that Howell could have possibly received was the Philos article—if he saw it at all. At best, the only useful information he received was a grudging confirmation of Ras Tafari's military and political power, which, to him, was conventional wisdom.

More importance was attributed to the Nya-Binghi story by other Rastas, like those in St. Thomas, or some that Howell's trial had inspired in Smith Village, a western Kingston ghetto pulsing with many spiritual sects, or those in Trench Pen, the new center for Pocomaniacs and other black cults. When Howell started preaching, there were men who agreed with him but stayed away because of his uncompromising personality. His trial gave a strong momentum to the movement, but Howell was not there to reap any benefit. He wanted the idea of Ras Tafari as the Black Messiah to become public opinion. Philos's article seemed to confirm this, and put it in relation to the apocalyptic news from Ethiopia. Suddenly, every Rasta in Jamaica wanted to join the Nya-Binghis.

And so began the first Rastafarian schism, only two years after its inception. The main difference between the Rastafaris and the Nya-Binghis stems from the fact that the "founding" text of the Nya-Binghis was virulent racist propaganda, written by a white man preying on white paranoia. There is a huge divide between the Black Redemption of the Garveyites and the race war that Philos fantasized. Garvey had, one must admit, denounced miscegenation

(*Philosophy and Opinions I*, page 16), but only as a struggle against the pernicious practice of "heightening" skin color by marriage—an instrument of human devaluation. But Garvey, by reevaluating the black image, restored to his people pride in their appearance and identity, and taught them that their fate was in their own hands. Philos's aim was malevolent. His goal was to persuade Europe to let Italy annex Ethiopia, so he invented an international plot among black Africans that described a racial hatred that Haile Selassie never shared—for the good reason that he considered himself white, as did most upper-class Ethiopians of his era. Howell spoke of love, Philos of hate. Howell spoke of rebirth, Philos spoke of death, claiming Nya-Binghi meant "death to whites." But the bitter irony is that this "hatred for whites," presented as a founding element by most white historians of the Rastafarians, is in itself the product of a European imagination. The logic is simplistic. "Isn't it normal that blacks hate us, considering how they suffered at our hands?" But Leonard Howell had no time for messages of hatred. One only hates what one fears. The Gong wasn't afraid of anything, least of all white people.

I remember, during my early visits to Jamaica in the 1970s, my embarrassment and hurt when some Nya-Binghi elders—embittered by lifetimes of oppression—took racist positions. Those stories of hatred and death were out of keeping with the human beauty of Rasta philosophy and the messages of love and redemption sung by Bob Marley and Burning Spear. Were not their messages of human dignity universal? Didn't they seek to show that racist theories, from whatever source, are wrong? But these prejudices were pernicious. Brown-skinned Rastas were barred from some Nya-Binghi celebrations because of their color. Two brothers would come to a meeting, one lighter than the other, and the lighter one would be asked to leave the yard. Intermarriage with whites was denounced as rank hypocrisy, but when they had the opportunity, the Nya-Binghis would marry blue-eyed American girls and disappear off to the States with them. But not all Nya-Binghis were racists. Some of their elders were my first teachers.

Like Bongo Puru. For years I called him "Granddad." He wore his long white dreadlocks tumbling down his back. One day in 1963 (if my memory is accurate), police tied his locks with a rope and then dragged him behind their truck. Then he was arrested with hundreds of other Rastas and imprisoned in a caged yard for days in the sun with no food or water. But Bongo Puru could never bring himself to hate whites. He tried in vain to reason with the police guards. "Why you do such a ting? We nuh human too?" Bongo Puru was an old gentleman with shriveled golden skin under immaculate white undershirts. His smile is ingrained in my memory. He died of a trifle, a simple cold complicated by malnutrition. He lived in a hut in Bull Bay and food was his only need, but a hard one to satisfy. When I learned about his death I felt somehow responsible. I should have been there to take care of him. My memory kept transporting me back to a quiet afternoon on the beach. Hot tropical sun, but we're sheltering in the shade of almond and tamarind trees waving in the sea breeze. When Bongo Puru finished his chalice of the holy herb, I asked him whether he had ever been to Africa. He first said no, but then he smiled toothlessly: "Well, I was there . . . in a vision!" And he started telling me of the magic moment when he found himself on a very narrow bridge leading to Africa, far above the abyss—"so narrow, it was just a simple tree trunk!" First he was afraid, and then he told himself that he had no reason to fear, and he walked straight home, back to Africa.

Symbolically, this is the history of all Rastas.

If the Nya-Binghis in Jamaica identified with a negative image of racial conflict, it is perhaps because they lived through a desperately troubled era. The mid-1930s were years of strife and hopelessness.

The effects of the Great Depression engendered explosive social conditions. In 1938 Jamaica would face bloody riots when trade unions demanded economic and political power. Howell was in jail, his followers persecuted, Ethiopia sacrificed to European political expedience. But Leonard Howell kept his cool. What was he up to in the depth of his cell? What was to come out of the chrysalis?

Gangunguru Maragh.

Leonard Howell transformed himself into a Hindu mystic.

11

The Hindu Legacy

Kingston, 1935. While Howell was still in jail, the Harding Commercial Printery published an Ethiopianist religious tract called *The Promised Key*. On the cover, under two crossed keys (a Masonic symbol), is the name of the pamphlet's putative patron, "Dr. Nnamdi Azikiwe, Editor of the African Morning Post, Accra, Gold Coast"—present-day Ghana. The work is credited to a "G. G. Maragh." The name Maragh is common among Jamaican East Indians. Mr. Ganga Maragh, a prominent businessman, had recently been a defendant in a well-publicized civil trial. His name made marijuana smokers laugh. In those days *ganja* was often spelled *ganga*.

The Promised Key comes, with little doubt, from the small group of "Ethiopians" in Kingston. Much of the text comes from Balintine, some verses come from the *Holy Piby*, and Annie Harvey probably contributed the description of Selassie's coronation. "G. G. Maragh" is Leonard Howell, Gong Maragh, the Tough King, publishing under an alias to avoid persecution. Did he compile his texts in jail? Was *The Promised Key* printed by one of his lieutenants to maintain a textual presence among his followers? Or did Howell publish it when he was released in 1936 and backdate it to protect himself? Released from prison, Howell assumed this new name, "Gangunguru Maragh,"—"Gong" for short. He was known by this name until the 1960s.

The choice of an Indian identity is significant. The Indian connection has been the most neglected of all the Rasta influences until it was documented in the 1980s by Laxmi and Ajai Mansingh of the University of the West Indies. Their historic work on Indian immigration in Jamaica, *Home Away from Home*, critically and convincingly restores important aspects of Rastafarian culture that later Afrocentric visions devalued or ignored.

They take us back to May 10, 1845, when Old Harbor citizens witnessed the arrival of the first shipload of indentured immigrants from India and their subsequent transfer to Halsie Hall, a sugar plantation in Clarendon. These laborers replaced emancipated African slaves who refused to work for their former masters. The *Falmouth Post* reported that the "coolies" "were not athletic, but active and wiry, and as good tempered and happy a set as were ever seen. The few negroes who were present at their landing seemed rather pleased, and mingled with them readily. . . . They were transported to allotted plantations by horse buggies, and greeted by the Afro-Jamaicans who often offered food and drink to them."[51]

Relations between "coolies" and Jamaicans never became antagonistic, and the limited number of women among the Indians expedited a quick absorption into the black population. As a child in Clarendon, Howell had contacts with this community. It is possible he, like many Jamaicans, copied their habit of smoking marijuana. *Ganja* is the Hindi/Urdu word for *cannabis sativa*, and it is generally accepted that successive waves of Indian immigrants introduced marijuana use to the island. Howell probably drank their sacred *bhang*, the refreshing ganja elixir. Above all he was probably most impressed by the power of Hindu culture, and by the strength they drew from daily contact with their gods.

At the end of the day's work on the plantation, the workers would retire to the barracks which were not far from those of the ex-slaves. After attending to personal and family chores, the "priest" among them would sit down with the children and adults and read the Ramayana and Puranic stories. Later the musicians would satisfy their urges by singing devotional and folk songs... Initially, these activities were restricted to Indians only, but as friendly neighborhood contact evolved with Afro-Jamaicans, the two cultures began to join in each other's rituals. . . . Almost at regular intervals, a few individuals in every Indian community would perform a "secret" Kali puja. Selected friends and relatives were invited to an unknown spot where a ram was sacrificed with a single stroke of a machete amid loud the chanting of mantras invoking the goddess Kali. After certain ceremonies which involved the smoking of ganja, the congregation would return to the home of the host, chanting and shouting "Jai Kali Mai!" Drinking of bhang (marijuana), smoking of ganja, hailing the goddess, and dancing and singing preceded the dinner of curried goat and bhat. Curious Afro-Jamaicans would always eavesdrop at a distance in hidden places. Some of them would join the festivities as guests.[52]

It is likely that Howell, the secretive child, the treetop observer, knew something of the Kali pujas. As a sailor, he met many Indian fellow workers. He later had children by an Indian woman and was an admirer of Mahatma Gandhi. He shared the Hindu fascination of his contemporaries. Hinduphilia had been a general trend in black America and the Caribbean for some time. In 1919–20, a Hindu revival under the flag of Kali took British Guyana by storm.[53] In New York, Indian medicine was highly rated by the black population. Occult books like *The Great Book of Magical Arts* and *Hindu Magic and Indian Occultism* were in vogue. A black dandy known as "Hindu" styled along the streets of Harlem in green satin pantaloons, golden slippers and a turban.

Meanwhile, in Jamaica, Howell absorbed teachings from the Indians. There were many in St. Thomas, and some reportedly came to him for healing. A big man called Laloo became his bodyguard and is said to have been responsible for the Hindi-Urdu part of Howell's prayers. But when Howell founded Pinnacle, Laloo did not follow him. Who was he? In 1934 in Seaforth, St. Thomas, one "Mrs. Laloo" was ridiculed in song to provoke the Rastas. But there were many Laloos, as it was a familiar Indian nickname for light-skinned people. Another coincidence: at the end of the nineteenth century an Indian-influenced Guyanese cult, the White Robed Army, had for leaders one Maraj and one Laloo.[54]

The Mansingh studies have enumerated Howell's innumerable borrowings from the Indians—his name Gangunguru Maragh (from *gyan*, knowledge; *guna*, virtue; *guru*, teacher; and *Maharadj*, King); his prayers' use of Hindi words; his concept of a God-King; the sacramental use of ganja, meditation, vegetarian cooking and spices, and even the holy salutation—"Jah! Rastafari!"

> One can hear the loud chants of Jai Bhagwan, Jai Rama, Jai Krishna, or Jai Kali (Victory to God/Rama/Krishna/Kali) at any private or community Hindu Pooja or prayer meeting. . . . As Ras Tafari gained the status of African Lord Rama/Krishna during the 1940s, phonetic usage of the word Jai was continued. But Rama, Krishna, and Kali were replaced by Ras Tafari. Searching the Old Testament . . . the Rastas found the word Jah, which is phonetically similar to the Hindi word Jai.[55]

Howell not only borrowed some exotic words and rituals from the Indians to feed the fancies of an illiterate audience, he also adopted a way of thinking. Indian thought—karma and rebirth—provided him with a system that resolved the western dichotomy of heaven and hell, Jesus and Satan, black and white, spirit and flesh. This different approach allowed Howell to recast the Rasta identity in a different mold, one both ancient and proven to work. Prisoners of the old dichotomy tried to turn an oppressive system around, to replace white supremacy with black supremacy—what Balintine called "the Anglo-Militant Upside-down Queen"—but Howell did not get caught in this reverse trap. In the Indian cosmology he found a third solution. Amid its innumerable lords and gods, the Hindu reality was cyclical. Nothing was "good" or "bad" forever. New causes brought new effects on a turn of the wheel of time. The flowing concepts of Indian thought allowed transformation from one state to another, from slave to king. This helped heal the injuries of slavery's Middle Passage, and reconciled black and white, God and man. Rama and Krishna were spiritual beings with perfect karma, kings who ruled their kingdoms with wisdom. The rituals, Mansingh says, had always aroused curiosity among black Jamaicans:

> The answer to every enquiry about Lord Rama or Krishna was that they were God incarnates, Kings of India. Weekly, if not daily exposure to services, music, dances, etc. in praise and honor of the God-incarnates-cum Kings of India resulted in the creation of a unique spiritual and emotional niche and vacuum among the forerunners of Rastafarians. Their minds searched and hearts craved an African potentate like Lord Rama or Krishna, just like Indian cricket fans wish for an Indian Michael Holden or Viv Richards.[56]

Joseph Hibbert, Howell's companion in St. Thomas, confirmed to Mansingh that "after learning about the Hindu God-incarnates Rama, Krishna, and Buddha, [Howell] was convinced that every nation had its own God—Jesus for the whites, Rama, Krishna, Buddha for the Indians, and someone in Africa (about whom he did not know) for the Africans." When Ras Tafari was crowned, Hibbert told Mansingh, Africans realized that "his title, given to him by the whole world, makes him a God, just like Ashoka, Buddha, Rama, Krishna . . ."[57]

After the coronation of Ras Tafari, Africans had a god-king and a promised land, but when would they be allowed to go there? Howell transformed Christ's verse—"My kingdom is not of this world"—into a more practical "My kingdom is not of this time." Things do change, and Selassie's coronation would be the dawn of a new age. Like the Indians, Ethiopians now had a king of their race to whom they could look for salvation, and a place in the world. "Jai! Ras Tafari . . ."

The Indian influence on Ras Tafari did not end with the foundation of Pinnacle. In Back O'Wall, the western Kingston ghetto that
became the main Rasta stronghold in the late 1950s, Indian elders
were shown the same respect as Africans. Exchanges ("reasonings")
took place around the "chalice," the water-cooled coconut-shell
ganja pipe. Dreadlocks, which some Rasta elders remember as
"zagavi" (from the Hindi *jatawi*) were possibly inspired by Indian
Saddhus, religious mendicants whose presence in Jamaica is confirmed by a 1910 photograph.[58] Some prefer to relate dreadlocks to
published photos of Selassie's tribal guards, the "Mountain Lions,"
or to Masai braids, but the Rastas' vegetarian diet likely has Hindi
origins as well, since traditional Indian dietary science holds that
ganja makes the body hypersensitive to toxins associated with alcohol and meat. Consequently, cannabis cultures like Indian and
Rastafari tend to avoid these.

Although the Indian influence was critical in its formative years,
Rastafari later erased much of it from communal memory. Howell
and his contemporaries were world travelers and looked for global
solutions. Ethiopia provided a spiritual nationality and a promised
land, but the first Rastas drew from the wisdom of many nations.
In later years, Afrocentrism prevailed among the Nya-Binghis, the
Emmanuelites (Bobos), and most of the small groups that formed
the Back-to-Africa Movement. These groups identified all strains
of beneficial and positive thought with Africa, and denied other
influences.

Howell had other reasons for his concerns with India. When he
learned about Mahatma Gandhi's struggle against British rule in
India, he became a fervent admirer and advocate of nonviolence,
according to his son Blade. In 1933, just before he went to jail, Howell probably read about Gandhi's positions that caste and color were
equivalent.[59] Howell understood, as did Gandhi, that the power of
the common people lies in their ability to refuse exploitation. When

a nation has no state to look to, no judicial protection, no army, it cannot attempt to "bring down Babylon" by force. The first thing is to establish an independent economic basis—the "green pasture" of Athlyi. This is what Howell was aiming for. But it was difficult to do from St. Catherine's prison.

At a bend in the shining green river, a bridge carries country folk from one bank to the other. Under the bridge the water is clear, and the small gravel beach makes a perfect swimming hole. A huge cotton tree growing there makes the wooden cabin beside it look like a doll's house. Cotton trees are mystical. It is said they come from Africa and harbor spirits; under them slaves would hold their secret ceremonies. They are also best for dugout canoes; their curious rocket-shaped roots and long straight trunks seem designed for forward motion. Beyond the shade of this cotton tree, ebony torsos shiny with sweat, two men work the dark soil of the valley bottom. I haven't seen Countryman in twenty years, and my memories are faint, except for his exceptional golden skin and glowing locks that blow in the wind. But the man walking up to me now, with his dark complexion and gray plaited hair, is definitely Country. Twenty years have passed since the movie that bears his name came out in 1982. He doesn't recognize me either.

Countryman is Indian with a tinge of African blood. His grandmother was born in India, near Bombay. She had three daughters. One day one of the girls was invited to a party on a ship. The mother, wanting to know what this party was about, went to see the organizer, a rich merchant woman. "Come with your daughter," cajoled the trader, "and bring your other children as well." So the mother went with the two daughters and a neighbor, all dressed up. In the middle of the party the boat set sail. Five weeks later the mother and three daughters disembarked in Jamaica, with dozens of other victims, and were placed as servants across the country. One of the girls ran away from Westmoreland and walked 150 miles to her mother in Kingston. The other married an Indian-African and they had a son—Countryman.

Country's journey to fame began one day in the late 1960s while hitchhiking on the north coast. He was picked up by Perry Henzell, a white Caribbean intellectual with sympathy for the Rastas. A promising young TV director, Henzell was a nonconformist who had spent most of his childhood on the Caymanas estate near Pinnacle, and he knew some of the first Rastas. He offered Country a ride to a hippie party at the home of Chris Blackwell, the white Jamaican who owned Island Records.

Country enjoyed a good time. He was at ease at the party, and made friends. Many years later, Island executive Dickie Jobson convinced his friend Chris Blackwell to finance a movie about various Jamaican intrigues around ganja, guns, and Rastas. Blackwell created Island Pictures and produced the movie. Dickie, brother of Bob Marley's longtime Kingston attorney, Diane Jobson, chose Country for the leading role. The film was entitled *Countryman*.

The screenplay was inspired by a youthful experience of Blackwell's. One day, cruising with some friends, Chris's boat ran aground near a beach where Rastas lived. Instead of the brutality commonly attributed to the Rastas (people said that "the Black Heart Men" tore the hearts out of children), he was surprised to find good people who rescued him, fed him, and took care of his stress with a smoke. This adventure was said to be the beginning of Blackwell's involvement with the Rastas. Bob Marley and Countryman, among many others, owe their careers in part to this experience.

Did Blackwell pay Countryman for the movie? Very little, some say. Country never had the means to leave his beach hut in Runaway Bay, and when he was finally evicted by developers, he roamed the country for a while with his family until Chris took pity on him and bought him a prefab house and a suburban lot. Others say Country got a big lump of money and blew it all. He's car-crazy, they said.

We swim in the river with Country and his grown son. The water is cold and clear. While the sun dries our skin on the gravel beach we eat Country's sweet oranges. I ask him about Leonard

Howell. The name is unfamiliar to him. "Gong? The first Rasta?" He's puzzled, but suddenly he brightens: "Ah—*Gonga!*" He was just a kid, but he remembers. Gonga was a great healer. He gave people all sorts of root juices and drinks, and cured their wounds. In those days many Indian plantation workers had sore leg ulcers from working irrigation jobs in the rice paddies and banana groves of St. Thomas. Howell would take them to Bath, a natural hot spring in the vicinity of Airy Castle and Port Morant, where he would wash their ulcers with the hot sulfurous water. (The hot spring in Bath is still very popular among Rastas. They go at night when no tourists are around, and the water beats the stress of Babylon out of their bodies.)

Gonga, Country continues, had a group of about sixty Indian followers who loved him. They called him Ganga Maragh, or Ganga. But when the churches learned what he was doing, they called out the police to stop him. The police found ganja and arrested him. This particular incident inspired Bob Marley to sing, "I am tougher than Gong," meaning that he was planting different seeds that would never die. According to Countryman, this is how Marley became known as Tough Gong. One of Gonga's best friends, Delahaie, was an Indian, but he ran when the police showed up. "Gonga!" Country laughs, "The police don't make him fret. Him never feel no way. Him was too strong in his head!"

The sun is disappearing behind the steep gully. Time to leave. I have some money to buy gas, so Countryman can take me home to Runaway Bay. But will we reach the pump with an empty tank? Country has a solution. Instead of going back up the main road we can ride downhill on the gravel back road. That way if we run out of gas, we can coast. After miles of bumps and ruts, we finally reach the coast road, safe.

By the time we reach Runaway Bay, night has fallen. Country left me at the Brownstown crossroads, so I walk the last miles in the dark. Compared to the lush vegetation and stony landscape of the hills, the coastal plain seems barren. Cars roar past me at a hundred miles an hour. Tourism has turned the narrow coastal road into a busy highway, and the night air carries the smell of exhaust mixed with the scent of jasmine. Big Japanese cars rush by in a hurry, air-conditioned bubbles vibrating with the brutal beat of the latest dance tune. Some young men sit on a roadside wall, killing time in the cool of the evening, and I feel their eyes on me, filled with dreams of sex and dollars. On a jukebox nearby Shabba Ranks is croaking, "I'm wicked in bed . . ."

Past the village, the road widens in front of Hotel Ambiance, a refuge for upscale tourism and always half empty. The thick lawn muffles my steps. White bungalows shine in the night. Silence. After a hundred yards the street lights end and I move into pitch blackness. Suddenly the grass is up to my shoulder and the moon disappears into a cloud. The only things that vaguely stand out are two pillars of a gate, half hidden in the dark mass of foliage. Entering the gate I follow a tiny white gravel path softly glowing in the grass. The track ends. The steps should be here. . . . This is the gate to David's empire.

At the top of the stairs a gust of wind showers me with the scent of iodine. The huge empty room is wide open at the other end. It allows the sea breeze in to softly caress you. At my back is Obia. It makes no sense to look at her. In the dark I feel her empty eye sockets on my back and my heart beats faster. Obia is one of David Marchand's murals, probably the most beautiful one he has ever painted. Magical. Some days I stand in front of it and it pulls me toward it like the little goddess at the bottom of an Egyptian sarcophagus, welcoming with open arms. The delicious, fragile arms of Obia under her veils and the wings and the strings and the talismans hanging all over her. On her head are two long antennae of shining red, gold, and green. Obia make you want to expire in her arms.

The old cane chair is still here facing the sea. My Jamaican friend David is sitting there with his back to me, his long elegant body molded to the curve in the cane. He turns to me, chuckling softly, and says, "I knew you were coming. I dreamt about you."

I sit on the step beside him. The jungle has reclaimed the property since I was last here, covered the walkways, cracked the concrete. Trees surround us with hushed restlessness. The sea is mixing several rhythm tracks—low, slow, and powerful rolls over the reef, crystalline waves crash on the beach. The moon reappears. A bat flies about our heads, and then plunges through the gaping windows (the fittings have been torn out).

"You haven't fixed the windows yet?"

Behind us the derelict villa looks at us with empty eyes. Moon rays penetrate the openings and reflect off old tiles against the dark. A firefly zigzags in the bush. On the hook where the lamp used to be, three bats are hanging asleep. "I told you I don't plan for the future," David says in response.

David asks if I like to dream. Dreaming, for him, is a sacred occupation. As soon as the sun sets, he lies down to dream. He sees legs that come out of the ground and cycle the big wheel of the sky. He sees the sun and the moon playing marbles, and hermaphrodite lizards. And he sees a comet falling into the sea. He has been waiting for the comet for many years. He's had the vision so many times, each time with so much clarity, that he knows the scene by heart. The horizon explodes, capsizes, and the sea turns to flame. "God is hunting us down. It will be the final flush."

12

From One Prison to Another

When Howell was freed from jail in the spring of 1936, the law thought the Ras Tafari movement had died. A police report declared

> The Ras Tafari sect is rapidly falling away; at the present time it is almost entirely destabilized. Followers have lost confidence in their leader; the result of this is that meetings are showing poor attendance. A collection has been taken up; it is on this that the leader subsists, but it is small. At the last meeting the collection amounted only to a sum of three and a half shillings. I do not think that the Ras Tafari threat need be seriously considered any longer.[60]

On March 31, 1936, an anonymous letter alerted the police that a Rasta gathering was planned for that very night. A few days later the same informer wrote again, reporting,

> on recent date they had a public demonstration with drums, fifes and emblems [banners]. This should serve as a revelation to the government to keep their eyes and ears open! In the streets [Rastas] preach sedition and assert that ere long Jamaica will have its own war. Negroes must rally to their colors and fight for their

rights. A black governor! A black colonial secretary! A black judge! A black inspector general, etc! If Britain has taken Africa from them, then Jamaica must be theirs, with the white men under them. . . .

Reacting to the letter, the head of the constabulary wrote to the colonial secretary that he felt certain "the white population of Jamaica have nothing whatsoever to fear. The only disturbances likely to occur will be because of rising unemployment and problems with the working class that feels unjustly treated."[61]

The chief of police was timidly echoing the bitter discontent of the Jamaican people, and warning the governor to consider whether or not he wanted to avoid the widely predicted civil unrest just over the horizon. Unemployment was still on the rise, and protest marches of the unemployed were becoming a common sight in Smith Village and other poor areas closer to the center of Kingston. After World War I, Europe had begun to produce its own sugar from beet crops, bringing the cane plantations, the legendary economic engine of the West Indies, to the brink of bankruptcy. With prices falling and layoffs pandemic, a large strike swept the St. Kitts plantations in 1935, and other islands followed suit—Barbados, Trinidad, St. Vincent, St. Lucie. In Jamaica the most vulnerable areas were, of course, planting parishes like St. Thomas. And this is where Howell—or Gangunguru Maragh—went back to work.

In jail Howell had had all the time he needed to develop new tactics. Since he was accused of disturbing the peace, he would no longer call public meetings. His sense of secrecy was stronger than ever. His reputation as a healer had begun to spread, and he made a habit of going to Bath. Miss L. remembers that he rented a cottage there to put up his clients and visitors. He probably did not use the regular hotel bath, but the natural spring farther up the gully, a favorite spot among Rastas today. He was reclaiming the old Baptist ideas of purifying the soul with water. ("Dip dem Bedward, dip dem in the healin' stream!") At the same time he used the sulfurous water to cleanse his undernourished followers' sores and aches. His fame as a bush doctor again began to circulate.

By Christmas he felt strong enough to call a big "Love Feast" just after the new year in St. Thomas, where he invited his adherents from Clarendon and Kingston. He made careful preparations at his tabernacle in Port Morant, erecting a tin fence around the yard so that only his Rasta people could enter. In front a string of big white shells spelled "King's House." On January 6, 1937, Rastas began streaming in by foot, donkey carts, and trucks. Each brought an offering: fruit, a chicken, a few coins. They entered the yard, where joyous hymns rang out in a bustling but peaceful atmosphere. The feast was planned for January 10. Three cows adorned with Rasta colors (again the Hindu influence) were to be led in a procession through town.

A reporter from the *Daily Gleaner*, probably invited by planter Ross and his gang to promote their cause, was in attendance, but what he observed left so much doubt in his mind that he felt compelled to present two contradictory versions of the same story to the public. Here is the first.

"Look at that truck full of Rastas." After this announcement there was a wild scramble of the curious and the idle to gain an advantageous position in order to check out the new arrivals. . . . Men, women, and children descended from the truck. Curious eyes followed them. They were mocking, disdainful eyes, and very angry eyes. A few stout lads eager for fracas and armed with switches and long sticks started towards Howell's devoted adherents. A nondescript-looking youth, bearded and whiskered in adherence with the Ras Tafari cult stepped from the vehicle. He was immediately accosted by the self-styled "vigilantes":

"A whay you come from?" This inquiry elicited no immediate response.

"Bway, you betta ansa."

Penned in on all sides and threatened, the youth lost his composure and began to stammer:

"A . . . come from . . . Clarendon."

"Clarendon!" came a mocking and amazed echo from a dozen voices. "Well, well, all the way from Clarendon. Bway, you bring anything for the ambassador [Howell]?"

"Yes," he replied rather diffidently.

"What? Speak up bway!"

"A foul." He blurted this out.

"Oh" said the chorus. The scared boy from Clarendon reluctantly surrendered a tired looking bird.

"Now bway," continued his interrogator mercilessly, "what you get from Howell? Anything? What he give you?"

"Him promise . . ."

"Neber mind what him promise, is what you get. WHAT YOU GET?"

"Nothing."

"Exactly. So you damn foolish enough to give him something for nothing . . ."

"Yes . . ."

"Well bway, Babylon is taking charge . . . Move . . . Give him the baton, boys . . . on with the lash."

The Clarendonian started to retreat. They pounced on him, lit his beard on fire, yanked at his whiskers, and kicked and poked him amidst loud laughter and noise.

A band of nearly a hundred proceeded to tear down "King's House."

A seething, heated, and determined conglomerate of men, women, and children. After that they moved on to the house of the ambassador. And god help the luckless "brother" or "sister" that was encountered on the way. It was wonderful, the marvelous intuition of the "vigilantes" in cases when a member bore no evidence of his connection with the Salvation Union, as they also called the cult . . . At the approach of the ever increasing mob, the Ras Tafarites took to their heels, those who were exceptionally fast gained refuge in the King's House.[62]

The reporter then claimed that the police, with help from the neighboring stations of Yallas, Morant Bay, Bath, and Golden Grove (all towns where Howell was feared), took charge of the situation "with great tact and diplomacy . . . circumventing the desire of the angry mob." After it dismantled the iron fence surrounding Howell's home, the mob entered the yard, pulled down the Lion of Judah banners, and abused and beat all they found. One brother surrendered and collapsed under the mob's violence. He begged for mercy. "I am a cripple!" The police, under Chief Constable Walters, again intervened.

The reporter has no problem relating how the mob could, under the benevolent eye of a full squad of constables, tear down the place and beat up the Rastafarians. When the mob had finished trashing and looting the Rastas' food, they demanded Leonard Howell's blood. Inspector Walters again intervened. "Enter the house," he warned them, "and as much as I should regret it, I will arrest you." Instead, he went into the house. When he didn't find Howell, he ordered the mob to disperse.

The next day, Howell turned up at the *Gleaner*'s headquarters in Kingston and insisted on giving his own account of the attack, which the newspaper published in its next issue.

Preparing to celebrate Ethiopian Christmas on January 7, Howell related, they had fenced their yard with zinc sheeting.

They were making uniforms for the ladies and gentlemen of the Ras Tafari faith and setting off firecrackers when the police inspector and a batch of men entered and read a warrant saying that they wanted to search for firearms. They searched, found none, and went away. At eight o'clock on Saturday January 9, about 500 Ras Tafarites and friends were at headquarters. The Ras Tafarites came for their uniforms. A crowd gathered outside headquarters and by 9:30 were throwing stones at us in full swing. The police inspector and his men were in the yard while the stones were being thrown by the crowd, but he did not demand that they stop. The crowd began to tear down the zinc fence and did not stop until they had demolished the whole thing. The police then left but returned shortly afterwards with more men and a lot of civilians armed with sticks, and began to beat the Ras Tafarians unmercifully. They ran in all directions. Those who were in the house ran outside when the police entered. I was in the house and they surrounded me. Many of my people were injured, but the police made no arrests because they took part in the floggings.

Howell described locking himself in a room, how he saw a policeman kicking down the door to the kitchen, and giving away food to the civilians. "What about my fifteen chickens, my 40 quarts of coconut oil, my 200 pounds of rice, and 480 odd enamel plates which were taken away in the presence of the inspector of police? . . . He told me that if I did not get out of the house immediately the people would set fire to it. They wanted me to get out of the parish. . . ."

Howell insistently stressed that the whole matter was started by the police and their "lads." "If the offensive was mounted by the civilians, as some people contest, why did the inspector not order them to stop? Why were no arrests made among civilians?"

Which version was true? The *Daily Gleaner* left the reader to decide. But in a trial two years later, a Sergeant Samuels of the Spanish Town constabulary innocently stated under oath, "I remember while in St. Thomas that I accompanied Inspector Walters to Howell's camp—and helped him to smash it."[63]

When he returned to Kingston on Monday, Gong Howell found the police watching his house. The pressure was on. They *had* to get him now. But this time they wouldn't give him a showcase trial. Within a year, while Jamaica was rocked by unprecedented labor strikes, they certified Howell insane and locked him up in a lunatic asylum.

A stairway to heaven, a pretty curving flight of pink brick leading nowhere, this was all that was left of the Bournemouth nightclub, just beyond the gardens of the psychiatric hospital. At the end of the 1970s, we would go there and smoke a spliff while watching the bay turn purple, exchanging news. My friend Sheppie told how the police had made another raid on his ghetto, firing at anything that moved, killing one of his brethren. On our left the long wall of zinc came down from Windward Road leading to the seashore. It served as a buffer for the ghetto, with emergency exits cut in the sheeting so the inhabitants could escape to safety during raids. Bellevue Hospital's park had become so dangerous that even the beautiful tamarind-lined pathways were deserted, and the big seed pods crackled under our feet. We caught sight of a man in rags sitting upright at the edge of the water, Zen-style, his handsome slender face turned up to the sun. He sat there every day, meditating. An inmate, a "nut." But who is really crazy in Babylon?

For decades Bellevue Psychiatric Hospital was used to warehouse the rebels and the head cases—people who freaked out under pressure from the system. In times of crisis they were jammed in the wards like livestock. A report at the end of the 1920s explained that most of the inmates were affected by job loss, general depression, "and other natural causes." Conditions in the overcrowded hospital were inhuman. In 1937, just before Howell's arrest, one Robert Lynsaigh sued the hospital superintendent, igniting a limited public debate. But the dozens of rebels and thinkers and ghetto "saints" locked away in Bellevue gave the place an aura of tattered glory. Bedward spent the last ten years of his life there. Howell was there at least twice, in 1938 and then again in 1960. During the 1960s and '70s several important reggae musicians had been there—singer Junior Byles, producer Lee "Scratch" Perry, and, most famously, the legendary Don Drummond. The premier trombonist in Jamaica, the composer of many cryptic and haunted melodies, Drummond spent two years in high-security N dormitory for killing his wife. He died there in 1966, allegedly with some help from the brutal guards. Howell also would have been in N dormitory.

The timing here is crucial. Howell came to Bellevue on February 15, 1938. Under what pretext did they lock him up? His disciples tell such a curious story that I thought I must have misunderstood. But when I asked again, they repeated that Mr. Howell climbed an electric pole and cut the wire with his fountain pen. Then he took the ends of the live wire in both his hands and the current went through him. It is no use asking what he was doing at the top of an electric pole with a fountain pen. That he lived was considered miraculous by the Rastas. The police, who didn't care about miracles, arrested Howell and put him in a psychiatric hospital, hoping they would never see him again. When Howell's wife Tyneth came, they would not let her see him. She came back the next day—probably with someone to help her—and was told reluctantly that now she could see him, but that he had gone into a coma. As soon as he heard Tyneth's voice, the supposedly comatose Howell "jumped up like a devil," sending the nurses running in frenzy.

This is a famous anecdote among Howellites. But this last portion of the story was no miracle. Howell was wisely playing dead in order to avoid the hospital's crackpot psychiatric procedures—electroshock and sedation. Ex-inmates testified that the sedation injections they received made them so sick for three days that they wanted to die. If you were not already crazy before, you had a good chance of being so after. (David Marchand has nightmarish memories of these injections.) By pretending to be unconscious until his wife arrived, Howell escaped the injections but not the confinement. After a while, though, his good behavior gave him access to the garden, and soon he was preaching again on Windward Road. Tyneth took a flat at Seabreeze Avenue, five minutes from the hospital, and came every day to see him, bringing what mail and newspapers the authorities allowed Howell to see.

Government intelligence agents were now watching Howell, and all of his mail was checked for "seditious" literature like *The Negro Worker*, the bulletin of the Red International of Labor Unions. Its editor was a Trinidad-born journalist named George Padmore, whom Howell met while abroad (as confirmed by a letter addressed to him in the Archives). Although wary of politicians, the Gong kept in touch with Marxist struggles, and in Bellevue he had lots of time to ruminate over their arguments. "We must combat," Padmore wrote, "the influence of the church . . . and the bourgeois and petit-bourgeois ideas and movements such as Garveyism, etc., who distract the negro workers from the anti-imperialist and anti-capitalist struggle at the side of the international working class."[64]

Howell would have shared the Marxist animosity for these "objective allies" of the establishment—the churches and a good portion of the Jamaican UNIA—but nothing proves that he adopted their conclusions. As Jamaica's nascent labor unions began to flex their muscles, the simple fact that he subscribed to *The Negro Worker* made him suspect, and for good reason. On January 5, 1938, a big labor strike began at Serge Island, a plantation between Seaforth and Trinityville, right in the middle of Howell's preaching territory, with an angry march by fifteen hundred workers armed with machetes and sticks. The Serge Island strike began a campaign of union actions that rolled through Jamaica like a social hurricane in 1938 and subsequently transformed the old colonial system. Only five weeks later (February 15), Leonard Howell was sent to Bellevue, leaving not much doubt about the reason for his confinement. He was considered one of the reasons for the unrest.

Nineteen thirty-eight was a critical nexus in Jamaican history. Did Howell and the Rastas play any role in it? Ken Post, a Marxist writer, claims that they did not.[65] But his research was based on the published literature and does not account for the actual facts that triggered the Serge Island strike and Howell's involvement in it. When scrutinized, the "fountain pen miracle" doesn't stand up. Was Howell trying to hook up a private electric line, as many ghetto dwellers do? But then he would have gone to jail. And Ken Post ignores the fact that for years the Rastas had been preaching in the area and preparing for a spiritual revolution. The fiery union bosses of 1938 were, like Howell, soapbox orators. In 1938, the labor unions began to morph into powerful political parties, which in turn gave birth to modern Jamaica, dragging the island amid gunfire and bloodshed into the twentieth century.

13

Bloody '38

Nineteen thirty-eight promised to be a tumultuous year from the start. The Serge Island strike was joined by dockers in Kingston; workers all over Jamaica shared their concerns. With Europe on the brink of war, prices of staples like flour and cooking oil were sky high. J. A. G. Smith, the great lawyer and politician, was leading fierce political attacks on the colonial government, which answered by tightening up "security." On Sunday evenings anxious crowds leaving church would gather, discussing unemployment, dockers' and cane workers' salaries, ghetto conditions, war veterans' pensions. Orators perched on ladders, barrels, and soap boxes, drawing crowds on every major street corner. One speaker thought this undignified and built a big platform, which he usually raised at the corner of Love Lane and the Parade, Kingston's main public square. Black skinned with strong features, he had "broad shoulders and the physical strength of a docker or soldier." His shaved head was dominant, and he wore a row of war medals on his uniform. He spoke out in a high-pitched voice, inviting anyone with something to say up to his platform. His name was St. William Grant, and this square where he once preached bears his name today.

St. William Wellington Grant belonged to Howell's generation. Born in Saint Andrew in 1894, he boasted pure African ancestry. Like Howell, "he reached Harlem, N.Y., after a stint in World War One (he had to stow away on an outgoing troopship to join)";[66] but Grant actually went to the front and fought courageously. Like Howell and Athlyi, he was in New York to witness the glory of Garvey in the 1920s. He joined the UNIA, spoke at meetings, cooked for the delegates to the conventions and for the poor in Harlem, and became an officer in Garvey's organization. In 1934, he went back to Jamaica to attend the UNIA convention—the year when the delegates attacked the Rastas. Grant also had disputes with Garvey, but he never left this great organization, even when he was selling fried fish and corncakes on street corners for a living. He was one of the first public speakers in Jamaica to condemn the invasion of Ethiopia in 1935, but he didn't make headlines until 1937.

Speaking in Kingston one evening, he saw a white Jamaican friend from his Harlem days in the crowd and called him up on the platform. The man was about fifty, well-dressed, and spoke in a powerful, high-pitched voice. The white man was booed by the crowd until Grant got down from the platform and grabbed the most disputatious offender by the neck. "He's not white," Grant said. "Him a brown man." At last the man was able to speak. He was Alexander Clarke, alias Alexander Bustamante, and this speech would lead to a political career that climaxed twenty-four years later when he became the first Prime Minister of an independent Jamaica.

William Alexander Clarke was born in 1884 into a family of planters who "passed" for white. His grandparents resented his father marrying a dark-skinned girl from the country and expelled him from the great house. The young couple built a cabin with a thatched roof, where their baby was born. To an American journalist who asked condescendingly about this thatched hut legend, Bustamante retorted, "Oh no, it wasn't me! That was your own President Lincoln. I was born . . . in a manger!"

The family's cruel rejection of his black mother helped determine this future leader's life. Bustamante loved his people. Sometimes this love served him more than it served others, but it was sincere.

At nineteen, Bustamante went to Cuba, where he was employed at a tramway company and rated a "good organizer." After three years the company sent him to Panama, where he married an English widow. In 1920, back in Cuba, he worked with the secret police. Between 1932 and 1934, he worked in New York as a dietician in a hospital—another self-appointed doctor. He went back to Jamaica in 1934, two years after Howell, and established himself as a pawnbroker. He soon made himself conspicuous by writing numerous and unusually articulate letters to the *Gleaner*, advocating the causes of workers, women, elders, strikers, and other marginalized groups. He began rewriting his personal history, claiming that he had been adopted by a Spaniard, fought in Morocco, and studied medicine. In 1936, reckoning that the loan business didn't fit his ambitions, he decided to go into politics.

He contacted one of Jamaica's first trade union leaders, A. G. S. Coombs, and offered to lend money to his union and drive him around in his personal car. In exchange he wanted only the union's presidency. Coombs accepted, but his Marxist lieutenants objected to putting a white moneylender at the head of a black union. Bustamante still made the rounds of labor and political rallies at Coombs's side, and he used this opportunity to make himself known throughout Jamaica. It didn't take long after the 1938 troubles began for Bustamante to position himself as the striker's advocate and spokesman.

Then the situation turned deadly on the great sugar plantations in Westmoreland. On May 2, 1938, four workers were shot dead and eight wounded on the Frome plantation, owned by Tate & Lyle. That next night an angry crowd of three thousand around Grant's platform began attacking journalists, and Grant had to come to their rescue. Under popular escort he took them to the Dungle, one of Jamaica's worst ghettos, so that the writers could see for themselves the inhuman conditions in which people were living.

All across Jamaica new strikes developed. At the Kingston docks, Grant again invited Bustamante to speak. While they were haranguing the dockers, a crowd rampaged through the streets, forcing Lebanese and Chinese shop owners to close. Until then both leaders had been protected by their aura and reputation. One was from the planting class, and the other was a decorated war veteran. At one tense confrontation between strikers and armed police, Grant was ever defiant. "Let them fire," he told Bustamante. "Better to die than live like dogs."

On May 23, a state of emergency was declared. Grant was arrested and beaten by the police, his famous skull all cut up. "Don't you dare touch me!" shouted Bustamante, when the police rushed to grab him. But arresting the labor bosses didn't help. The strike went on, and Jamaica was in turmoil. Who would come up with the solution? It was at this moment that a young lawyer named Norman Washington Manley crossed the threshold of Jamaican history.

Like Bustamante, who was his first cousin, Manley was a "high color" bourgeois. Unlike Bustamante, Manley was an intellectual. He enlisted as the strikers' counsel and—less confrontational than his fiery relative—actually obtained a wage raise from the government for the dockers, who still refused to go back to work until Grant and Bustamante were free. The two leaders were let out of jail on June 19, 1938, and immediately founded the first great Jamaican union, the Bustamante Industrial Trade Union (BITU). Embarking on his historic destiny as a Jamaican national hero, Bustamante assumed control, a pistol on his hip. Grant was shouldered aside and only given an honorific position as a street organizer. The two light-skinned cousins, Bustamante and Manley, shared Jamaica's political spoils for decades, while Grant—black nationalist, learned Garveyite and Afro-historian, cook and prophet—ended his life as a night watchman in 1977.

Many of Leonard Howell's character traits can be compared to Grant's—the energy, the physical strength, the love for Ethiopia and the Jamaican people. Like Grant, Howell understood that "before you can educate the people, you must be able to capture their attention." He also wore striking outfits and uniforms. But Howell, who was watching the 1938 revolution from behind the bars of Bellevue, did not want to commit Grant's error of putting himself at the mercy of politicians. As soon as he was out of the hospital, he had to carve out a kingdom for himself, a place far away from Babylon. The Promised Land, here and now! But how could he buy land? He had hidden away some fine pearls that he could sell, but he couldn't find a suitable buyer in impoverished Jamaica. So he wrote George Padmore a confidential letter asking him to sell the pearls in London. This letter was intercepted by Scotland Yard and ended up in the colonial secretary's files. Howell's wife Tyneth, who took care of his mail from her little flat on Seabreeze Avenue, discovered this through the International African Service Bureau, who confirmed that they had sent books to Howell's address that never arrived. The Gong told her not to worry, he would soon be out and able to take care of business himself.

14

Pinnacle

During the 1990s, on my visits to Jamaica I would rent a room at the back of an auto body shop on Kensington Road, just across from Bellevue Hospital. In front of the gate, young men perched on the rusted hulks of big American cars and played cards. Inside the yard, workers moved among piles of old jukeboxes, dead machines, and cars. Amid the scrap and junk you could still see the beautiful carved wooden veranda of an old colonial mansion. But the neighborhood had declined, and the place had been turned first into a seedy nightclub, then a brothel. It eventually became a warren of rooms and workshops creaking under a rusty tin roof.

Mr. Winston Chang was the prince of this dusty lair. A cellular phone attached to the belt of his trousers, wood dust sprinkled over his black cloth slippers, he directed the work of two dozen employees. Most of them were local youths, for whom Chang's place served as a safe enclave amid the senseless hell of its ghetto surroundings. For lunch, an Afro-Chinese lady cooked an enormous pot of rice and beans, which she mixed with a delicious oxtail stew. Even if the youngsters burned away their salaries on ganja and games, they still had something hot to eat. This lunch kept the employees working.

Work appeared to be the local religion. Mr. Chang would occasionally get angry and shower his employees with insults, but they bore his tirades in good humor, knowing that the storm would pass. It was comical to hear the Chinese gentleman indulging in the most obscene Jamaican patois; never would a white man dare to speak like that to a black man in modern Jamaica. Never, for that matter, would a white live anywhere near this eastern ghetto. But Mr. Chang was a Jamaican-Chinese, and his soul was deeply Jamaican. "The Chinese got on well with the blacks," Perry Henzell told me. "They managed to work together like whites and blacks could never have done."[67]

When Leonard Howell got out of the psychiatric hospital, he managed to get help from a Chinese merchant whose name was also Chang. Albert Chang was born in 1891 in Hong Kong and worked for the Kwan Tung railways and then for a construction company before immigrating to Jamaica in 1913. In 1916 he opened a grocery store in Bog Walk, just beneath Pinnacle in the Rio Cobre gully. He later moved to 49 Princess Street in Kingston. When Howell got out of the hospital, Chang was the proprietor of a big grocery store at 96 King Street. It was directly across the street at 75 King Street that Gong opened his first office. Albert Chang is remembered as a pioneer and a philanthropist. He opened the first supermarket in Jamaica and was elected chairman of the Chinese Benevolent Society. He helped start the Chinese Athletic Club and was a prominent member of the Chamber of Commerce and the Imperial Association. The reasons for his association with Leonard Howell are unclear. They did share experience in traveling and a concern for social welfare, but little else is known. Winston Chang, my landlord, denied any relation. In Crossroads, where Albert's heirs still manage a supermarket, I was confronted by a wall of indifference.

But there is no doubt that in 1939 an agreement was reached between the Chinese businessman and the black preacher. Gong Maragh always had good relations with his Asian compatriots. It is unclear as to how relations between the two men evolved. In any

event, it was the Chinese businessman who gave Howell the chance
to realize his dreams.

In 1939, when he got out of Bellevue, Gong went back to St.
Thomas. By then the trade union movement was in full swing. On
January 23, Bustamante had legally registered the BITU. On February 10, he attempted to launch a general strike, but the governor
answered by declaring a state of emergency. Again Bustamante had
to rely on his cousin Norman Manley to get him out of a sticky situation. Manley persuaded the governor to recognize a new federation of unions that would incorporate the BITU. This federation,
the Trade Union Congress, would alleviate the necessity for a state
of emergency. Gradually, life on the island went back to normal, but
the police were still watching.

Howell arrived in St. Thomas during this state of emergency.
On December 3, 1939, the police reported him preaching in Port
Morant; on January 7, he was in Chapel Hill. But the next meeting,
planned for February 11, 1940, was banned by police because of
rumors that only armed men were invited. The intelligence service,
still shocked by the unexpected militancy of 1938, saw communism
as a threat—and with some reason. England entered the war, and
Russia was still on Hitler's side. The government decided to finish
off the Rastafarians. All their meetings were prohibited.

But it didn't matter, for the Rastafarians had their Promised
Land at last. On January 7, 1940, on the day of Ethiopian Christmas, Howell announced to a gathering of some five hundred people that a large estate would soon be at their disposal.

The land register shows that on April 25, 1939, Albert Chang
bought Pinnacle, an abandoned estate above Bog Walk, the area in
which he established his first grocery. What were the businessman's
intentions? Pinnacle only had water for a few months a year. It was
a highland wilderness with few fertile areas and no road. The estate

was too far from Spanish Town to make a practical housing enterprise. With the exception of fruit trees, bat manure, and an abundance of gravel, Pinnacle had little to offer. Was it the price of £900, a fantastic deal for 153 acres? Was he aware of the lack of a water source? Surely Albert Chang, one of the brightest businessmen of his generation, had done his research. There had to be a good reason why he bought Pinnacle.

The truth was that he already had a buyer. For £1200, at a forty percent profit to Chang himself, Leonard Howell bought Pinnacle to resurrect his dream.

Members of the family state that Howell gave Chang a down payment of £800. His father had died in 1935 and Leonard, like each of his eight brothers and sisters, had a share of the ancestral land. According to his nephew, he sold it. Perhaps he found a buyer for his pearls after all. Maybe his followers helped with contributions. He told a journalist in 1941 that Pinnacle was not his, but belonged to all the members of their cooperative, the Ethiopian Salvation Society.

Chang wasn't taking a big risk with the purchase of the land. As long as Howell didn't pay him the remaining £400, Chang held the deed. If things turned bad, he would keep the estate and the down payment. If things went well, he would pocket £300 and would also be the sole provider of goods for the community settlement. He knew it could be a profitable enterprise. His store most likely provided the 480 enamel plates and 200 pounds of rice stolen by the mob in Port Morant. The Rastafarians could provide him with fresh produce—mostly yams and fruit. Like my landlord Winston, Albert Chang hoped to put the Rasta community to work for profit. This was exactly Howell's plan; he wanted Pinnacle to be a utopian example of collective self-determination and hard work.

News of Pinnacle spread like a jungle telegram. Rastafarians rushed to the Sligoville hills. The land seemed totally barren. There were no huts, and only a trickle of water. But they were thrilled. No more taxes. No land tenure. No police. No crooked politicians. No hateful neighbors to su-su pon you! Overnight thatched huts sprang up, and people started cultivating the land. Luckily it was spring and the brook was still running. While corn sprouted, Rastafarians burned charcoal and sold it in town. A tannery sprang up. A cobbler began working at the entrance of Pinnacle, and ran his little enterprise there for many years. He never actually became a member of the sect, but he provided many of its members with strong sandals made of rawhide and tire rubber—the famous "power shoes" that Pinnacle veterans still remember.

Families poured in from Clarendon and St. Thomas, mainly women and their children. They sold their possessions and put themselves under the protection of the leader. For a long time women outnumbered men at Pinnacle, and many bachelors were asked to join. "When you go there, Gong Howell gives you a woman. But you have to work for him!" At first everyone was in high spirits. John Carradine, a reporter from the *Gleaner*, came to visit and subsequently published an enthusiastic account of his experience. It was a perceptive, unbiased piece of journalism published on November 23, 1940, one of the deepest and liveliest portraits we have of Howell. The double-page article takes the reader on a tour of Howell's kingdom, through the villages of wattle and thatch cottages, among workers of all trades. "Men in the fields with cutlasses weeding, women attending to their household duties, shoemakers plying their awls, carpenters sharpening their tools, men preparing to burn coal." The dining room was "very commodious." There were two huts built apart from the rest to quarantine one patient with yaws and one with tuberculosis. The community had its own doctor, A. Phillips from Kingston. Children were fed and clothes provided to members of the community.

Carradine then follows Howell up a rocky road to Pinnacle's summit. There, sitting "on the ruins of an old house which legend says was once owned by Sir John Peter Grant, a former governor of Jamaica," Howell explained his vision. "The Rastafarians are not essentially a religious sect," Carradine reports.

They are rather an economic community. In fact, they struck me as extremely irreligious. It was my intention to go up to Pinnacle in the afternoon and stay for one of their ceremonies or prayer meetings. When I brought this matter up with the leader, I was greeted with loud laughter. "We have no form of worship here. There is no minister. As for those people who baptise and so on, I personally have nothing to do with them. We are not religious fanatics. All we want," he said, growing vehement, "is cush, cush, cush." But wait, I thought to myself. Did they not regard Selassie as the son of God? "We all believe that Haile Selassie, as King of Kings and Lord of Lords, shall in time take up his righteous reign for the people of Israel, wherein all oppressors shall melt into the ocean of forgetfulness where they can be seen no more . . ." But he didn't mention anything about how this was to be achieved. "We shall serve Haile Selassie to the end, and all clear-thinking men and women, regardless of color and creed, should do likewise."

Ras Tafarians believe that Haile Selassie was a minion of God. But apart from that belief, they were not enjoined to live in any specifically religious way or follow any moral code apart from obeying the laws of the land. Their moral lives were to be handled individually—there was no prescription. Howell has witnessed the eruption of war and had been much impressed by the government appeal for greater food production efforts. He and his followers believed that very hard times were ahead. Many would suffer while the King of Kings conquered the earth. If they should live to see that day, they must plant and store what they reap. Pinnacle would be a place of safety.

Carradine was impressed by Howell's achievements. But in his analysis he also ventured to take a good look at the man behind the force.

When the men see Gong they stand erect and resume their labors. We wanted a picture and we saw some men sitting around. . . .

Addressing one of the number, Howell ordered in certainly not respectful tones, "Put those loafers to work!" and the men humbly scrambled to their feet and did as they were ordered.

There was too obviously one voice at Pinnacle, and that voice was Howell's. All the people, big and little, old and young, called the leader "Gong." He confided to me that he did not like to be addressed "Sir" or "Mr.," so he dispensed with such formalities among his flock. But there the leveling process seemed to end; no one was allowed to forget who was the boss there.

Carradine concluded his report with a question. "But the lover of Democracy will, after a visit to Pinnacle, say, 'Long Live Democracy'; for loss of personal freedom is a very inevitable and necessary evil, the sine qua non of advanced socialistic states. The man himself must receive our admiration; for his initiative, his strength of will, his ability. Further we must not delve into his character. His people? Should we condemn or praise? Suppose we leave it to time."[68]

Summer came and the brook dried up. Pinnacle's residents had to trek down to the Rio Cobre, two kilometers below the village, to wash and "catch" water. News of Pinnacle had spread, and crowds of destitute, downtrodden people were streaming in. When food ran short, Howell had to find supplies while waiting for the crops. Every day, twenty cooks prepared oatmeal for hundreds. Stocks began to diminish. Epidemics spread. In November alone nineteen members of Pinnacle arrived at the Spanish Town hospital. Eight died and the others were sent to the poorhouse. Malnutrition, anemia, tuberculosis, foot ulcers, and neuritis could all be fatal at Pinnacle.

In January 1941, health inspectors went to Pinnacle and concluded that it presented "unsatisfactory conditions: the shacks were not weatherproof; the rough beds were made of sticks with no mattresses and scant, filthy bedding; the latrine accommodation was entirely inadequate, and the water had to be brought from some distance away." One would think that health inspectors intended to improve the well-being of these impoverished, starved people. Instead they tried to stamp out and destroy what they described as a primitive jungle camp. The assistant director of medical services "advised the clerk to instruct the Chief Sanitary Inspector to make another visit to Pinnacle. There he will tell the owner that he must service the construction of many latrines. This will be the first step in getting him to abandon the camp. I also suggest that systematic inspection and inquiry should be undertaken to identify the causes of the Pinnacle illnesses. This would help weaken the leader's grip on his inmates."[69]

The winter of 1941 was wet and difficult. But the Rastas did not give up. Planting time was nearing again, and the first crops began to flourish. But then relations with the neighbors deteriorated after several incidents, Howell recalled, when "undesirables had seeped in. These incidents involved campers who left at night and stole from the neighbors who promptly stigmatized the whole camp." So he flogged them and expelled them from Pinnacle. But some illiterate residents took literally the idea of Ras Tafari as Earth's Rightful Ruler, and they trespassed beyond the boundaries of Pinnacle.

But what were the boundaries? The vast expanse of hills had only vague landmarks. A hundred and fifty acres is a lot of land. When Howell bought it he was told—and subsequently told his followers—that Pinnacle went "from the top of the hills to seaside." Maybe this was true in the days when Pinnacle was a Crown property, with a great house for the overseers. But when it was sold in 1932, the most habitable areas were subdivided for settlements like Spencer's Pen and Tredegar Park. What was left of the original Pinnacle was the most rugged part, roamed only by herds of goats and charcoal burners, who were tolerated because they cleared the land. A group of charcoal burners had worked freely at Pinnacle, but when the Rastafarians came there was trouble. Charcoal was one of the few ways of making cash. Every time they discovered charcoal burning on their territory, Howell's men would wait for days and then raid the campfires and confiscate the charcoal.

Two men from Gordon Pen, Jeremiah Simpson and Nathanial Osborn, had been treated this way, and they went to ask Howell to pay them compensation. Howell came down on his horse surrounded by a crowd carrying sticks. The two charcoal burners were beaten. The eldest had to be admitted to the hospital. The police finally had an excuse to crush Pinnacle. These were the events leading up to the first raid of 1941.

15

Life in the Hills

At four o'clock in the morning I wake from a dream to the familiar sound of the ironing board being set up on the other side of the cottage. The iron is being heated on a small butane burner. Soon a hand will grab the hot handle in a rag and the smell of hot cloth will float through the door. The khakis are being pressed. Sharon has three boys; every day she hand washes and presses all three khaki school uniforms. While the creeping dawn slowly reveals the shapes of the sleeping boys, arms and legs across the double bed, Sharon sings her favorite hymn. "Though my boat may be rocking and my sail may be torn, he holds me in his arms so safe and warm. Here I find peace in the eye of the storm." She displays a particular energy in the chorus. "He holds me in his arms, so safe and so warm . . ." and I curl up under my sheet, wondering about Sharon's divine lover until she calls to me, "You wake up yet? You can press the khakis for me please? I going to cook water and make tea, and after we go wash."

It's daylight now, and Sharon blows out the kerosene lamp. Behind the cottage I hear the big drum can being opened and water being pulled. The sound tells me that it is almost empty. It has not rained in a while. Today we must carry fresh water from the spring;

the boys will bring it down. The sight of a city woman struggling up the stony path with a tub of wet clothes on her head will be funny enough for the neighbors—at least I don't have to carry a jerry can on top, too.

At Pinnacle, which was located two miles below Sharon's place at Mountmoreland, water was always a problem. Many Jamaican visionaries have stressed the necessity of a proper irrigation system. Water was one of lawyer J. A. G. Smith's greatest struggles. "The People's Champion" was one of the most inspired and dedicated black leaders of the island. "Xaimaca," the Land of Springs, as the Arawaks called it, might really be a paradise if only the drinking water could be properly distributed. Pinnacle was one of Jamaica's most arid spots. It ran from the plateau edge to the plain below, its rugged (and porous) limestone canyons, caves, and holes unable to retain any water.

A cistern still stands at the north corner of the Great House. Before the house was destroyed in the earthquake of 1907, the cistern gathered water from the roof. But by Howell's time the house was long gone and the adepts had to bring water up from Rio Cobre, some two hundred meters below. They would leave the village at dawn and head for the river where they would do their washing, bathe, and comb out their beards; then they would come back up, carrying water for the day. It was not an easy climb up a steep and rocky path, especially under the hot morning sun. But, Amy says, there were always children with nothing to carry, so they took one bucket for Counselor Howell. It must have been hard for a child, I said. She protested vigorously. "Oh no, it *light*. We *use* to it!"

On the northwestern slope behind Pinnacle there was an old cement reservoir, but the water, even in Howell's time, was only good for the cattle. There was also a pond to sustain gardening. It lay at the bottom of a large bowl of red soil trapped between the hills where water seeped into the porous lime underneath. Gardens

Miss Amy Fairweather, born 1930. She came to Pinnacle in 1940 with her parents and sister Vinette (who died in 2000). © HÉLÈNE LEE.

surrounded it on three sides; on the fourth side was the main village, which was composed of several dozen thatch-and-wattle houses. The town was intersected by East Avenue. The large "Mess Hall" (a term borrowed from the ships) could hold seven hundred people. Huts and cottages spread across the property and deep into the neighboring hills and valleys. (Howell claimed, and the valley people confirm, that there were as many as five thousand people at almost all times.) When summer arrived and the pond went dry, people and animals suffered.

But Ras Tafari was watching, because in the early 1950s the pond began to fill, and it became a full-fledged lake. Blade says he could never figure out where this water came from and why this pond got bigger. Maybe the cattle had made the bottom broader with their constant stamping. At first the water was muddy, but after a few years it became clear and could even be used for cooking. Blade brought up some small fish from the river that fed on mosquito larvae, and they proliferated to the point that he could actually go fishing on a small raft.

Nowadays the pond has dried out. In the 1980s, development of nearby housing subdivisions was hampered by the negligible water supply. The developers eventually had to dig a well and set up a tank. No more microclimate, no more raft fishing. Now a copse of trees grows where the pond was. A rusted old metal pan, relic of the old sugar industry, lies among the reeds.

Water remains a huge problem for most rural Jamaican communities. Although rain isn't scarce in these parts (at least not on the eastern and northern slopes of the plateau), most water rushes down to the sea through steep gullies, disappearing in the dry season. Sometime a politician looking for votes will bring water to a community. Then he is replaced by someone from the other political party and the piped water is directed somewhere else. This is probably what happened in Mountmoreland, the community that Sharon and the boys live in. A few years ago clean water ran all the way down from its source; we only had to walk a hundred yards or so to the public standpipe. But the pipes were not properly maintained and the water cut out. The spring up the road, tapped with Canadian funding, is the only water available to nearby villages. This is where we do our washing.

Seven thirty. Sharon, her sister, and I squat by the spring, hanging dripping laundry over the wire fence. School children in uniforms pass us in small groups en route to Seven Miles school. Men in baggy pants riding low on their hips are washing their cars on the other side of the fence, sometimes addressing us in mocking tones. The women answer brazenly. Few Jamaican women expect anything from men. Even those men who have jobs (some of the youngsters here operate "taxis" along the Sligoville route) do not bring any money home. They just come for lunch, leaving behind their children and their dirty laundry. Bitter, only half joking exchanges fly from one side of the fence to the other.

The sun is now high. Sharon has to rush to work. While she waits for a "taxi" at the curb, her sister suddenly comes running down the hill, telling us that the source has stopped. Where are we going to fill the cans? I climb the hill to the cottage. Gladdy, Sharon's children's father, is sitting on a bench outside rolling his first spliff of the day and watching the mist melt into the valley below. "Gladdy! We must fetch water. The spring mosh up." Gladdy looks up with red eyes.

"We haffe go to Five Miles fe water but me no have no taxi money."

"I'll pay for it."

"When Sharon come tonight she go get to it. Taxi drivers nuh like carry water you know."

"Sharon be *mad*! She works all day . . ."

"If me had me a car, me could go! Me could carry for everybody! But from me was in a car accident last year, me nah drive again."

"All right—let's walk to Five Miles then. You carry two cans, me carry two, and that will be enough for tonight."

"Walk? No man! Me nah walk. Dem would say look how I'm broke."

"What do you care what people say? We just need water for your kids to drink and wash."

"No man, me nah do dat. If me to walk carry water me better run away, me better go back to the States. Me have one big son in the States you know."

Run to the States? Same old story.

That night when Sharon got home she was furious, and in the wink of an eye Gladdy found a solution and brought back water. So much fuss for what? Water! Gladdy likes Guinness better. So to cheer up my buddy (if not the best of husbands, Gladdy is a sweet, good-hearted man) I take him down the road to buy a few bottles. We started drinking on the wooden steps of the country store with a couple of old-timers.

Uncle Hugh lived in England for many years. He has the manners of a dandy and calls me "lady." He speaks in a mixture of country patois and cockney slang sprinkled with sucking noises from his false teeth. He bore witness to the rebirth of Pinnacle. "When me just left school, Pinnacle was a place where me mother go buy nisberries. There was a man there, you give him sixpence or a shilling for the nisberries, you just load your donkey of it! Any amount you want to pick! And sweet! That time Howell no come here yet."

"Some say Howell a fool the people," Gladdy ventures. "Me no say so. You see a man go spend his own money to feed the people, me say a good man dat. Even if him have dem flogged sometimes. Government have dem *hanged*, you know!"

Gladdy's neighbor, an old man with big rugged hands, sucks on his teeth. "Sometimes him hang dem too."

Deacon is the leader of the small revivalist church in the valley. As a child in the 1940s, he helped his family burn coal when trouble started between them and the Pinnacle community. He never forgave the Rastafarians for the floggings and the "stolen" coal. "Howell," he said, "he had dem as slaves up there!" According to Gladdy, people say that when someone did something wrong, they would catch him and put honey all over him, and tie him up next to an anthill. "Me no know if a true. A people tell me," he says.

"They no like people come and sneak up dem place," Uncle Hugh says. "You could not go inside. They had guards and they lick your ass! Once when me brother Cuban that built my likkle shop in '53—a nice brother, look like half-Indian—him sneak up to see a woman from Pinnacle, and one day dem ketch him and put him on the cross sticks. Dey gone slice him balls with dem razor and they dig him grave to bury him whether dead or alive! And him bawl, 'Lord! Help me!' and dem get a bush whey dem call cowitch, and they put it up him backside and let him—is a plant make your body itch. It itch so much you bleed."

Sipping their Guinnesses, the company shakes their heads in unison. A car rushes down the bend coming from Sligoville, glaring headlights in our faces. The toad and bug chorus stops singing, and then begins again.

"But afterward you see, man, when dem settle in—me tell you the truth, me nuh fool you—they change up to the nicest best people. They were quite honest people. They were so gentle to everybody. And when the police come back and raid them again, everybody miss them."

"When did the police come?"

"First time police come is because people die. They bury them all around, it stink up the roadside! And they don't bury you in a coffin. They just tie you up, dig in a hole. One hole carry four people."

"More than dat. The deeper dey can get it."

"So they dig a hole twelve feet deep, and put one down, settle dirt, and put another on top—up to six in one hole!"

"They bury them same place, in front of the doorway?"

"They bury dem anywhere. More than a million grave bury there!"

Why did so many die?

"At that time when they come up, they have nothing for them to eat, and they have to beg banana. At that time Bona Lodge plant bananas, Caymanas dem plant bananas, so certain days they have to go down and beg bananas, and plenty of time some of them have to beg working, all pon the road, mosh up deyselves."

But the *Gleaner* says Howell cooked for them.

"You tink if go bring four thousand people in there . . . where you gwaan get feedin' fe food dem?"

"Him buy some old cornmeal and people have corn," Uncle Hugh explains. "You see this corn? When you pick him off so, and trim him in de mill, you gage the mill to certain way that you get the best part outta it to the first class of people. You go back again, you get certain grade outta it, that the second class have. That time all the corn is done with, you know, the last part of it is like trash, him have to use that for the third class, you getta cup a it, it may be sweet and a little salt ina it, and if you don't drink it down fast, dem whip your ass!"

Deacon, the old timer, shakes his head. "Sometimes it stay there three days and it get spoiled, and the people get sick with dem belly and many die."

"I hear say Mistah Wisey live over their burying ground too."

"Somebody lick down the tombs, dem build house pon top and live ina it! That's the reason why the owner sell it, that the fool-fool run!"

Night is darkening around us—the right time for "duppy" stories, a favorite pastime of country life. As the dark stout flows, the local folklore about Leonard Howell gets down and dirty.

"He was a powerful man! Mystical!"

"Sometimes him have a sacrifice in dem caves," Deacon throws in. "Dem sacrifice *children*, you know!"

"When the police come, to fool dem him turn people into trees. Him turn ganja into gungo peas!"

"And him become invisible! The people see him, but the police cyan see him!"

"People say him disappear, but him go hide in the caves. Plenty of holes up there you know. One hole—you throw a stone into it, it come out at Spanish Town!"

"Him have books whey him take him science. Him have *whole heap* of magic books up there. When police take dem away, him lose him power."

We all venture a look around, checking the hedge across the road for suspect shadows. One more Guinness, please, just to keep the duppies at bay.

16

The First Raid

On Saturday, July 12, 1941, the *Jamaica Times* published a report on the "Ras Tafarian reign of terror in St. Catherine," detailing the floggings of people caught planting and burning charcoal on Pinnacle lands. According to the report, the attacks on these people "bore a close resemblance to the ruthless Maroon era . . . and Pinnacle has no respect for the law: any member of the force with business in Pinnacle will be escorted to headquarters by a guard with a club." There was no comment or explanation from the inhabitants of Pinnacle; the article was unusually blunt and sensational anti-Rasta propaganda.

The next day, Sunday, Howell gathered his followers. He'd had a dream. "Tomorrow we are going to have visitors. Do what they say," he insisted. "Do not resist. Ras Tafari is with you." The people listened to their leader and sang hymns until the late hours to boost their spirits. "Shout thy glorious tidings / Swell the strain of gladness / Look for Haile Selassie / For he shall make us free . . ." At one or two o'clock in the morning, Howell went back to the great house and retired into meditation. Around three o'clock he silently disappeared down the narrow path leading to Rio Cobre. A few minutes later, Tyneth heard the heavy boots of the police com-

145

ing up the same path that Howell had just taken. When the captain asked to see Howell, she realized her husband had escaped.

The police had anticipated taking the Howellites by surprise, but because Howell had foreseen the raid and warned his followers about it, the raid had lost its psychological effect. Instead it become a big game, and it was remembered as one of Howell's most miraculous deeds. Pinnacle elders, all children at the time, remember the day as something of a lark.

"Every morning we wake up at four o'clock and go to the river to bathe and the man dem brush their hair and fix up them beard

Tiken Jah Fakoli, Ivory Coast's reggae superstar, visited Miss Amy at Tredegar Park. © HÉLÈNE LEE.

and all of that. So we going to the river in a line and the army drive up, come up on we. The people a reverse, and everybody turn back uphill. We retreat and retreat, and we reach back up, we did have a big life skill, the likkle ones and everybody, nobody get hurt. When you hear boot a run down through the river road and come up, it sound like an earthquake! When we come up here now, police come up from behind too, so no escape. They gather us all up on East Avenue. The police nuh take away all of us. Dem take seventy-two men and carry them fe Spanish town. And the seventy-two men— when dem release from jailhouse, they go out to seventy-two nations and His Majesty message scatter right around to every nation."

The police wanted to arrest Pinnacle's leader, but Leonard Howell was long gone.

"That day they search for Mr. Howell til dem weak," Amy laughs. "They say he hiding under the floor under the baker shop, and they lick it off and throw down a whole heap of something to ketch 'im. And they hear him shout this way and that way, and when they run down, they don't see him!"

But late in the afternoon, after a whole day of eluding the police, Howell suddenly materialized near the mess hall where everyone had gathered. He was wearing an old dress and scarf and riding Baby, his donkey. He began chatting with his people in an ordinary manner. The police, weak with thirst, hunger, and frustration, failed to note the peasant woman riding by, her bare feet against the donkey's flanks. No one made any sign of recognition except for a silent shiver that went through the crowd. When the police ordered Howell's followers to search for him in the hills, the disguised Howell joined the party. It was then that he vanished into the stony landscape. It was an Anansi tale come to life, an instant legend.

"And him a dem look for, you know!" Vinette explained. "Because they want him bad! And him was there and they no see him! He walk in the middle of dem. Pon *donkey*. A donkey we call Baby. And him walk pon the donkey back in the middle of dem; me and you see, but they don't see him! When they take us in captivity, they tell us, 'you nuh see God and live.' That's what Europeans teach us, you know. We can't see God and live. It nuh go so. You love to see God at the time you live! Yes! Anytime you live! But up till now people hold it up to you. Definitely, some of them cyan really see him. Cause God has chosen people on earth you know. You did not know? When you have God within you, you see God."

How Howell "work to that" is a mystery to Amy, but "the likkle what me know me know," she says. "Him have a glass, me don't know what kind of glass, them say it control something ina air. They come down with force fe come kill 'im. Him never deliver himself until *November*. When him ready, him tell dem to come fe him, him ready," she laughed.

"A November them ketch him?" my friend Donovan interrupts.

Vinette and Amy jump up. "No! Them don't *ketch* him, me tell you: him send for them. Him send two sisters from his home—it was a home where you have plenty of us sisters there, some work and some cook and some . . . you know? Nuff people were round him. Him send two sisters call the police to come to see him. You don't understand what me tell you? Is him *set up* the '41 raid!"

And so the raid of 1941, "remix" version, becomes one of Howell's many legends. The police riot was transformed into a mystical experience, with many awe-inspiring episodes, a prophetic dream, the leader appearing and disappearing at will, and a masterly third act where he was visible to some, invisible to others, as he went out to search for himself. In this legend the seventy-two prisoners taken to Spanish Town became the seventy-two nations present at Selassie's coronation; while serving their jail sentences they became the ambassadors of the faith to the outside world. In this version, the raid appears deliberate—a way to disseminate the philosophy. But it was also the start of the legend that Howell was himself an incarnation of the King of Kings. Heaven after death was a notion that the Howellites rejected—they had found the Promised Land at Pinnacle. Wasn't the notion of a faraway and invisible God another European trick? The image of this man parading on his donkey among police was a revelation to the Howellites. Their leader was, like Rama and Krishna, an aspect of the godhead.

But then God vanished. The following day the police still nosed around, and seventy-two adepts were in jail. The community took care of the children who were left behind, but spirits were low. Some families gave up on Pinnacle and left. The *Jamaica Times* reported the exodus: "Old men with white beards, lame women with undernourished babies, young girls with half-exposed bodies. Their belongings were few—a mattress, an old grip, and a three-legged chair perhaps. They passed in groups of two to twenty, all bound for nowhere."

One Kingston reporter who followed the police up the hill went over to the great house, but all he found was desolation. A police officer indicated

a frail woman sitting on the door of the deposed chieftain's home. "That's Howell's wife over there," he said. "He also left her behind."

Her head was dropped in sorrow, her courage was given way to despair. She did not stir as I approached. Since morning she had become used to strange and heavy footsteps. Those of hostile civilians. Those of the law. At her skirt a little boy tugged. Howell's and hers.

She raised her head slowly as if hoping that the scene had changed—a seemingly un-ending nightmare of men moving about swinging sticks, batons, machetes. Her thoughts were not of herself, of her humiliations before the eyes of the serfs who had once comprised her "Kingdom," but of the man who they believed was their king. The man she still loved—her husband. And yet, she accepted her plight. For she believed in Fate, in God. Perhaps she could have been a school teacher, and he a doctor. But as Miss Bent, the promising "young miss" of St. Elizabeth district, she had deserted the schoolroom; he had tossed aside the medical books. Subsequent developments were guided by a hand which could not be detained.

When her eyes finally came to rest on me, they held a blank stare; were red and a bit swollen—due to crying no doubt. But bereft of their sadness, her features were those of a stern woman. Perhaps not a cruel one, but a woman who could issue orders to many a man and see them carried through.

This was the *Times'* class revenge on the almost-white girl who gave herself to a black man. He knew more than he would say; in town he had probably heard the story of how this upper-class girl turned down a rich cigar manufacturer to marry Howell despite rigid social taboos. The journalist asked her for something to drink, but no water had been carried up the hill that day and all she could offer him was some fruit. When he asked her where her husband was, she answered "I don't know" in a way that left no question about her sincerity. "Looking far into the distance, as if into a world beyond her gaze, she muttered softly, 'I believe only in one man, and I have faith in Him; so long as he stands by me I shall have no fear.'

"Who's that?" the journalist asked.

"The Lord God Almighty."[70]

The Japanese poet Terayama Shuji wrote, "Behind the laughing mask is a crying mask / Behind the mask of drunkenness is the mask of wisdom / Behind the mask of a criminal is the mask of a sojourner / Behind the mask of the revolutionary is the mask of a movie director." The charismatic Rasta preacher Howell, champion of the poor, was also a great director. As soon as he came back from the United States, he carefully shrouded himself in the proper amount of shadow and light to manipulate the drama of his life. He had many women, which is not a surprise. In Jamaica, lonely single mothers are plentiful. Slave society left its imprint on the cultural mentality of men who could be sold away from their women and dispossessed of children. Many Jamaican men came to see themselves as nomads, and women became the hub of the family. Of course the strong African sense of family also survived, and the various churches did their best to encourage these values. But still today a vast majority of Jamaican men see themselves as rootless, and they leave familial responsibility to their children's mothers.

To those mothers Howell proffered Pinnacle, a utopian community where economic support was part of his protection. There were many women who loved him for that. John Lennon used to sing "Woman is the nigger of the world," reflecting the sense of exploitation felt by women in almost every society around the world. Religious passion has traditionally been a way for women to restore their dignity and spiritual privacy in a society like Jamaica's, where women are a majority in almost every denomination. The Revivalists, for instance, were mostly women. By 1921, war and emigration had taken such a toll on the male population that the ratio of men to women was 8.8 to 10; women began joining cults en masse. "The mystics, mainly women, sublimated their sexual desires and directed their energies toward the Christian trinity, particularly towards Jesus. Extravagant emotional behavior usually accompanies this relation with Jesus."[71]

At Pinnacle, women found a Jesus of flesh and blood. Of flesh, mainly. And just as he offered them a paradise on earth, he opened to them the heaven of his arms.

17

Howell and the Women

At shop counters and the little bars in the valley, a favorite conversational topic is the women who loved Gong Howell. Old-timers still chuckle at the number of women who lived at Pinnacle. They were the majority, and they gave him every bit of money they earned when they went out to work every day.

"Why they love him so?" was a frequently asked question.

"Him have a straight nose, him have a dimple, pretty boy, and glass in him eye, and him have a gold ring that whether you fancy him or not, ketch you long time. Science, y'know? As soon as she sees him, she finds herself in his bed later that afternoon. Women said, 'He could have been a ghost!' I don't know if him power come from God or from the devil."

"I heard a story 'bout man and a woman living in Kingston. They had a fight and the woman packed her bags and moved straight up to Pinnacle."

"Yeah I hear dem tings! And whenever a woman go missing, them first come look for her up Pinnacle. And when the man come, Howell take him too!"

Uncle Hugh, in a salacious tone: "Him sleep with him married woman, till about eight o'clock. He leave that one, then him gone

to him young girl in there. Every one a dem that's good looking—
dem a fe him. May I tell you, young lady," he says to me, "If Howell saw you tonight, unless he don't fancy you, he nuh leave you!
Miss, he was a good man. But he could have up to forty of them—
in one night! Him most like to be with five women at a time. One
a fan him, one a kiss him, one a love him, one a feel him up . . . and
one a fuck him good! I know! I almost lost my raas in there one
time. I did have one girlfriend from up there, but I didn't know she
was him direct woman that! He woulda kill me man!"

"Him have two sons with him married woman, Monty and
Blade. They lived with him in the great house. I know them, they
come buy things from me sometimes. Him also have some black
pickney, and one set a pickney with Chinese woman, and with
coolie woman. She was wild!" he laughs. "Independent woman—
only Howell control her. She was so bad, that one. She fling out a
ting, chip me face so! Blood claat! That same woman, I told her me
get her, but me cyan because Howell love her and him protect her.
Lawd! He put some kinda science on me. Him take your money and
him take your wife and you turn up and you see him loving your
wife and you cyan say nothing, or else your behind a-go get it. Him
boil the medicine and the medicine work in dem belly, and what it
makes is love. A woman drink him potion, all she think about is sex
with him. That the type a medicine he boil!"

"One time him have a case in Spanish Town. When he come to
the court house, him wear a long robe, and him go to the judge, him
bow before the judge. 'Yes me lord.' The judge name is Miss P. Of
course him put a science on her to draw Miss P. come and sleep with
him that night! The judge! She must excuse herself from the case
and dem set Howell free."

"Dem catch him a lying wit' five dawtas [Rasta word for *unmar-
ried women*] a one time!"

"Fe him dawta?"

"Him tell the judge, say a fe him dawta them and dey no vex.
The pickney dem dawtas, dem tell the judge: if him put dem daddy
in a prison, where they get a man to sex?"

Tiken Jah Fakoli visited Pinnacle and found one of the bottles of roots or medicine Howell stored at the back of his house. © HÉLÈNE LEE.

Fantasies, legends, or no, it is clear that Howell had many "queens." One of his many aliases was "Honeyman"; he even had a bank account in that name. But this amorous career must have started long before Pinnacle. In the United States, at age twenty-six, he mentioned a Jamaican woman named Myra, saying that she had been his wife in Panama. To his children he mentioned at least one "babymother" in the States, plus the "beautiful wives" he had in Japan. A woman in every port? When he arrived back in Red Lands at the age of thirty-four, he probably had many children already, but nobody, not even Monty or Blade, knows anything about the first part of his life.

In Red Lands he was the center of all the young ladies' attention. One of them, a teenaged cousin, became the housekeeper in his new Kingston home. At first it looked like a good deal. Life in the capital was exciting to a country girl. They had all sorts of visitors—even Mr. Garvey came to visit them—and Cousin Howell was a loving man. But soon she found that she was not to be his wife, and this out-of-wedlock relation started burdening her with guilt. Miss L. was raised in the very strict Church of God, and even at eighty the memory of her relations with the Gong is painful. She insists her name not "be in the book." She has excuses, she says. She was so young! Her mother, she adds bitterly, pushed her into the arms of the good-looking doctor. When Howell was arrested in St. Thomas, Miss L. went back to Red Lands, but when he was released he came to fetch her. The girl did not want to go. If she came, Howell promised, he would send her to sewing school. Miss L. gave in, but the school he sent her to was not a proper one, she complains. "The lady just make dresses and only make us work for her. She don't show us nothing."

Unfortunately this was not the only deception awaiting her in Kingston. While she was away, the Gong had married Tyneth Bent. Was it a legal marriage, as everyone claims? There is no trace of marriage registration in the legal archives, but Miss L. saw the wedding picture. Tyneth made it very clear who was the mistress and who was the housekeeper in the home. A journalist from the *Gleaner* noticed that the Bent heiress was used to giving orders and having them obeyed. Tyneth was from an upper-class Jamaican family based in St. Elizabeth, with a mixture of Irish, Scottish, German, and Jewish blood. She had some African blood too, which gave a glossy touch to her silky black hair and wide dark eyes. Tyneth was beautiful. She had been dating the well-off Cuban owner of Machado Cigar's Jamaican operation, where she worked for a time. Howell was of another class altogether—he was black, she was white (almost), and the future Mrs. Machado was not even supposed to dignify his presence with a glance. But Tyneth gave up everything for the handsome rebel. As soon as he got out of jail she married him. Friends and family sneered, but she was strong. When he was sent to Bellevue, she assisted him. The year he got out of Bellevue, she had their first son, Monty (Martinel). As soon as Pinnacle was up and running she went to live with him, and settled in the servant quarters beside the ruin of the great house. It was a tiny, three-room brick cottage without water or electricity.

Tyneth took upon herself the responsibility of caring for Pinnacle's many pregnant women, and women with young children. By all accounts, she took this seriously. Even today, her sons Monty and Blade are remembered fondly in a sort of folkish tribute to their mother. She was truly a queen—and she acted like it. But she also had to live with the rumors circulating around the island like poisoned blood that Howell had thirteen wives. This was even printed in the *Gleaner*, to the shame of her family. She had been passionately in love with Howell, had given up her comfortable future for him, but by the time the first raid occurred, the marriage had begun to go sour.

Where did Howell go when he disappeared after the 1941 raid? Probably up to one of the hidden caves in a remote jungle canyon. After a few days (not a few months, as his adepts say), he was back in the Great House. On July 24, two women came to see him. They may have been his contacts in the Spanish Town Police who had warned him about the raid, or maybe they were informers. Howell sent them to tell the police to come and pick him up, for "he was ready." At midnight he was relaxing on his veranda when the police came. Now he preferred to face them rather than hide. Gong Howell was not a man to hide. Imagine him dragged down to town to be arrested like a common thief! Perhaps he took the advice of his white friend Bobby Alexander and got a lawyer. After all, he was just one of many land owners who dealt harshly with people he found deforesting his property. Everybody did it. But Howell still wasn't the right color. On August 20, 1941, he was sentenced to two years in prison, his third jail term. He had spent five of the past ten years behind bars.

When he got out in 1943, Howell went back to Pinnacle. In the meantime, Tyneth Howell had another child, Bilbert William, nicknamed Blade. Up in Red Lands, where Miss L. lived for the duration of Howell's detention, she gave birth to his daughter Daphney. Miss L. did not want to leave Clarendon to go back to Pinnacle, but her mother insisted. "I gave up. I thought, this is my destiny." She tried to settle in between Tyneth and the concubines. There she had another child, Cardiff. But this was too much for Tyneth, who started acting strangely. There were several other women in Howell's harem—Pearl and Ivy, two sisters with beautiful shining skin, one named Enid, and many others. When Howell went to them, Tyneth would smoke a big spliff and lock herself up in her room, or else go out and roam the rough wilderness around Pinnacle.

One night, in a rage of frustration, she grabbed a knife and threatened to cut her own throat. The Gong got down on his knees and swore that he loved her. She finally surrendered the knife. Then she wandered off. They found her in the forest, alive but dazed. Two nights later, she disappeared for good. Howell organized a huge search party at Pinnacle, but after five days of looking for her, someone noticed vultures hovering over one of the remote valleys. Her body was down there, all torn to bits by the birds. One arm was missing.

So, in 1943, Leonard Howell was sent back to jail for the murder of his wife. When he went to the police to report her death, they arrested him. Everyone in the valley murmured that he had disemboweled her. Several months passed before all the witnesses were heard. Miss L. was the first. "He did *not* kill her," she told the court. "He *loved* her." All the witnesses confirmed this. And since forensic evidence could not determine the cause of death, Howell was freed. In April 1944, the attorney general advised the colonial secretary to release Howell. Appended to this document was an unusual recommendation.

> If, as I believe, Pinnacle belongs to, or is leased by, Leonard Howell and his organization, the government should take no steps to break up the settlement of his followers upon that property, despite the fact that their habits and customs do not conform to those usually adhered to by civilized communities. The foregoing, of course, does not imply that if evidence of breaches of the law by Howell and his followers is forthcoming, that those breaches should not be punished, whether they take place at Pinnacle or elsewhere, but merely that so long as Howell's followers observe the law, they are entitled to continue to live unmolested in whatever way they please.[72]

Victorious, Howell returned to his redoubt to continue his work.

18

Ganja Plantation

There were a number of reasons why the attorney general advised the police to leave the Rastas alone. One of them was that 1944 saw an important shift in Jamaican politics. Thanks to the 1938 strikes and the unrelenting struggle of people like J. A. G. Smith, the Clarendon lawyer against whom Howell had once refused to testify, universal adult suffrage was established at last. Alexander Bustamante left his cousin Norman Manley's Peoples National Party (PNP) to establish the more conservative Jamaican Labour Party (JLP). The difference between the two was not so much in their agendas, but in the way that they pursued their goals. Bustamante's JLP depended on its leader's charismatic ability to rally support from both sectors of the establishment and the uneducated masses. The better organized, more liberal PNP analyzed and planned everything, sometimes failing to understand the needs of the people. In 1944, with the advent of voting rights and the new JLP, the modern Jamaican political structure was now in place.

In the first general election in November 1944, Spanish Town candidates looked up toward Pinnacle for its thousands of potential votes. The JLP candidate, L. W. Rose, was a black man of humble origin. The son of a watchman, he had been a shoemaker before becoming a union leader (the BITU's vice president) and faithful supporter of Bustamante. But Rose was not Howell's candidate. Howellites claim that in this first election their leader supported PNP candidate Bobby Alexander, the owner of neighboring Tredegar Park. Bobby Alexander often visited Pinnacle, and the black leader and white land owner spent hours discussing their positions. Perry Henzell, who knew Alexander, describes him as intelligent and open-minded and definitely not a ganja smoker.

Howell allowed ballot boxes to be set up at Pinnacle. This was the only time that Pinnacle voted. Apparently, most of the votes went to the PNP, although Howell himself did not vote or give any instruction to his followers. This tally annoyed the local JLP majority. In the next election, they carried the ballot boxes first to Seven Miles, farther up the hill; they managed to get back too late to allow Pinnacle to vote. In 1944, Spanish Town became one of twenty-three districts to elect JLP candidates, out of thirty-two. The PNP won only four. Bustamante was riding high.

Why didn't Howell support Bustamante? Their views were fairly similar. Both loved their black brothers. Both believed in hard work, free enterprise, land redistribution, and opening economic opportunities to more people. Bustamante had created a loyal political network by lending money to enterprising working people whom his intuition told him would succeed. Howell could easily have been one of his clients, but it was Albert Chang who had provided the Gong with the only credit that he had needed. Pinnacle was the type of enterprise that Bustamante admired. It put the unemployed to work without public money, and in 1944 there was no money to fund social programs anyway. Of course Howell and Bustamante knew each other from New York or from Panama, but they had a tacit agreement to steer clear of each other. Whatever their relationship was, it would have been improper for a national hero and future prime minister to be linked to the biggest ganja planter in modern Jamaican history, for this is what Howell became after he returned to Pinnacle in 1944.

Perry Henzell says that the Rastas' true stroke of genius was to make ganja a religious sacrament. The idea was clearly borrowed from the Hindus of St. Thomas. Most academic studies and police reports tell us that the use of ganja began in Jamaica among Indian indentured workers in the nineteenth century. This accounts for the many Hindi and Urdu words in the ganja lexicon (including the famously potent "kali weed," also spelled "collie weed"). But Howell was probably smoking herb long before he went to St. Thomas. Although no proof exists that he used it in Clarendon, as his father was a stern Anglican and ganja availability was still limited, Clarendon was one of the first areas of Indian immigration and Howell had perhaps tasted *bhang*, the sweet drink made from ganja, there with his Indian friends. Surely he smoked on his trips around the world. In Howell's Harlem, the police reported over five hundred known "tea pads," as they were called in local slang. (The dealer was the "tea man.") Howell was said to have run a tea room on 136th Street. Let's just say that we can hardly imagine him serving Lipton to old ladies.

The fact that he first chose St. Thomas as a base might have had something to do with the availability of ganja in this particular parish. In August 1941, one Francis Howell was tried for ganja in Bath, where Leonard rented a house and brought his followers to heal in the hot springs. This other Howell claimed that he started selling ganja in 1908 and would continue "until the trumpets of the judgment." Although Francis Howell probably had no link to Leonard, he helped make ganja readily available in the area. The Athlican network that Howell used for his first meetings in Falmouth, Morant Bay, and Bath was probably accustomed to smoking. At any rate, Balintine must have been a heavy smoker if we judge by his writings. Even Marcus Garvey is rumored to have been a ganja user.

Until the 1930s, Jamaican ganja was grown mainly in two neighboring parishes, St. Thomas and St. Mary, where many Indians lived. Until the beginning of the twentieth century, the colonial establishment appeared to take no notice of ganja users, but in 1924 a law was passed banning marijuana. Nineteen twenty-four was, as many remember, an important year for the Athlicans and their friends, and the police probably noticed that ganja was beginning to reach beyond Indian immigrant circles.

As long as ganja was an Indian prerogative, the "sacred herb" was associated with their folk customs like their food, music, and dress. It did not accelerate violent behavior; on the contrary, it made workers happy, and they imported shiploads of it from India to meet their needs. In 1894 a British commission studied the effects of cannabis on the Indian population. Their conclusion was that there was no reason to prohibit it. "The fact that many witnesses testified to the peaceable and orderly character that is exhibited in the consumption of ganja goes far to prove that these drugs do not tend to evidence crimes of violence."[73]

Why did the establishment change its mind and outlaw ganja? Was it because they feared that control of the herb would fall into "dangerous" hands?

Fear is the system's closest ally—Garvey hammered this down in his most stirring speeches. He struggled with his own fear with such energy that during his first speech in America he had a seizure and fell off the stage. In an article in the *New Jamaican*[74] he advised, "Whatever you are afraid of, you must walk right toward it!" This could have been the motto of the times. Who were those "Ethiopians," Athlicans, BWIR veterans who wrote impatient letters to the government and the press? Who were Garvey, J.A. G. Smith, How-

ell, Saint William Grant? Who were they but black men who conquered their fear?

Unfortunately medical science has not studied the role of ganja
in conquering one's fears. The reason is that fear is not considered
a malady. But what were the sons of slaves suffering from, if not
from fear? The crack of the whip still haunted their dreams, their
songs, their culture. But gnawing away at one's humiliations is no
use. "If you think of one thing too long you begin to 'go sour,' you
lose your sense of proportion, you become morbid. . . . Learn to
relax—study the art of turning your attention to something else."
This was Garvey's advice.

This is exactly what Rastas practice when meditating. After
smoking ganja they sit and read the Bible attending "creation learning," as Balintine put it. "How worlds are built, and upon what trig-
ger Kingdoms are set." They observe reality from above—they are
"high." If they call their king by his old name (Ras Tafari), they love
the "I" at the end of Haile Selassie I. And even if it was meant to be
read "the first," they read it "I," like "high." In the 1950s, the "I"
became a watchword in Rasta parlance. Since, in Jamaican patois,
"I" (the pronoun) was replaced by "me," the Rastas got hold of the
proud "I" and made it their war cry.

From a chronological point of view, the wider dissemination of
ganja in Jamaica can be seen to correspond to the rise of the Rasta
movement. In 1935, the Jamaican Central Board of Health observed
that "more than three times as many Jamaicans as East Indians"
were using ganja, and that the offences, previously limited to the
eastern part of the island, had now spread to the rest of the country.
The Board illustrated the situation with a press release, in which a
typical Jamaican couple, "John and Mary Brown," expressed their
virtuous indignation.

John: "Two young men from up the valley . . . run wild and beat
up two Chinamen in their shops. One struck down an old woman
and the other nearly killed a man over 70 years old. . . . They did
not hurt these people for any reason; they just sort of ran wild and
the unfortunate victims were the ones that they happened to meet.

It would have been the same if you or I had met them . . . they'd have been smoking ganja!"

Mary [exasperated]: "John Brown, you are certainly one to worry about nothing at all. Here you look solemn and depressed and have worried me to death. And all because a couple of Coolie boys been smoking ganja!"

John: "But they are not Indian boys! They are Jamaicans and the sons of respectable, law-abiding folks—just like us!"

The respectable, law-abiding folks of Jamaica had their worst fears confirmed in 1938 when the police claimed that the union strikers were using ganja to strengthen their resolve against rational negotiation. Another report noted that ganja was found in the possession of certain labor agitators, who claimed to use this "dangerous plant" to give themselves what they called "french pluck."[75] Detectives in Portland reported that public ganja smoking had been present at every riot or violent outburst. People found possessing marijuana claimed that they had never taken it before, that strangers gave it to them. Detectives reported that ganja was distributed in the area by two men on bicycles.[76] But after the troubles of 1938 had ended, ganja use just grew. Between 1939 and 1940, the year Pinnacle was established, convictions for ganja possession increased by forty percent.

Were the Rastas responsible for the invasion of ganja? It seems as likely that the movement developed in its wake, perhaps carried by the ganja wave. In January 1939, the year Albert Chang bought Pinnacle, St. Catherine parish already led in ganja-selling convictions: ten out of twenty-three nationally. And Pinnacle was situated on the southern slope of the St. Catherine hills, where some of the highest grade ganja is still grown today. Could it be that the honorable Mr. Chang was a grower of the sacred herb? This seems doubtful, but Mr. Howell was another story.

Howell loved to smoke the holy herb, as he is remembered to have called it. He also advised his adepts to smoke it. It not only had psychotropic and healing effects, it was an excellent way to make fast cash. When ganja became the main crop at Pinnacle, the community suddenly became quite prosperous. But Howell, who never cultivated or sold the ganja himself, never opened the envelopes handed to him by the growers of Pinnacle's famous kali weed whenever they made a deal. He did not like to touch money. Sometimes, when he needed money for his personal use, he asked someone to wash the bills with soap and leave them to dry in the sun. When the wind would scatter the money, he told his nephew Lesford, "Leave it, God is making his distribution."

The Golden Age of Pinnacle had begun. In ten years the community transformed itself into a successful ganja plantation. By 1950, Pinnacle owned several trucks and cars. There was still no water and electricity, as the politicians said that their "handout" budget was insufficient to get water running up there. It didn't matter, the Rastafarians could now pay people to carry it for them at a few shillings per bucket! The kids in the valley made pocket money that way, and everybody was content. The local peasants could now sell their produce at Pinnacle's market, avoiding the long journey to Spanish Town. No longer did the forty-five hundred residents of Pinnacle "bust dem shirt" trying to grow vegetables on the dry land. The ganja grew tall and oily in the tropical heat, and money flowed into the Rasta commune.

It was at this point that Uncle Hugh built his shop. He built it with Pinnacle money for Pinnacle's people. Monty, then fifteen, often came in a truck to buy groceries, half a bag of flour, a quart of oil. The whole valley now depended on Pinnacle, and Rastas suddenly became pillars of the community—as long as you did not mess with their women.

Howell was living alone now. After Tyneth's death and Miss L.'s return to Clarendon, Tyneth's boys, Monty and Blade, whom everyone called "the princes," had been raised by one Miss Ethlyn Nichols ("the only mother image around," Blade remembers), but she did not actually live at the great house. He spent some of his time in

Kingston, where he kept his office and two typists. He never learned to drive. When he had to get to town, he had either Granville or Lennard—his two devoted chauffeurs—come and pick him up. Inside the property he still rode around on his donkey Baby, just as Selassie sometimes did when he visited his people upcountry.

On his thriving ganja farm at Pinnacle, Leonard Howell was like a king.

19

Like Children of God in Paradise (Interview with Blade Howell)

One day when I was about eight or nine years old, an older friend said to me, "Sir Blade, don't you know that your father is a god?" I told him that I'd never heard anything like that. He was amazed. "You really don't know how powerful he is?" He laughed so hard that he almost fell over.

My father's attitude was not exactly a "Back-to-Africa" stance. One of his first tenets was that the black man is as good as the white man, and made his contributions to the world just as the white man had. But this philosophy was ridiculed. In the nineteenth century, when my father was born, the black man was always the last in line. He was almost nonhuman. Dadda (this is what my brother and me called him) did not like this; the black man is just as important and just as talented as the white man. In those days, such a statement was revolutionary. The first time he was arrested it was because he made a statement like, "This whoring queen of England [Victoria], who raped the non-white world . . ." They arrested him for sedition.

I have never met anyone with such strength of character. My father was not afraid of anything. I remember one incident where we stopped the cars at a shop in Thompson Pen [a suburb of Spanish Town on the road to Pinnacle] and there were a lot of people there who were very hostile toward my father. Several men in the crowd had machetes and they were cursing at the people in our party who went into the shop to buy something while we remained in the car. Suddenly Dadda got out of the car and walked toward the hostile crowd and shouted at them, while focusing his gaze on one person who seemed to be the ringleader; and that man literally fainted! I have seen this happen several times. He would zero in on a man and the man would start shaking, looking like he was about to have a heart attack. My father had such an unbelievable presence. No one ever touched him. He would go into any area, any time, anywhere, and I would see grown men backing away from him. He had a presence that you could not ignore.

On the compound [Pinnacle] his word was like the word of God. When he gave an order, there was no arguing and his words were always carried out. People would say, "Counselor said this" or "Counselor said that," "Counselor can I cultivate this plot?" and "Counselor can I sell this wood?"

Dadda was not very involved with the everyday running of the property. He had a string of lieutenants. Delahaie was one, but Delahaie went to live in Kingston sometime in the late forties. Every now and then this [manager] position would change depending on what the need was. I don't think anyone ever relinquished the position as my father's lieutenant or spokesperson unless they were asked to, but many people had the chance to be important to him at different times. For a long time Walker was in charge, and the last one was Edgar Reid, who died in 1997. When Reid got the position over Walker, Walker was a bit upset.

I grew up believing that this place was paradise. It was a beautiful life. I don't know if I could have been happier growing up anywhere else. We had the freedom to do as we pleased, with no pressure. We met our friends, we would go into the bush and the mountains, enjoy ourselves, play games and catch birds, go to the river, or indulge in my favorite pastime—a game or two of cricket. It was a fantastic, idyllic childhood . . . as long as Dadda wasn't around! He was a very strict man, an autocratic type, very alert, and well dressed at all times. Whenever he was around we were always well behaved. I remember making donkey noises and him scolding, "Don't whinny like jackass, try to roar like a lion!" We didn't always want him around because he would interfere with our fun. When we were off playing he would call us back to the house or send for us, but as soon as he turned his back we went back to the village about two miles from our house. You should have seen us running through the shortcut behind the house. It was a dangerous path, very steep with sharp limestone rocks, the type they call "honeycomb," but we could almost fly down there anyway.

Pinnacle was an ancient site, an old Spanish lookout post from the 1500s. [Spanish settlers arrived in Jamaica in 1509.] When we came to Pinnacle, we lived in a house with two porches. The main porch looked out on the ruins of the great house that was much bigger than the one we lived in. The other porch led to our rooms and overlooked Spanish Town. When we first moved in, one side of the porch was made of wood, but it was blown away in the big 1951 hurricane. Dadda rebuilt it with concrete. He bought a concrete mixer and used iron bars to cement it and make it stronger. It was from this porch that we used to watch the trains traveling to and from Spanish Town and Bog Walk or Linstead.

We also watched planes take off and land at Palisadoes Airport, and the boats coming and going into Kingston Harbor. We could see a 270-degree panoramic view. This was probably why the Spanish got up here in the first place—it was an ideal lookout post.

The ruin was very old with five large arches around the back. The arches looked more British-style than Spanish. The only one still standing is the smallest of the five. My father did some reconstruction on the ruin; I remember helping the stone masons cut stones. But my father never rebuilt that great house. During the days of slavery there must have been a rich family with children living there. We found the heads of several porcelain dolls lying around. Sometimes we would find clay pipes with long tubes, and fragments of pottery and old tiles.

When the British took the island [in 1660], the Spanish buried their treasure, thinking that they would come back at some point to claim it. Once, two kids dug up a jar full of gold coins and old jewels by the Rio Cobre. They sold the stones for next to nothing and melted the gold coins to sell. These were very valuable old things and the kids didn't even know it. I can't even imagine this, but some Jamaicans have no sense of history.

As kids we had a million things to do. We used to catch birds, roast them, and eat them. We had stone throwing contests to see who could throw the farthest. We set traps, all kinds of traps. I brought some small fish and put them into the pond in the village compound and they proliferated. We made a raft, and during the last years that we were at Pinnacle, I would go fishing in the pond. We had hundreds of animals—goats, donkeys, mules, chickens, cows—everything but pigs. We had parrots too, and not the small green parrots that are common in Jamaica. We raised a different species of parrot with bright colors that came from abroad. When the police attacked us, we had to let the parrots go. I still wonder if they mixed with the local species. I loved to experiment, and I would graft orange and grapefruit trees, sometimes putting more than one graft onto one tree. I wonder if they are still there.

The hills were rich in vegetation. I never saw so many different plants that could be used to make tea. I knew them all, or most of them at least. In those days, we wouldn't go to the doctor unless we were dying. When someone was sick, the lady who knew all about plants would tell the patient what to take. My father was like a doctor for the entire community. He knew the different plants too. Sometimes he would concoct a mixture, but not too often. No, I never knew what he put in the mixture.

We used ganja for everything, including spice, to make soup, for tea, and of course for smoking. Not the children though, we never smoked. Would you believe me if I told you that the first time I really smoked marijuana was in the United States? When my half-sister Catherine went to England and someone offered her a smoke, she protested "But I am not sick!" To us ganja was medicine.

Dadda used to smoke. Sometimes a lot, and sometimes not at all. He said smoking was good medication and he advised people to try it. Among the rare types of herb they had was one they called *makuoney*, or something like that. Very rare, impossible to cultivate because if you planted the seeds, you just got ordinary ganja. It was dark, almost black, and very strong; it was certainly special. When the herbsmen could find some, they brought it to my father as a gift.

My mother, who died when I was young, was considered a saint among the older people. People had much goodwill toward me because of my mother. They would say, "Your mother was such a nice person, she visited us at night and made sure the baby and everybody had something to eat." As a kid I found it embarrassing when people would rub my head and say, "Oh, your mother was such a nice woman." I would always shy away from that.

Once I asked Dadda how many children he had. He said women love money and power; when you treat them well they don't want to leave. His other name was Mr. Honeyman. He had a bank account in that name. When people brought him money he would say, "Put it in the bank and tell them it's for Honeyman, Mr. Leonard Percival Honeyman." His last passport application was under this name. I still have it.

Music? We had all kinds of music at Pinnacle. I had a gramo-
phone—"His Master's Voice"—and when my father was away, I
went down to East Avenue [in the village] and we had parties with
the kids my age. Sometimes I would go to Kingston, to the dime
store. I would buy records—Bull Moose Jackson, Big Joe Turner,
Louis Jordan, Clarence Henry from New Orleans. This was the
kind of music I loved.

We had our musicians too. They didn't play all the time, but
they liked to gather on occasions—like when someone died, they
had a festival for several days called Ninth Night. They played fifes,
different types of fife: straight, side, recorder. There was one man
named Hood who could blow the flute through his nose. He could
stoke up a big spliff and blow the smoke out through the flute holes.
(After that no one dared to use his flute.) There were several gui-
tarists too, but only one of them—Brother Barrett—was a real
genius. He was a fantastic guitarist, even greater than Chet Atkins
or Ernest Ranglin. He could pick and strum at the same time, he
could make the guitar sound like three or four guitars playing at
once. I loved to listen to him. It is unbelievable to me that this man
was never recorded. He was ten times better than anyone that I
knew. He died a very old man at Tredeger Park. His son Toots is
still alive.

My dream was to learn to play the guitar and play like him, but
I had an accident. One day a wild pig rampaged through the garden plots and the men cornered it. We had to kill it. I took a straight
machete and planted it vertically in its heart, but the machete did-
n't have a hilt and my fingers slipped. I cut my left hand. Now my
two middle fingers won't bend. I suppose I could have played the
drums, like we did sometimes. We had St. Thomas drumming, you
know, not like Rastas play today. It was the old African style,
Kumina. I wish I could reproduce those sounds. I wish I had recordings. Once in a while I hear Kumina recordings, but they are nothing like the sounds we had up there. Some of these men were
famous because of the different drums they played. Malabre was

supposed to be one, I think. So long ago! I think he was from St. Thomas. I remember asking people where they came from. There were a lot of people from Manchester and Clarendon, but I would say the majority were from St. Thomas, because the whole movement had its roots there.

Dadda never claimed to be God. He was a believer; he often spoke of the Almighty. Sometimes he would have us recite prayers from *The Promised Key*—"King of Kings, Lord of Lords." He was not a great Bible reader, but he knew a lot of it. He also read other things, and wrote a lot too. He was always scribbling. When he found something interesting, he wrote it down. Many of his writings were taken by the police. I had some of his notebooks in a trunk, but when I went to America and eventually returned to Kingston, they told me that insects had gotten into it and they had had to burn it. We even had an encyclopedia at the house called *The Book of Knowledge*. It was a great book and dealt with all sorts of things, Egyptian history, Africa, colonization; a book that was not afraid to speak out against the establishment. That is why I think Dadda knew so much. We had a formal library, but the police took everything. Once when Dadda was charged with ganja possession, he asked the judge what "ganja" meant, because he did not have the word in his dictionary. He began to explain to the court that the closest word to ganja described a small bird indigenous to East Africa, but the judge grew annoyed and banged on the table.

The one thing I could never understand is why he did not pay more attention to the question of education. Sometimes tutors came to teach us, people like the pastor, Gobatto Jackson, but it was not until the Mountmoreland school opened that some of us went to school. Perhaps he did not want outsiders that might be spies on the compound, or maybe he didn't want us to get brainwashed by colonial teaching.

I am sometimes invited to speak about my father, but I don't like to take part in public discussions of his personal life. I also believe that some amount of mystery is worth keeping. It forces people to think for themselves.

20

A Stroll in Paradise

"See that?" Gladdy points to the bright blue sky. Black specks drift down aimlessly like butterflies, landing lightly on the ground all around us. I bend and look at the delicate velvety sculptures, which crumble at the slightest touch. They are tiny pieces of carbonized sugar cane, torn from the burning fields by the wind at harvest time.

Last night the black goat gave birth to two kids. If we play with them, Gladdy warns, the mother will smell our scent and reject them. We only looked for a bit, but the mother goat still refused to touch them. "No worries," Gladdy says. "I tell her to get up and she feed them." From a distance the goat hears his words and slowly gets up, allowing the kids to suckle. Gladdy smiles proudly. At least his animals obey him, if not his women. The goat was born wild. Gladdy thinks that goats were brought to this area by the Spaniards and freed when the English came in the seventeenth century. There may also have been goats at Pinnacle that escaped at the time of the first raid. In any case, goats roam these now forbidden hills freely.

I often watched a man in work clothes disappear down a narrow path, his machete slapping his leg as he walked. Where did this path lead? Once Sharon and her sisters followed it to check out an old mango tree at the bottom of the hill, and I went with them. The

177

mangoes were mostly worm-eaten, so I left the children perched in a huge tree, their chins dripping with orange pulp, and walked on. After a while I got to a crossing, then to another one, and yet another—a whole network of paths. Every minute the view became more beautiful. I sat and caught my breath, high on oxygen. I could see Pinnacle Hill looming high above the plain like a watchtower.

I ran down the hill when I heard voices calling my name. Sharon's nieces were searching for me and seemed quite worried. It turned out this area was a no-go zone near the ganja fields. Look up there, at the enormous white villa—up on top. See? The house belongs to the big man. I should never come here alone.

Deacon has promised to show me the Pinnacle caves. One afternoon I walk down with Mark, Sharon's brother, following the sound of Deacon's machete slashing through the gully. Deacon is getting ready to burn coal. Since Hansy (Howell's brother, who controlled the coal business) is long gone, the valley's charcoal burners have come back. Deacon carefully builds up his furnace, placing split wood and branches one by one in an artful pyramid, the thick ends outward, smaller branches squeezed into every gap. When the pyramid is about the height of a man, he covers it with earth and sets fire to the straw at the pyramid's core with a burning rag. For three days the wood will burn slowly while he looks after it, making some small openings and closings to even the combustion. He's eager to finish this one, since the day before he had mashed his thumb under a log and his hand was swollen to twice its size. I was horrified. Deacon laughed.

He leads us along one of the old wagon tracks in the wilderness around Pinnacle. At the turn Deacon heads up a narrow ravine called Coolies Gully because Indians lived there. On the left is a rugged limestone cliff, covered with a blanket of trees and vines. After a while he stops and points toward the cliff. I step onto a path that he cleared with his machete, watching out for poison ivy, and suddenly my heart jumps. Something massive is looking down at me—right there! A huge scaly-skinned gargoyle lunges toward me, a prehistoric dragon with menacing features. I step back to get a better look. It's only a weathered stone outcrop, but its stark white silhouette against the dark cave entrance made it come alive. And no, I'm not smoking anything.

For Howell's adepts, this cave was a mysterious place where no one went unless summoned by their leader. I suspect the Gong would have discouraged nosy visitors. Amy once told me that Howell had them build a "hawk"—could that be my gargoyle? Behind me Deacon sucks on his teeth. "They do obeah in here. They sacrifice children—burn dem alive." Strange hissing noises come from the cave. Suddenly a brown cloud of bats hisses out of the cave, brushing past us toward the fading daylight. Mark picks up a rock

The entrance to the caves where Howell used to hide. In front is the "hawk" head that some adepts say was made on Howell's order.

and throws, killing a bat. He runs to it, pulling out his ratchet knife, and cuts open its belly, triumphantly brandishing two little pieces dripping with blood: the bat's testicles.

"What's that?" I ask.

"I-mon *eat* it. It make mon *strong!*"

The cave is large enough to hold a hundred people. Just beyond the entrance sits a big round rock covered with white crystals, formed by eons of dripping water. "Him stand up here when him preach," Deacon says. Behind the white rock a natural hall opens into the size of a small church, with a pool of clear water in the middle. The astringent smell comes from bat droppings, Deacon explains. "Cross Pen people come here for bat manure all the while. Best fertilizer you can have. See dem donkey droppings going down?"

Back at the entrance, Deacon shows us a hole in the cave wall. It has been obscured by a pile of rocks, but when the rocks are cleared, the hole is big enough for a man to pass through. "There is another room down there," he says, "bigger than this one. People hide in there. Put a rock 'pon the entrance and hide in there." I put a torch into the hole but all I see is a pile of rocks and detritus. "One crazy man live here long time. He throws plenty of garbage, you cyan go down again. But down here is big! People been living here since Arawak times! When police raid Pinnacle, Gong come hide in here. And him hide him ganja too!"

The sun is setting on our walk back to Mountmoreland. We find the children playing football on the road—the only flat area. When they see us they leave their game and climb the path to the cottage ahead of us. Each of them carries a plastic toy that makes all kinds of shrill noises. I follow their techno path in the quiet sunset. From time to time one of the boys hides in the bush by the side of the path and jumps out, startling me, then he runs to catch a firefly and offers it to me for forgiveness, a tiny greenish light pulsing from the cup of his hand.

Spanish Town. I don't like the dust and heat, the bumpy sidewalks and crumbling bricks. There are three prisons here and one reform school, along with a soaring crime rate. But when I see Miss Amy's familiar silhouette sitting with her basket in front of the hospital, I feel safe. Everyday she is here selling oranges and sweets, piece by piece, and single cigarettes. From behind a tree she pulls out an old battered paint can and motions me to sit beside her. As the day idles on, I stand by taking notes. Amy spent eighteen years at Pinnacle and she loves to remember.

"It was like a family. Each one help one. We never have no violence in there. One and one argument, but no violence."

"Mr. Howell came to settle disputes?"

"No miss, him nuh come, him here all the while, even now him here with us. You believe me?" Her strong penetrating eyes rest upon me, her beautiful chocolate face bending to the side.

"I wonder, do you love me?"

I smile at her. "I was just thinking, you must have been a pretty young lady."

Amy's eyes sparkle. Was she one of Howell's women? Perhaps, but how could I dare to ask her?

Eventually I convinced her to come up with me to Pinnacle. We said we'd meet on Sunday morning at her home in Tredegar Park. Although I came very early, she had been ready for a while; the wooden cottage was spotless, the lamp glass wiped clean, the floor waxed. Her dresses hung inside out (to avoid dust) under an Indian sari in a corner. All her clothes seemed to be yellow and green. Miss Amy may not own much, but everything in her house expresses dignity. Amy and Vinette are coming with us to Pinnacle together with a third sister, Lovie. They are all friends from childhood.

When the taxi leaves us at the entrance to Pinnacle the three women glance around with distressed faces. The two pillars at Pinnacle's entrance are gone, and two or three houses are being built where the market once stood. I feel a huge sadness filling them. We walk on in silence. After a while Miss Vinette says in a low voice, "So they sell it fe true," then she lets out a huge sigh. "Everything is for a reason." The other two nod. They most likely had not believed the rumors about Pinnacle being sold, about the housing project, about the trials that deprived them of their paradise. They were probably still hoping. Pinnacle belongs to one man, and it will belong to him until the Day of Judgment. Time stopped on that afternoon in 1958 when they watched their houses burning from the top of the hill. Amy recalls, "That same morning, I pick up a basket of nisberries and go sell them a market. Ken Watt said, 'The nisberries belong to me. I could have you arrested for stealing!'"

At the first crossing the sisters go left, toward "home." But nothing is left of East Avenue. The spring is completely dry, the wattle walls have crumbled, children have picked up the last piece of wood. Vinette points to the spot. "My house was here. When they started mashing everything down we had to run to the hills and watch the houses burning. My daughter was three month and a half; I sit and feed her and watch. The houses were going down one after the other. One police guy see me with my baby and him cry. Him say it too unjust. Him ask me what I gonna do."

"So what you did?"

"Me spent the night under the rocks, and the next day me go a Tredegar Park and ask one friend to put me up."

"You were happy here."

The old lady looks down in silence, then lifts her face again, full of anger.

"Of course we were happy. *We never know happiness* since we leave Pinnacle."

21

Howell and Bustamante

Pinnacle enjoyed relative peace and prosperity during the ten years between 1944 and 1954, but the police raids of the 1950s were approaching and with them the demise of the community. This is still a mystery to anyone seeking the roots of the Rastafarians. Why was Pinnacle tolerated for a decade and then suddenly destroyed? It couldn't have been for sanitary reasons—the health inspectors who visited the camp noted decent living conditions and "fly-proof latrines." There weren't significant problems with the neighbors either; the people of Pinnacle had gained the respect of the local population. No, there was peace in the valley. The problem was in Kingston.

For the four or five thousand community members, the world was divided into two different realms: Pinnacle and the "outside world," "Zion" and "Babylon." Howell went from one to the other, altering his appearance in accordance with his moves. At Pinnacle he was God incarnate, the High Priest with the Chalice.[77] In Kingston he always played another role, but which one? It is hard to pinpoint exactly. Always dressed in a three-piece suit, his necktie in an intricate knot (never hanging lower than the third button), he could be seen riding around town in a chauffeured Humber, the type of car used by government ministers. Howell maintained extensive contacts up and down the social ladder and kept an office in town with two secretaries (one was Miss Gertrude Campbell) and four servants.

For several years his office was situated at East Queen Street, right in front of the police station. On Sundays the community trucks would bring down loads of followers dressed in immaculate white costumes for a "mass" that served as his showcase for the "outside world." He took particular care of the decorum for the event, and the ghetto onlookers crowded in to watch the white-garbed assembly, sometimes mingling, listening to the sermons and the music. Rastafarians were black and poor, they demonstrated, but they took charge of their lives and their destinies. From them emanated a strong sense of dignity, and every year hundreds of new adepts flowed to Pinnacle. Some liked it, some drifted away, but the Rasta shepherd never had any problem replenishing his flock.

In 1939 he had registered an association called the "Ethiopian Salvation Society" to promote goodness, salvation, and unity of Jamaicans. According to the registration form, it was formed for the purpose of "assisting the propagation of the Christian religion and the message of spiritual redemption," and "to receive money via membership fees, subscriptions, donations, charitable grants, tithing of members, and by interest and capital of the mailing members." The purpose was to "insure sums of money to help with the burial expenses of members, their wives, husbands, and children" as well as "granting temporary financial aid to members during periods of illness and other distress circumstances that merit."[78] It was patterned after the older Jamaican burial societies, community-based funeral cooperatives once numerous in Jamaica. People held onto horrible memories of old slaves abandoned to solitary deaths, the deceased stripped of their rags and thrown naked into a hole in the gully.

Burial was a serious matter in Jamaica. Some believed that, provided the correct ritual was performed, the souls of the dead went back to Africa, where the indignities of slave life were repaired in death. Howell simply copied the regulations of one of those burial societies. The eighteen pages of Ethiopian Salvation Society text aren't very interesting, and they don't seem to reflect Howell's usual positions. Section 51 states that "No female member shall be entitled to sick benefits during times of pregnancy or child bearing until thirty days after delivery, and only if sickness intervenes." We know how Howell cared for women; he put Tyneth, his own wife, in charge of the welfare of pregnant women and young children at Pinnacle.

But the regulations also contained familiar, Gong-approved features such as the references to the toxic effects of alcohol, and the unlimited powers conferred on the Ethiopian Salvation Society president—himself. What about the monthly dues of two shillings—a day's wage for cane workers? Ex-members laugh, "We never paid them!" But the Ethiopian Salvation Society still managed to survive as a legal front against the authorities.

The political situation was becoming blurred. In 1944, as we know, Bustamante was elected chief minister, but he retained little executive or financial power. The army and police were under the direct control of the British, as were foreign affairs. Between 1944 and 1962, Bustamante slowly spun the web that would eventually enable him to be elected prime minister of an independent Jamaica in 1962. But in 1944 he was already the key man in Jamaican politics, and an astute one at that. The timing of his election and the beginning of the Golden Age at Pinnacle makes us wonder—could there have been some kind of understanding between Alexander Bustamante and Leonard Howell? Both had acquired a similar, slightly foreign accent and adopted similar organizing methods aimed at the same clientele, the illiterate masses impressed by their extensive travels and self-granted doctor's titles. Both knew their Jamaican people well, and knew exactly how to talk to them.

What did the people want? Love and bread. As soon as Howell arrived in Jamaica, his first move was to help the Red Lands hurricane victims. His niece Daphney remembers how the children spent nights putting money into small brown envelopes to bring to the poorest and oldest of the village. During World War II he was there again, and she remembers how he rode into Red Lands with cart loads of cornmeal and salt fish, a rare treat in those days of austerity and rationing. "As soon as they saw him come up the road, people left work in the fields and came up to greet him. There was a party, a feast. He gave to thousands!"

Bustamante's method was similar. He either lent money or gave it away. His party, more concerned with economic efficiency than with social justice, was famous for flashy handouts at election time, but in 1938 it was his cousin and future adversary Norman Manley who won wage raises for the workers, not Bustamante. Independence itself was engineered by Manley and J. A. G. Smith more than by Bustamante. The trade union movement was less an instrument of social change and improving working conditions than it was a political tool. Whoever wasn't with him was against him; if you didn't join the BITU, you couldn't get a job. "Since the labor disturbances of May last year, I cannot get permanent work. I just drift from place to place, which is actually against my faith," wrote one Frank Warren to the colonial secretary in 1939.[79]

Another unemployed man, Egbert Charles Smith, wrote to the governor, "For the past six months, I am totally victimized because I refused to support the dictatorial Bustamante Industrial Union. . . . We did not know that there was two governors in this island, Sir Arthur and Bustamante."[80] The dark-skinned individual, even with an education, had no place in industry except as the servant of brown masters. "Bustamante publish on Thursday 12/9/46 through the press what he thinks and only offer us gully work, road work etc. Pick, axe, and shovel again!"[81] All kinds of favors and privileges were rewarded to trade union leaders and political associates of Bustamante, while the people scrambled for crumbs. "The minister of social welfare is now living in a palace and we in cardboard huts!"[82]

What could have tied the two leaders together? Each read the other's intentions like a book. Bustamante probably did not feel any menace. The Rastafarians only wanted peace, and from him they would have it. In exchange, Bustamante wanted their votes. How-ell's white friend Bobby Alexander, who spent many tropic evenings discussing the political situation with the Gong, apparently chal-lenged Bustamante's candidate in the election of 1944, and brought the ballot boxes up to Pinnacle. If Howell was pro-PNP, how did he manage to protect his followers from the next decade of JLP power? Did he make a compromise with Bustamante? Did he join the Jamaican Labour Party?

22

The 1954 Raid

The spring of 1954 proved to be fruitful for Pinnacle. The ganja crop was exceptional. The herbsmen had never seen plants so tall and green. The buds were huge, oily, and abundant. Chief planter Elijah Powell told Leonard Howell that, if the weather held, they would never have to work again. Powell invested everything he had in this crop. In early April the planters began to harvest.

On Tuesday April 6, 1954, in Kingston, Howell was "dictating a letter to his secretary" in the early afternoon. He was in the upstairs room of his East Queen Street office when plainclothes policemen barged in. They searched every corner and found a bag full of money, a dozen grilled chickens and other meats in his fridge, two bottles of bush medicine with an acrid smell, eight thermometers, and two stethoscopes—but no ganja. They arrested Howell on charges of illegal practice of medicine. On trial, on April 13, Howell testified that he had studied medicine at Antwerp University in San Francisco from 1920 to 1924, and that he had practiced medicine in the army. He admitted having neglected to register himself as a doctor with the Jamaican authorities. He said he hadn't practiced medicine in Jamaica except in family emergencies. The judge asked him to spell the name of the university, but he declined.

Spelling, apparently, "was not his strong point." "Very interesting," the magistrate sneered. "Isn't it?" Howell replied. But his lawyer had a different line of defense. He explained that Howell had led a Back-to-Africa movement, and that all the medical instruments were to be sent there. Even if he had been practicing medicine, the lawyer remarked, why else would he need eight thermometers? Howell was let off, but this was only the beginning of the trouble that year.

Howell had been away from Pinnacle too often. Discipline had become loose. All kinds of people came, and open land became scarce. No one knew exactly the limits of Pinnacle Estate; some newcomers decided to settle on the other side of Sligoville Road, on Williamson Run, a steep gully bank that no one really took notice of until the adepts decided that the land on that side was theirs as well. People say that one Sunday a preacher from Sligoville named Parson Chambers was coming down from Spanish Town when he was suddenly confronted with a fallen tree in the road. The Rasta-farians wouldn't let him pass onto "His Majesty's Land." He had to ride all the way back to Sligoville and take the longer route through Orange Grove. When he eventually reached Spanish Town, he went straight to the police to complain. Other witnesses swore that there was in fact no fallen tree, only a confrontation at the gate between a parson and the Rastas. Since the raid happened the very next day, the Rastas blamed the parson. In fact, Parson Chambers had little to do with the raid. It had been planned for weeks.

At three A.M. on May 22, 1954, a large Kingston police force mustered at Half Way Tree station. They were later joined by more than a dozen Spanish Town officers. In all they numbered five supervisors, five detectives, 116 policemen, and a number of technical assistants. They had been thoroughly briefed and were equipped with rifles, tear gas, riot batons, walkie-talkies, two car radios, and an HF radio unit, supported by a mobile water tank and canteen. Taking Pinnacle by surprise was not an easy task, since, as a police journal later reported, "the main entrance from Sligoville Road was the only access available to a large party; the rest of the property was ringed by an almost impregnable barrier of precipitous honeycombed limestone, and covered with a dense overgrowth of shrubbery. Only one other approach was known, but this was a narrow foot path capable of accommodating only a small party in single file."[83]

The police reached the main entrance at four-thirty in the morning. They bumped into two women on their way to Spanish Town market, one of whom they arrested for the parcel of cured ganja they found in her basket. When they reached the marketplace where the guard's hut stood, they said they found two loaded revolvers in his possession.

From there they followed an uphill path that led to the "main settlement of some 150 huts [East Avenue] still sound asleep and completely unaware of police presence." Awakened by the police bullhorns, the inhabitants began to come out of their houses. This is when the house-to-house search commenced. "Ganja was brought out in every conceivable form of container: in suitcases, paper parcels, cardboard cartons, crocus bags, barrels and packing cases." Money was also produced in "staggering quantity; no less than £3000 in cold cash was handed over to the police for safekeeping. One woman alone produced £803 in cash, a clear indication of how lucrative the ganja trade has become, for either local consumption or illegal export."[84]

After the mobile canteen arrived and the police had breakfast, they fanned out to search and destroy all ganja cultivation on the property. Nine thousand plants were uprooted, with three tons burned on the spot, but the work was too much to be done in one day, and twenty men were then employed for this task over the course of the next three weeks. In all, close to one million plants were destroyed and 138 people were arrested, among which 110 were sentenced to prison terms ranging from nine months to two years of hard labor. If Police Superintendent C. A. Mahon, who wrote the report, remembers the day as a jolly occasion, such is not the memory of Pinnacle's inhabitants, especially Howell's teenage sons, Monty and Blade.

The 1954 raid, East Avenue; police gathering evidence. Houses on fire on the left; the large building in the center is the "mess hall." This photo appeared in the Jamaica Constabulary Force Magazine, *1955.*

COURTESY OF THE LIBRARY OF THE UNIVERSITY OF THE WEST INDIES.

Blade, who later went to art school and became a graphic designer, tried to fix his memories on paper. His drawing shows the superintendent sitting arrogantly at his desk on the hillside, while a long file of prisoners in handcuffs wait to be questioned. Policemen with machine guns mill around; huts burn in the distance. The people were stunned and silent. This was the biggest ganja bust in Jamaican history, "if not indeed in the hemisphere," Superintendent Mahon proudly noted. Pinnacle's prosperity was annihilated. "Law and order" had prevailed.

But there were flaws in the operation, and questions were asked. Why did the police wait until the middle of the harvest, when Pinnacle was bringing in huge sums of money? Why now, on the eve of a crucial election, when for a decade the police and the government had turned a blind eye on Pinnacle? Can we believe that such a major operation remained outside an intense national struggle for political power? Howell had bought off politicians and bureaucrats in the past, but now it looked like he had been playing with the Big Men and had lost the game.

My friend Donovan Phillips, who shares my passion for Howell, eventually convinced me that the only person who could shed light on the Gong's political alliances was the legendary Rasta elder Mortimer Planno, famous for encouraging Bob Marley to join the Rastafarian faith. Planno was hard to find. His health was failing, his financial situation unstable. He lived quietly up in the hills with a doctor friend from Guyana, and only emerged in his wheelchair for important meetings or conferences. Planno was a man of few words, and he didn't welcome visitors. I was not enthusiastic about the idea of disturbing him in his retreat, because I had a bitter memory of a stormy encounter with him at Tuff Gong, Bob Marley's headquarters, many years ago.

But Donovan was right. Mortimer Planno was the only Rastaman to have a thoroughly sophisticated vision of Jamaican politics. Raised on Fifth Street in Trench Town, he had friends all over the political spectrum, and he knew more than he would ever reveal. In 1960, he was the one to contact the university about researching the history of the Rasta movement. The following year, he led a Rasta group on a mission to Africa and met Selassie several times. As close to a maximum leader as the Rastas had in the decades when the movement became the Third World's spiritual nationality, it is Planno we see standing beside the emperor on the plane steps in the famous film footage of Selassie's state visit to Jamaica in 1966. In the late 1960s, when he was managing Bob Marley's struggling career, Planno envisioned Marley's role in spreading the Rasta message and encouraged him to use the power of show business to spread the word. Mortimer Planno is the author of one book and several pamphlets that put the Rastafarian movement in a very original light—including a memoir, of which he owns the only extant copy[85]—but even the university's copies of his publications are missing from its library.

Willing or not, I had to seek him out. Early the next morning, I found myself on a Clarendon bus in the company of Donovan and reggae singer Winston "Flames" Jarrett, en route to an uncertain interview.

It was noon when we stepped off the bus in Porus, a town hidden in the Milk River valley. We entered a blue house on the corner. At the end of the corridor was a big room with several windows. A warren of beds separated us from the ailing Planno; we walked around them, acutely conscious of his scrutiny. A foul smell of sickness added to my feeling of unease. Donovan embarrassed me by introducing me as "a white woman, but black in her heart." I am clearly white, with no apology. But Planno does not seem to take notice, and starts firing questions at me. I answer cautiously, knowing that a single wrong word could be my exit cue. Eventually he smiled. "You are right to do this research. Leonard Percival was a fascinating character . . . a *crucial* part of our history."

He begins by confirming my doubts concerning the ganja trade. In the 1930s, he says, ganja was not yet illegal. The British even advised Guyana, with its big international debt, to plant and repay. But in 1953 Winston Churchill (who had been reelected prime minister in 1951) decided to put an end to the ganja trade. Norman Manley, Planno says, called him into his office and told him, "Morty, you *must* tell your half-Indian brothers to quit the ganja business."

Morty looks at me. His ugliness is powerful, a kind of monstrous, fearsome beauty. His face looks like an unfinished sculpture, a moss-covered rock with one swollen lip. But from under the mass of entangled locks his eyes shine with intelligence. Mortimer starts shuffling through a pile of papers on his small bedside table and extracts a notebook dated 1976. Under the title "Leonard Howell" was a series of questions, more or less the ones I wanted to ask him. What was the relationship between Howell and Bustamante? Where was Howell when Garvey was in jail? What was Howell's role in the ganja trade? What were his relations with Lucky Gordon?

Lucky Gordon! The Profumo Affair!

Lucky Gordon was a Jamaican-born London pimp and drug dealer who was a minor figure in the Profumo scandal, supplying women and ganja to a group of influential political figures. The presence of a Jamaican ghetto toughie on the fringes of high government circles deeply shocked the English and contributed to the resignation of Minister of War John Profumo in 1963. The media complacently relayed the lurid details of the affair, and the scandal helped reveal the size and ramifications of the ganja trade, especially to the Jamaican public.

There is no doubt that Pinnacle played a pioneering role in establishing the industrial cultivation and export of ganja. Rasta elders still remember their trips to the Friday morning market in Pinnacle to buy ganja and yams, and their trips back home with the ganja hidden under the yams in the donkey cart. It was packed in burlap "crocus bags" for local shipment, and even in the legs of old trousers. Blade remembers witnessing huge international deliveries. The buyers would come with two trailer trucks and a police escort. Since 1934, the government knew of the corruption within the police department, and admitted that "Crown bailiffs and district constables apparently connive with the cultivators."[86] In the 1940s, ganja started circulating in small standardized packages that suggested industrial production. East Indians were the main retailers. Coolie Boy, Baïwadem, and Sital are remembered among those big dealers who came to Pinnacle for major loads of herb. Their gang, the Kapatula, controlled the western ghettos and the Spanish Town Road traffic.

Like any mafia, they had protection and informers. An old Rastaman, dubbed Humphrey Bogart for having appeared in *The*

Harder They Come, told the following story about Coolie Boy, one of the biggest dealers in the Spanish Town Road area. In the 1950s, Coolie Boy made a juicy connection through his girlfriend, who worked at the Normandy Hotel on Bond Street. Among her customers was Joe Goldburn, the first Jamaican helicopter pilot, and Coolie Boy and Goldburn became friends. When the government dispatched his helicopter to search out ganja fields, Goldburn told Coolie Boy, who went up to Pinnacle to exchange the info for some high-degree bushweed. Sometimes Coolie Boy would also ask his pilot friend to delay a trip for a day or two until the crop was secure. "Coolie Boy," Bogart said, "became *very* rich. But then [Norman] Manley called him personally and asked him to quit, and he did. Coolie Boy dead now." Bogart himself died in 2000.

Pilots, constables, politicians—all kinds of people were linked with ganja traffic. What about Bustamante? His energy and pistol-packing aura became insufficient to ensure his control, and the Jamaica Labour Party became known for crude strong-arm tactics. Guns began to appear in the ghettos, but in the 1950s they mainly came from the police. In 1954, Elijah Powell, the chief ganjaman at Pinnacle, was arrested for the illegal possession of a firearm, but he was freed without prosecution; his weapon had been bought from a policeman.

There is little doubt in Jamaica that the 1950s saw the rise of an international ganja trade controlled by local businessmen, and that when Jamaican political parties started arming their ghetto fiefdoms around election time, the guns came mostly from ganja profits. Marijuana, the new gold of Jamaica, was fueling this terrible system, putting the country in the hands of criminals.

That ganja paid for the weapons that permanently disrupted a contentious but generally peaceable society is an open secret in Jamaica. Several books on the history of reggae note this, although no "J'accuse" has ever been published. The two rival political parties drove (and still drive) thousands of Jamaican youths to violent death, but the Big Men of both parties never betrayed each other. (Many were related, as Bustamante and Manley were.) In 1978, under a Peoples National Party government, seven gunmen were executed in a notorious army ambush in Green Bay. The lawyers tried to bring the Green Bay killings to trial when the Jamaican Labour Party re-took power in 1981, but once again the case was dismissed. Jamaican *omerta* is just as sacred as Sicilian.

In a country of often daring newspaper reportage and savage radio talk shows, journalists become cautiously silent as soon as the Big Men are concerned. Most trial records concerning Howell and Pinnacle were destroyed in the criminal arson of the Spanish Town courthouse. And now, who would dare to speak out? We'll probably never know what role Pinnacle played in the financing of which party. But we can look at the roles played by different protagonists, especially the police, and try to draw some speculative conclusions.

At first glance, the 1954 raid on Pinnacle had all the aspects of a normal police seizure of a ganja plantation. The official version is even generally corroborated by information from Mortimer Planno. It has long been said in Jamaica that Winston Churchill personally pressured Jamaican officials to destroy the ganja trade. But we also know that for years the Spanish Town police got on well with Pinnacle, and not for humanitarian reasons. The police officers would come to the big house expecting handouts from Howell. Blade nurses a particular grudge against one particular officer who showed up at regular intervals. He sat in the big chair waiting to be served. He had a huge belly and loved to eat. When he came, Howell would kill a goat and have a curry prepared for him. One day he ate so much that he had to unbutton his pants. He belched, and when he did the chair beneath him gave way and he fell to the ground. Everybody hated him, Blade says, even the other policemen. There was one Spanish Town officer who was an honest guy and tried to do his job with some sense of justice. One day he got fed up, grabbed a gun, and began firing at random. Several people were killed, and among the dead was the fat cop.

The government couldn't entrust the Pinnacle operation to the Spanish Town constables, so they assigned the regional superintendent, C. A. Mahon. This is an indication that the government was aware of the corruption. But the raid meant the end of easy payoffs for the Spanish Town officers, so they quickly arrested the teenage "princes," Monty and Blade, and told Howell that if he didn't pay £2000 (the price of a nice house back then), they would charge the boys with ganja offences. Howell paid up. The boys were tried for possession of stolen goods—two gold watches their father had given them as birthday presents—and were easily discharged upon presentation of the jeweler's invoice.

Police corruption was rampant and unashamed. After the raid, the valley people remember seeing constables sneaking back to Pinnacle at night and early in the morning for loads of ganja they had stashed in the underbrush during the daylight hours. Clearly, if the chief of police had been earnest in his fight against ganja, things would have been much different. It is hard to believe that the politicians and trade unionists of the area were uninvolved, considering what we already know.

We naturally turn to the Spanish Town delegate L. W. Rose, an old Garveyite turned trade unionist and Bustamante loyalist. If he were using ganja money to finance his electoral campaigns, Rose would have left Pinnacle alone. But his PNP opponents may well have instigated the raid to cut off his resources. Jamaica's military, police, and executive branches were still under direct British control. The erudite and sophisticated Norman Manley was socially more in tune with the colonial authorities than the rough-hewn Bustamante. It is possible that Manley, who had the ear of the British and spoke in their name against ganja, found a way to kill many birds with one stone. His righteous anti-ganja stance demonstrated his dedication to British policy while it weakened Bustamante's position by cutting off a crucial cash supply. Pressured by Churchill (according to two witnesses), Norman Manley—the only significant opposition leader—personally contacted ganja dealers in 1953 and ordered them to quit.

Why would Churchill favor Norman Manley over the more conservative Bustamante? It has been posited that the JLP was too thuggish for the postwar colonial sensibilities. Although the PNP later demonstrated its own abilities in the field of corruption, the JLP opened the floodgates as early as 1947 when scandals forced two of Bustamante's ministers to resign. Bustamante himself boasted that he had a large bank account and was quoted as saying, "This money, some say I stole it, but then I was wise enough not to get caught!"

There is another element indicating that the JLP was the main beneficiary of the ganja trade, and that Norman Manley was well aware of this. His journalist son Michael had just returned from Britain and his studies at that socialist hotbed, the London School of Economics. In 1952 Michael Manley began his career as a trade unionist in Spanish Town, where the Ariguanabo textile factory workers were on strike. He spent months at the factory, discussing and promoting the PNP-linked union in the evenings. In the union elections of 1953, he won his first victory against the Bustamante BITU. If, during the battle, Michael Manley discovered that Howell's ganja was fueling his opponent's finances, he would have tried to stop it. His father, who knew how important it was to curry British favor to eventually gain Jamaican independence, had already placated the British in 1952 by expelling Marxists from his party. In 1955, after breaking much of the ganja trade, he went on to win the general elections. Two years later, he obtained a kind of quasi-autonomy for the island.

Howell's political connections remain unclear, but it was always obvious that the ganja trade was backed by politically connected businessmen, the only men who could have financed a big purchase, sent trailers to transport it to the wharves, and obtained a police escort to guard their investment. This was the inference made in an editorial in *The Star* on August 24, 1954.

> It seems obvious that an export trade exists and is highly organized. No doubt the planting is financed by a gang. Indeed, we could say a great deal more were it not for the laws of libel. We

must at present time confine ourselves to stating in public a small part of what the C.I.D. already knows. Some very well-known and "respectable" people have been organizing the growth and export of ganja for some time. The same people have extended their activities locally to include the running of an exclusive gambling house and a very expensive brothel for the not-so-tired businessman. The police even know the names of these men, but have not yet succeeded in finding proof against them. One good reason for this is that the gang gets tipped off about police activity in good time.

Needless to say, the gang never got caught, and names were never revealed.

My research had a major benefit for me. I made my peace with Mortimer Planno. The visit to Clarendon convinced me that this man— the most powerful chief and theorist of the Rasta movement since Leonard Howell—was in fact a genuine prophetic visionary. When I met him in the 1970s at Bob Marley's uptown Kingston compound, he appeared to match the stressed and paranoid feeling of the place. Now, though ill, he shone with an aura of benevolence. As I was leaving I instinctively knelt by his wheelchair to take his hand in mine, and asked him if sometimes he felt dispossessed by all the writers who, like me, were reviewing the history of the Rasta movement.

"Dispossessed?" He smiled kindly. "Of what? I never possessed *anything*."

23

The Ghettos

At the trials after the 1954 raid on Pinnacle, 110 residents received prison sentences ranging from nine months to two years at hard labor—relatively light by contemporary standards. But suddenly the very existence of Pinnacle was at stake. Now unprotected, the Rasta community soon had to deal with shakedowns by gangsters as well as corrupt policemen. A slow trickle of army weapons had invaded the ghetto, along with a serious influx of guns in ganja circles. The ganja planters had to be armed to protect themselves. "The Counselor told them to stay away from guns," ChiChi Boy remembers, "but dem did not listen." All Pinnacle's weapons were confiscated during the raid, so there was no way to protect East Avenue. Soon after, the papers carried the news that Pinnacle was up for grabs.

When Albert Chang died in 1946, it appeared that he had never officially registered Pinnacle's land to Leonard Howell. Had Howell neglected his payments? Doubtful, his son remarked, since several times the price of the property was seized at Pinnacle. Howell probably had paid, but his lawyers neglected the paperwork. Howell wasn't big on details. Once he bought a beautiful house in Kingston, spent two years fixing it up, and just when he was ready to move in, the real owner appeared and claimed it.

Albert Chang, journalists reported, left Pinnacle to the Boy Scout Association, which wanted possession. In July 1953, local representative L. W. Rose saw Isaac Barrant, the minister of agriculture, and asked that the government buy the land. What was Rose's purpose? To befriend the thousands of Rastas living at Pinnacle? To enhance his chances of winning the next election? To keep the flourishing ganja trade alive? Or to divide the estate among his political allies? As Planno told me, the politicians were getting bolder, with wealthy constituents whose cravings for land needed to be satisfied.

Rumors and strife crushed morale at Pinnacle. Those who had run away did not dare return. It was the end, and the dawn, of an era. The Rasta movement, Jamaica's new spiritual nationality, shifted from Pinnacle to the slums of West Kingston. A new culture—flamboyant and eventually world-shaking—developed in this hothouse urban environment.

The ghettos. Shanties. "Dat where de *people* live," a taxi driver explained to me on my first day in Jamaica. Derived from the Ashanti people of Ghana, the word *shantytown* came to describe the ramshackle squatters' districts that grew west of downtown Kingston. Whites seldom go there. Once, after visiting a good neighborhood uptown, I was offered a lift home. I politely refused, explaining that the number 59 bus line went straight to my place. "The 59? But it goes through Maxwell Avenue and Spanish Town Road! You'll be riddled with bullets. You *can't* go there, Miss."

I never had any trouble on the Spanish Town bus because, as a friend explained, "In Kingston, is not just anyone get shot. We only shoot people for a reason." One might get caught in the crossfire, but I was ready to take this risk to get to my friend's house.

There are different types of ghettos in Jamaica. The Whitfield Town apartment I stayed in during the 1970s, on Maxfield Avenue, was an old tenement yard surrounded by half a dozen wooden shacks occupied by poor families. There was a water standpipe in the middle. This, in fact, was luxurious. Most Jamaican ghetto dwellers have to walk a distance to the public water standpipe, sometimes very far. Slums generally follow the same pattern of evolution from cardboard boxes to rusted tin sheds to scrap wood cabins to concrete block cells—until someone brings in the bulldozers. One threads quickly through narrow zigzag alleys between walls of rusted tin; pink clusters of *serosee* flowers climb everywhere and provide a colorful touch and a bitter tea for those with nothing else for breakfast.

Kingston's slums began to spread as rural people moved toward the electric lights of the city in the beginning of the twentieth century. They grew larger in the economic depressions of the 1930s, and progressively invaded the coastal plains until the rich moved into the hills above the city, creating their own exclusive ghetto, leaving the plains west of Kingston to the poor. Plagued with heat and dust when not drowned in mud, the ghettos offered a desultory welcome and a life of ruthless competition to successive waves of migrants. And after every deadly hurricane, with every new crop of refugees, the shanties have crept farther and farther along Spanish Town Road, consuming the western plain in bites.

The first ghetto sprang up in the 1900s in Kington Pen, just west of Kingston's city center. It spread all the way to Smith Village behind the market, one of the biggest haunts for African preachers. W. F. Elkins describes some of them in his fascinating study, "Street Preachers, Faith Healers, and Herb Doctors in Jamaica: 1890–1925."

In 1897 the semi-crazed prophet Warrior Higgins returned from England, where he had joined the Ethiopianist movement. He went around announcing the end of the world at the turn of the millennium. He paraded through the streets with his Millennium Band, declaiming the most menacing and ominous Christian hymns—"There is a fountain filled with blood . . ." He claimed to have fought in Africa against the Boers. He made and sold herbal tonics to cure "cramps, pains, rheumatism, nervousness, and loss of appetite"—probably using ganja. He announced that he intended to marry a white woman "to spite the white folks: they would all want to cut their throats because seeing a black man like himself with a white wife would be such a shock." He pronounced all clergy and judges corrupt. He was seen one night riding on horseback with a hundred of his followers armed with sticks. In 1902 Higgins was severely beaten by baton-wielding men later described as "vigilantes." He died shortly after.[87]

In 1914, another prophet named David Bell came from May Pen to settle in Smith Village. Bell was also a healer; he made medicines from roots and herbs. The banner above his gate read "Faith Healing Church of God—Fret Not Thyself because of Evil Doers." He was fighting against fear. Bell could exorcise bad spirits, even coolie (Indian) spirits. He quoted Revelation, saw the mark of the Beast on the foreheads of government officials (666 is the number Rastafarians recognize as emblematic of the anti-Christ and the Pope), announced The End was near, and called for "more fire" ninety years before Sizzla, the fire-belching DJ of the Bobo Tribe. His fearless manner is reminiscent of Howell. "Who are *you* to be heard?" he asked a preacher and justice of the peace who interrupted a meeting. "I don't give a damn who the hell you are. You are nothing but a little white boy." He then picked up some trash and said, "I don't count the man as I count this trash."[88]

Revivalist Solomon "Sal" Hewitt gained fame by predicting the huge earthquake of 1907. He came from Boca del Toro, Costa Rica, and cautioned his followers to beware of deadly earthquakes—which duly shook Jamaica with much devastation. Although Ras Tafari had not yet been crowned, Hewitt sang, "The Lion of Judah will break every chain," one of the Rastas' favorite hymns. He even had himself "crucified" on a cross like a black messiah. His language, half religious, half social, was the language later used by the Athlicans. The first Rastas were not the inventors of the symbols that came to mean so much to the movement: the parables, the hidden histories, and even the three colors were prefigured by the prophets of Smith Village, Jamaica.

These proto-Rasta characters were not the only Africanist preachers in the area. At night the sound of hymns and drumming rose from the Pocomania and Kumina yards, the latter a transplanted African American sect from St. Thomas. Many area residents didn't appreciate the noise of these "ignorant practices." "They indulge in loud singing, jumping up and down, and rolling around on the ground."[89] They were apparently "howling and grunting like animals," according to the police. In June 1936 "someone set fire to the spot where these people have meetings and it was completely destroyed." But nothing was done about the ritual and noise, and the "good Christians" who were "disgusted by these savage practices" had no choice but to move eastward, which was almost as poor but "decent" at least.

In the 1920s and '30s, Smith Village—today called Jones Town—became the new center of Kingston's ghetto culture. Inhabited primarily by war veterans and Garveyites, workers deported from New York and black clerks denied advancement at work, the area had more of a radical slant. On Elgin Street in Smith Village, the first stone of the Athlican church was laid. On Asquith Street, Smith Village, we find Sam Radway and his Reform Club. Founded in 1923 by two alternative healers (one a homeopath, the other a radiologue), the Reform Club represented the restless fringe of Kingston's black intelligentsia. Its founders, Samuel Radway and Alfred Mends, had worked as doctors in New York and brought many unorthodox medical practices with them back to Jamaica. After multiple efforts to be accepted by the Jamaican establishment, they realized that the root of the problem was that they lived in a colonial state, which prevented them from practicing the same form of medicine that was being legally practiced in England at the time. So Sam Radway, defender of alternative medicine and freedom of worship, turned to African nationalism.[90] In 1949 his Universal African Nationalist Movement, based in Jones Town, Smith Village, probably played an important role in convincing the Rastas that any struggle within the political system was useless. He also propagated his critical views on established medicine, vociferously denouncing vaccination, contraception, and all chemical products.

As the ghetto moved further northwest, it claimed Denham Town, then Trench Pen. In 1939 the government built the ghettos' first low-income housing. These "government yards" were one-floor dwellings. The kitchens were outside, with fourteen families in each yard. But most people preferred to cook inside their rooms, and the outdoor kitchens became hangouts for homeless youths like Bob Marley, who—when his mother left to work in the United States— took refuge with his young singing companions "in a government yard in Trench Town" in 1959–60.[91] Trench Pen, renamed Trench Town, was on its bitter road to planetary fame.

Salt Lane, Back O' Wall, and Ackee Walk, two ghettos south of Spanish Town Road, were the first ghettos in which the Rastas found refuge after the 1941 raid on Pinnacle. Others went north and founded Rasta yards along Sandy Gully, a large, mostly dry riverbed. In 1941, the government started building a concrete gully there.

There was a large wilderness between the railway and Spanish Town Road, which served as the city dump. Called Dung Hill, or the Dungle, it ended at the graveyard wall. Fear of ghosts and duppies kept squatters away until the non-superstitious Rastas began to reclaim certain zones and built crude dwellings. This became the famous Back O' Wall ghetto, a kind of haven where the Rastas spoke of love, self-sufficiency, and solidarity, and where ganja overcame the persistent dread of ghetto living. Rastafarian communality spread; their self-respect proved, even to the poorest squatter, that dignity wasn't something money could buy. This idea sparked the curiosity and interest of much of the city's youth in the early 1960s.

The new, younger generation of Rastas was different from the older, founding generation. Most were country boys who had never been to war and who hadn't ever traveled. But they lived in constant contact with the generation of war veterans and travelers, healers, prophets, Indian gurus, and Pinnacle veterans. Joseph Nathaniel Hibbert, the old mason from Panama who worked with Howell, lived in Trench Town. While the Gong was in St. Thomas, Hibbert formed the Ethiopian Coptic Church, but Howell declined to support him and Hibbert went on alone, steeped in a dignified Ethiopianism of his own design. American researcher G. E. Simpson, who visited Trench Town in 1953, photographed him in his ceremonial red jacket adorned with cabalistic signs of crown and sword—also a masonic symbol.[92] Joseph Myers also lived in the vicinity, another ex-worker from Panama who was close to the Athlican group. His King of Kings Organization operated in Denham Town in 1947. In 1950 he moved to West Road in the heart of Trench Town with a new denomination, the United Ethiopian Body. Altamont Reid, founder of the 1936 "Ethiopian King of Kings Salvation" in Jones Pen, was the one of the few prophets who escaped the ghetto. After his involvement in the strikes of 1938, he became the personal bodyguard of Norman Washington Manley in 1940.[93]

What happened to Archibald Dunkley, the Bible-reading sailor who compiled all the scriptural references that identified Haile Selassie as the Lion of Judah? He was arrested several times in 1934–35 and eventually spent six months in an asylum. Nineteen thirty-eight brought him into business with Hibbert and Paul Earlington. They established "Local 17" of the Ethiopian World Federation (EWF) at 22 Bond Street, Smith Village.

The EWF was founded in 1937 in New York by Malaku Bayen, a cousin of Ras Tafari. Bayen had studied medicine at Howard University and had served as a surgeon in the Italian war. He was sent to New York in 1936 as Selassie's personal envoy to black America.[94] In New York Malaku organized an Ethiopian relief campaign, selling "Save Ethiopia" stamps, publishing a newsletter, and creating the Ethiopian World Federation. When the news of this hit Jamaica, local Ethiopianists sought affiliation and created their own (unofficial) Jamaican branch, Local 17. The president, L. F. C. Mantle, another self-appointed doctor, was a bizarre character who became famous in 1935 for a series of authoritative letters about Ethiopia to the newspaper *Plain Talk*. It finally came out that the "doctor" was a Kingston ice cream vendor who had never set foot in Africa but had worked in Cuba and had read many books. His main sources were most likely the three issues of the American magazine *National Geographic* devoted to explorations in Ethiopia, published in 1928, 1930, and 1931. Through the EWF and with the help of Archibald Dunkley, he tried to reunite all of Jamaica's myriad Ethiopianist groups, but this goal was above human achievement and Local 17 soon dissolved in personality conflicts and doctrinal schisms. (The Ethiopian World Federation was not officially established in Jamaica until 1955, when American delegate Maymie Richardson visited Kingston on behalf of the organization.)

There were also several Africanist groups in Trench Town that were set to emigrate, not to Ethiopia but to Liberia. This is where Marcus Garvey had planned a new colony of repatriated Africans that never came to fruition. One of these groups was the Afro West Indian Welfare League, started by Claudius Barnes and Scarlett Monroe in Whitfield Town. Each of the groups eventually broke up, divided by personalities or small doctrinal differences. In these millenarian circles, the debate centered on a central question—was there still any hope to straighten things out in Jamaica, or was it more fruitful to look to Zion?

While waiting for beards to grow long enough "to part the waters to Ethiopia," Leonard Howell had created the semblance of a Promised Land in Jamaica. It was hellish in the ghettos, and Pinnacle's downfall crushed the hopes of its survivors. The two general elections of 1944 and 1949 had brought about no change. The trade union movement's only contribution was a new mafia with a monopoly of sorts on unemployment. The ghettos operated on an almost feudal spoils system of jobs for votes. In general, the Rastas were too realistic to play that sort of game, and gave up voting in 1954.

Bustamante's economic "achievements" were pathetic. After ten years, Norman Manley calculated, workers' weekly salaries had only gone up about the price of a pack of cigarettes. Meanwhile the island's population was exploding. One G. Robinson (possibly ex-Howellite George Robinson) summarized the situation in a letter to the Colonial Office in 1950. "The population of Jamaica is growing at a fast pace; the island is still the same size. Year after year Jamaican unemployment grows. And what does the government do about that? Nothing. No amount of tear gas or bullets will stop the unrest. There is but one solution: go back to Africa."

24

Pinnacle's Last Days

On the morning of March 19, 1958, Miss Amy's sister, Vinette Fairweather, woke before dawn and set out to sell nisberries at Spanish
Town market. At the main road, her baskets full, she met a white
man leading a gang of armed thugs. "Those nisberries are *mine*,"
the white man hollered as he passed her. "I could have you arrested
for stealing." The white man and his goons continued uphill toward
East Avenue, beginning the final raid on Pinnacle.

Pinnacle's new owners now conducted a violent eviction of the
Rastas. There was no search for ganja, just destruction and arson.
Amy and her sisters escaped into the hills, but they paused to watch
the burning cabins go down, one by one. Gong Howell's house was
seized and looted. In the days that followed, the inhabitants of Bog
Walk, located in the Rio Cobre valley beneath Pinnacle, saw many
Rastas desperately fleeing the area. One even quarreled with a taxi
driver and ended up smashing his windshield.

Pinnacle had finally been sold out, once and for all.

How could such a thing happen? Dozens of people have
recounted Howell's assessment of the situation. Miss Gertrude,
Howell's trusted secretary, insisted that Howell bought the land not
once, but twice. "Mr. Howell was in America when he bought the

land from Mr. Albert Chang. And then he leave America and come to Jamaica, and the property was in the hands of another Chinaman. And him buy it again! So him have to buy the property two times, so you can't take Pinnacle from him. His name was Mr. Leonard Howell. So Pinnacle belong to Mr. Leonard. If you buy it, part it a thousand times, it still belongs to him!"

Blade wasn't actually that surprised. "He was very trusting. He make an agreement with you, he gives you a thousand pounds and you gone do that thing. And they used to rip him off. As a kid I remember he would contract people to build things, and they would come and take the money and then he wouldn't hear from them. They sell him cars that they don't own, and then two days later someone comes and takes the car. This went on month after month after month. When it came to money, he didn't have no . . . I would say, no use for it."

But if Howell had no legal title to the estate, his enemies would have dismantled it earlier, since they had tried for years to destroy the community. The 1943–1946 tax registry in the Spanish Town archives attests that Howell paid twelve pounds a year in land taxes. But Jamaican land taxes in that era were not paid exclusively by owners; they also could be paid by lessors. Only the Central Land Registrar in Kingston could tell us more.

The history of the estate has only been recorded since 1932. This was when Pinnacle, previously a Crown holding, was sold for the first time. There's no hint about who gave the place its mystical name. ("Pinnacle" was the heavenly temple to which Jesus was transported after facing down Satan's temptations.) Local legend says that Sir John Peter Grant, the reforming governor who replaced E. J. Eyre after the Morant Bay Massacre, used the estate as a country retreat. It was in the Pinnacle great house, destroyed in the 1907 earthquake, that Grant had his famous vision of a modern Jamaica living in peace and prosperity.

The registrar tells us that Pinnacle was sold for the first time in 1932. It changed hands several times between 1932 and 1939, when it was acquired by Albert Chang for the sum of £900. When Chang died in 1946, Pinnacle was "acquired by transmission" by the General Administrator of Jamaica. But then in February 1947 ownership was transferred ("by the will of A. Chang, deceased," the registrar says) to two important Kingston businessmen of Lebanese descent, Honan Fletcher and Edward Rasheed Hanna.

It would be interesting to have access to Chang's will to explore this strange transfer. But it is now certain that the Lebanese merchants were the rightful owners of Pinnacle during her glorious ganja career. And what a revelation! Edward Rasheed Hanna was a Jamaican legend. What comes to mind is the Lebanese character in Perry Henzell's novel of Jamaican political intrigue, *Power Game*. Powerful, smart, hedonistic Eddie Azani rules an empire of shops and businesses, runs a big gambling ring, lends money, and keeps girls. When Jamaica's biggest Rasta community is threatened with destruction, the Syrian businessman finances its survival by converting it into a huge ganja plantation. He arranges export shipments by plane, and on his last trip he sends the whole crop to herb-starved Miami.

The gambling, the girls, the Rasta community, the ganja export—the whole scenario instantly reminds me of that editorial in the *Star* in August 1954. Could Hanna be one of the "respectable businessmen" about whom the Kingston newspaper's cautious editorialist wrote?

Edward Rasheed Hanna was a big man. He had lived in New York, and served in the American navy during World War I. He returned to Jamaica in 1919 and succeeded his father as head of the trading firm Hanna Enterprises. From the early 1930s he was president of the Boy Scouts Association and also one of its main benefactors—along with Chang. Why would Chang have willed Pinnacle to him? Was his motivation philanthropic? Did the merchants throw a community of four thousand people out on the street so the boy scouts could have a playground? Or did Chang give Hanna a ganja plantation in exchange for something?

It seems strange that the two Lebanese owners of Pinnacle never claimed their land, or even let anybody know that it was theirs for ten years—and then suddenly sold it.

Hanna became one of the biggest businessmen on the island. Only a man of his stature could have organized big ganja shipments by truck and trailer; only a man like him could have arranged the international connections, bribed the dockers, paid the police escort. Hanna had the means to buy silence from witnesses and government officials, and he had friends all over the Bustamante administration.

Suddenly the crypto-historic connections swim into focus. Using the Boy Scouts Association as a front, some people were clearly running an agro-industrial commercial enterprise, which—as well as making some key people very rich very fast, as contemporaries attest—also served to finance the electoral campaign in exchange for government leniency. We can guess that the traffic was organized primarily by the likes of Hanna, but there is little chance that any definitive proof will ever surface. Drug traffic, the Star said, was organized by the local mafia, who were informed of police activities every time a search was planned. But after the raid of 1954, when corrupt policemen and street-level Kingston hoodlums started launching "freelance" raids, the operation became too risky for "respectable" people.

On July 17, 1957, E. R. Hanna sold Pinnacle to Joseph Linton Watt. It was the death of Leonard Howell's dream.

Watt, Howell's nemesis, is another of Pinnacle's many legends. He had two daughters and two sons. The girls went to live in Canada, and the elder son died, but the younger one, Joe, agreed to talk to me in his beautiful villa in Red Hills. It was a difficult decision for him. But finally, after much prodding, gentlemanly Joe Watt decided to share his version of what happened.

He reckoned that his father was a peculiar character. The son of a black housemaid and a Scottish overseer who had arrived in Jamaica at the end of the nineteenth century, Watt belonged to the Plymouth Brethren, a fundamentalist Christian sect. His four children were raised in accordance with the strict rules of the order: no music at home, no makeup for the girls, church four times a week and twice on Sundays. Joseph L. Watt, a hard-working entrepreneur, founded many enterprises, including the famous Spanish Town dairy that provided milk for the Cremo factory, and numerous cattle farms. He owned stone quarries and bulldozers. He speculated in land, developing Forest Hills and a large part of Red Hills, overlooking Kingston, into residential districts for the well-to-do. In Spanish Town he bought all the hills in back of the city: Orange Grove at the top, then Tredeger Park and Waterloo, Hillview and Crosspen (which abutted Pinnacle) at the foot of the hills.

But what use could Pinnacle have been to Mr. Watt? "There wasn't much land there," Joe Watt admits. "Not very good soil. Just a few pockets. Very rocky place. It's a big enough property, but there's very little arable land to cultivate on it. To be honest, I was no longer working for my father at that point, but I would occasionally go and see him and we would walk together and he would show me what he was doing. I think he bought it for the stones. He was in the quarry business, and Pinnacle had a lot of stones. He did not have to blast or anything—the stones were there to pick up. But he would have had to blast out roads to haul them out."

This Plymouth Brother was a builder through and through. His roads are still there, just a bit overgrown and discolored by time.

Did Joseph L. Watts have any known political sympathies? His son answers with a definitive and resounding no. What were his relations with Howell? "As far as I know, though I can't verify, my father bought the place from him. I remember meeting this fellow Howell on one occasion. They called him Gong. You would see him riding down on his donkey in a full suit. He always had two or three outriders. It was a funny sight—a person in a dress suit riding a donkey with a saddle. But it was very charming, as charming as he was in fact. Very friendly. My father eventually knocked down the building on top of the hill. It was Howell's residence, but really not much of one. There was no road leading to it, only a footpath. When my father bought the place from [Howell], his house, it stank like hell! They had to take off the roof, and the crows [vultures] came in. It was awful. I don't know if they murdered people there, or what."

At his death, Joseph Watt willed everything to his daughters, leaving nothing for his sons. Ken, the eldest, had already bought the Waterloo dairy farm from him, and Joe had his own bulldozer enterprise called Earth Movers. In his later days, the elder Watt decided to live in England, but he didn't like the climate and came back to Jamaica to die. He'd been cursed, Howell's disciples say, by the fate of Pinnacle and the thousands he had rendered homeless. This, they say, also explained the untimely death of his son Ken, who was one of the leaders of the 1958 raid and probably was the man who had snarled at Vinette Fairweather.

According to Joe Watts, certain Howellites were offered jobs on his father's quarries and farms and were permitted to stay at Pinnacle. Some others—stone masons, cattle tenders, guards—found employment at Caymanas, the enormous estate to the east of Pinnacle. Caymanas' administrator was Perry Henzell's father. Perry remembers the old night watchman from Pinnacle, who used to sit under his window with his big stick and tell Bible stories. The director's interest in the Rastas was triggered by his encounters with such characters. His famous film *The Harder They Come* was the first to spread word of the movement into the international cultural arena.

There were Howellites living at Pinnacle until 1980, when there was another trial over the estate. Witnesses claim that one Henriquez, a friend of Bobby Alexander's son, was going around selling off parts of Pinnacle. The whole file for the trial was destroyed in the Spanish Town court fire. Kingston attorney Ras Miguel Lorne knew the judge in charge of the case, but she refused to give him any information and pretended that she didn't remember anything about it. Even now, people still come to local estate agents' offices, brandishing what they insist are ownership papers and deeds to Pinnacle.

In November 1958, Howell no longer resided at Pinnacle, having settled at South Camp Road, Kingston. His two sons, Monty and Blade, had been studying in town, the elder at the technical institute and the younger at art school. Uncle Hugh describes the youngsters as carbon copies of Harry Belafonte, Jamaica's international superstar. They were both six feet or taller, with broad shoulders like their father, piercing eyes, golden skin, and regular features. At school they were at first ridiculed for being "God's sons," but very soon they had become the most respected pupils in school. Brother Sam Clayton of the Mystic Revelation of Rastafari, who was in school with Monty, described him as "a kind of mystic: whenever someone said something about his father, he would smile a certain smile and say nothing."

Blade remembers that once his teacher in art school asked him if he didn't find it strange to drive to school in his own car while his teachers had to walk. Blade was surprised. "It was only a small car that I bought with pocket money." Monty had another passion—motorbikes. He got his first big one in 1956. After his father was arrested and fined in 1954, the police came and seized four of his vehicles—trucks and cars owned by the community. They were sold and the money given to Mr. Dayes, Howell's attorney. Dayes paid Howell's debts and fines, but there was some money left over. Monty found out about it and approached Dayes, threatening to tell his father. Dayes agreed to buy Monty a bike. "I took the biggest one," Monty reported with a laugh. "Now I could outrun the police." But one day he crashed with Blade riding on the back. After four days in a coma, Blade barely survived.

They were privileged and sought after. ("I changed women as I changed shirts," Monty admits.) The boys kept to themselves and didn't let people know who they were. They gave up trying to defend their father. They had inherited the Gong's aura and some of his moral authority, but also his deep sense of isolation and wariness.

In Jamaica, in 1958, a new mento/calypso song told the story of the raid. "Before the sun rise in Sligoville, they mash down Pinnacle..." It was a dark year for the Gong. Chang had betrayed him, and his people were scattered and homeless. He probably sensed that the movement was drifting away. Rastafarian yards were spreading out over every corner of the Kingston slums. In the 1930s, when he was preaching in St. Thomas, Howell had claimed to be Ras Tafari's envoy to Jamaica. His group was the first to be called by the name of the emperor—"Rastafarites." But now Ras Tafari had entered the public domain, and dozens of cults were referred to as "Rastafarian." The dreadful term "Rastafarianism" was invented by academics and journalists, a nonsense word for people who like the meaningless "ism" tacked to a word to put it in context.

The Rastafarians had come a long way from the first community of rural women flocking to Leonard Howell. The Rastas of the 1960s were ghetto dwellers with an urban agenda. In March 1958, Prince Edwards Emmanuel, a young Rasta from Ackee Walk, just south of Spanish Town Road, organized a convention of Jamaica's Rastafarians. He convened some three thousand "beardman" for three weeks of reasoning and drumming around huge bonfires, an important event in Jamaica.

Howell didn't show up.

Some say he was sick. Some say Emmanuel didn't invite him. In any event, faithful Howellites were now on their own, separate from younger, dynamic elements of the movement in Back O' Wall and Trench Town. But each shantytown Rasta yard or camp was in effect a miniature Pinnacle, where the community's restive youth gathered to reason, seek fellowship, smoke the holy herb, and sing.

On Second Street in Trench Town, a fourteen-year-old country boy from the rural parish of St. Ann listened to the stories told by Pinnacle veterans and other Rastas. He shared Howell's dream of a paradise on earth, but promised himself never to be wiped off the slate like the first Rasta. "I am tougher than Gong," he sang, so his friends began to call him Tuff Gong. The world knew him by another name—Bob Marley, prophetic star of reggae music.

25

God or the Devil?

Walking up to Pinnacle one last time, I looked at the old entrance pillar to see if the "Pinnacle" sign still existed, but years had passed since my first visit, and the last traces of the letters had been washed away by time and weather. In the place of the footpath that once led to the great house, a road had been gouged out with a bulldozer. The huge aloes that had protected the great house with an arsenal of green cactus spears had all been cut to the ground. I'd felt a surge of hope when I heard that the estate's current owner, Ms. Lois Sherwood, had been an artist in her early days, and so I went to see her at her office on Hope Road.

Ms. Sherwood is a handsome woman with golden skin and an authoritative air. I was told that she is a partner in the firm that owns Jamaica's Burger King franchises. She bought the property from Canadian resident Dorothy Louise Ramsden, the daughter of Joseph Linton Watts, without knowing the history of the estate, whose name had been changed to "De La Vega Heights." Perhaps everyone agreed it was better to erase all traces of the Rastafarians, so the historic name "Pinnacle" no longer exists in the land registry.

Recently a Rasta friend of Ms. Sherwood had told her of the history of the land, and she thought she might restore the ruins for tourists and pilgrims. (She had originally planned to subdivide the property for housing.) But now she wasn't sure what she would do. She seemed frightened by the idea of Rastas making pilgrimages to the spot to smoke herb and god knows what else. There was also some talk of the government buying her out and declaring the place a historical monument, but heritage conservation doesn't have a great record in Jamaica. Rita Marley built a souvenir stand next to her husband's mausoleum.

At dusk, I meditated on the veranda of Howell's house. The plain was far below, and from my spot I could see the entire coastline. My friend Donovan, as usual for him, was swept away in visions. He talked of the Arawak Indians who took refuge in the caves while the Spaniards built their lookout post at the top of the hill, the "Temple Ridge." He remembered Governor John Peter Grant, the visionary who began his work in Jamaica by closing down a prison, saying it was an unnecessary entity as he would entirely take care of his people!

Pinnacle. What a beautiful choice of land for the first Rastas. Howell certainly had a dramatic a sense of history. Donovan showed me the old road leading from the bottom of the hill down to Spanish Town. "No surprise he always got away from the police. He could see them coming two hours in advance." To my left spread an ethereal blue-green expanse of cane fields. From our lookout, we could see the two ghettos, Spanish Town and West Kingston, crawling toward each other like two hands trying to shake. The Spenser's Pen housing development hung onto the plateaus beneath us, and the Rio Cobre glittered far below. "He had all of the Jamaican landscape right before his eyes," Donovan remarked. "How could anyone have expected him to stay away from the political arena?"

Donovan has guided my research on the political front. With his knowledge of contemporary Jamaican history, he helped unravel the intricate threads of many of the political and social machinations pertaining to Pinnacle's demise. He encouraged me to put them together, because no one else had ever tried. But the result puzzled me. Could Howell have been a player in the Jamaican political power game?

This wasn't pretty. That the money from ganja grown at Pinnacle funded crooked elections, armed union enforcers, and eventually the ghetto gunmen is an idea that revolts me. I want to believe that the Gong would never sell out. Didn't he refuse to vote? Maybe some of his herbsmen fell into the political trap, but hadn't their leader tried to ban all weapons in the community? Chi-Chi Boy had insisted it was the growers' fault. They brought the weapons into Pinnacle. Howell? No, Gong would never countenance gunmen.

I stood and took a few steps back across the black and white veranda tiles, now almost all a uniform gray. Dry leaves cracked underneath my sandals. One brick step led to what had been the rooms of Monty and Blade, but the partitions have fallen down, and bushes have cracked the tile floor. At the back was Howell's bedroom. It is whitewashed and so small that there is barely room for a bed and chest. Where did he put all his books? Where were the meals served to the corrupt policemen? Clearly not here.

I sat against the wall in what was once Howell's room. Rain has washed away the white coating from the walls, and in some places the brick structure is apparent. Where was the bed? By the tiny window? What would have happened if I had met the Counselor? Would I have sat on his bed like so many others? Would I have watched in the darkened room as the light played on his broad shoulders? Would he have turned back to look at me? Would I have seen his eyes? Something builds inside me, a tension, a longing. Then the vision evaporates. Against my back the wall is damp and cold.

His eyes. In the maze of "facts" about Howell, I see that he has many faces. I am not sure which one to trust. "God or the Devil?" asked Uncle Hugh. I feel that if I could see his eyes for just one moment then I would know. I suddenly feel discouraged. The shards of "evidence"that I have been patiently assembling will never

give me what I truly crave—just one glance at the legendary Howell, one glimmer of his soul. It is he who holds me. He seduced me
like all the others. And I followed him.

Donovan laughed when I told him this. "Rastas say that woman
see Jah through man," he taunted from the porch.

"It's about time they plug into the direct line," I answered
thoughtlessly.

Donovan put on his sorcerer's smile. "How is that? Isn't that *you*
I see here, humbly following the path of a notorious macho man—
with all those ladies around him? You would never have put up with
it!" My mind goes instantly to Tyneth. Older people here always tell
me that I look like her. Would I have thrown myself to the vultures
instead of sharing my king? The other "queens" apparently accepted
sharing. But the Counselor was unique. Never before had so many
women known and been looked after by such a courageous, confident, loving, and free man. They loved his freedom above all.

Miss L. never succeeded in wiping Howell from her memory,
though mixed feelings about him still trouble her at the end of her
life. Howell was her greatest trauma and her greatest love. What
does she hold against him after all these years? "He said that Christ
was black," she answers. "Christ has no color." I looked at the shriveled knot of her fingers in her lap, her cloudy gaze, the shadow of
bitterness at the corner of her mouth. I can't help but think she
broke herself against him too. She believed that he was Christ, and
she got caught.

Leonard Howell's career as a prophet and leader lasted twenty-five
years, from 1933 until 1958. After the destruction of Pinnacle, he
drifted into the shadows and other leaders took his place as spokes-
men for Jamaica's alternate spiritual nationality. The conventional
wisdom was that Howell had believed he was God. Maybe it was as
the African reggae star Alpha Blondy sings, "See that God's chair
was empty—he sat down in it." But there's no evidence or testimony

that Howell ever thought that way. It was his followers who called him a messiah. He led Pinnacle with a dignified attitude, visionary ideas, and indomitable authority. He put his talents and charisma in the service of the poor. His powerful image at the top of the hill protected East Avenue. He persevered through police beatings, prison terms, and stiff fines. He transformed the lives of thousands of people. Who but a larger-than-life being could have done all this?

But if God is in everything, why incarnate this force into human form? Bongo Sheffan answered, "When you cry for help, it is a man who comes to the rescue."

Howell answered countless cries for help from the abandoned mothers who came to live at Pinnacle, from jobless workers, from landless peasants. He guaranteed their dignity at Pinnacle for no less than eighteen years—long enough to raise up a new generation.

The new generation became the one that launched Jamaican music and Haile Selassie into the planetary consciousness.

Before plunging back into Kingston's hot atmosphere of diesel fumes, smoke, and dust, I wanted to breathe some salt air, so I popped in at David Marchand's place in Runaway Bay, on the north coast of the island. David had just painted a life-sized Christ, complete with white robe and flaming heart. In the place of the face and hands he left three open holes so he could pose as Jesus, eyes turned toward the sky, right hand covering his burning heart. David is quite serious about this image. For years he has been connected to Christ by direct line. He says he has Jesus' private cell phone number.

That night I went up to the roof and lay down, listening to the jungle broadcast of tree frogs mixed with the symphony of waves and wind. From somewhere nearby I heard a preacher raising his voice. It was impossible to catch what he was saying, but his voice was deep and rhythmic, and had a lyrical note. Inspired, I jumped up and ran to the road. The voice led me though the fields and past the village to Brownstown Road. The words began to make sense now—he spoke of Revelation and the second coming of Christ. His expert cadences grew in intensity as I came nearer to him. I ran through an alley, a chapel at its end. Its gates were wide open, and a profusion of light spilled forth from inside. At first I saw only the garden of colorful hats—muslin, orange, ribbons—all moving delicately in the breeze. Inside were only a very few men but a whole flowerbed of devoted ladies who stamped their feet, moaned, and cried out. On the platform at the front, a flush-faced man was yelling into a microphone, his arms wide open. "Are you ready now? Are you ready for *him?*"

"Ahhhh!" sighed the flowerbed.

"He's getting *closer*! I feel him *coming!*"

"Ahhhh!" The pink and yellow breasts exhaled.

"He's coming! He's coming! He's here! Creeping up on you! Penetrating you! Do you feel him coming? Do you feel him? Do you feel him? Do you feel him *coming?*"

The amplified voice burst into a high triumphalist shout. "He's INSIDE!"

The flowerbed, enraptured, swooned in the embrace of the Holy Ghost.

26

The New Culture

On a warm day in 1958, two boys, both in their middle teens, walked down Molynes Avenue toward Trench Town. They were thrilled by the prospect of spending a "sabbath" in the yard of the respected elder Brother Ira. The boys, one of whom was the future Jah Bones, had encountered Rastafari for the first time a week earlier when they took part in a Rasta fast at Fire Key. Bro Ira's yard was enclosed in corrugated tin; five small houses sheltered several couples and a few children. The ceremonies always began with a prayer from Brother Ira, Jah Bones recounted.

> Bro Ira would quote any amount of prophecy. He quoted from *Promised Key*, Revelation, talked about Selassie I, Garvey, Africa. . . . Once as the man opened his mouth, words flew out like a million birds released from a gigantic sanctuary. That was the first time that I had ever heard a black man pray so positively and realistically. Everyone was free to chip in from time to time, for example: "fire burn!," "Rastafari!," "Selassie I," "Thunder! Lightning! Brimstone! Fire and blood!" was the favorite rhetoric along with "ertquake." . . . These were rhetoric or slogans that were filled

227

with sound and power. Words, sounds, and power had special significance to Rasta—and so prayer meant a great deal.[95]

After the prayer from Brother Ira, the scripture was read and hymns sung. Every participant could read, pray, and bring forth his own vision. Somebody prepared the chalice while Psalm 18 was read. The brother in charge of the lighting the water pipe first blessed it by reading from Revelation. Then the sisters chanted and the brothers played drums for hours while the chalice passed in and out of the hands of the participants. "After three, four, five hours everyone would be blacked [on herb]. At this point Jah was strictly in charge."

Fasting ended at six o'clock, after reading Psalm 91. Everyone rose for the psalm with difficulty, as no one had eaten anything for the previous twenty-four hours. "You held on to the bed with your knee or even on the chair back with your hand or anything, but one must stand up." In a loud chorus, as everyone drew on reserves of energy and willpower, the room filled with the verses of Psalm 91. When the assembly reached verse 13—*Thou shalt tread upon the lion and adder; the young lion and the dragon shalt thou trample under feet*— "everyone would stamp their feet as a symbolic gesture, signifying the actual grounding to dust of Babylon."

> Jah! Rastafari . . . Haile Selassie I! Man and woman must hail and greet each other in righteousness, and who must move must move, who wants to stay, stay, and cooking, drumming and more reasoning in a "free" form . . . into a triumphant celebration. . . . The fasting duty is seen as a way of cleaning the spirit and the flesh which is badly corrupted by Babylon. It served an educational need, as well as allowing I and I to identify and utilise I and I psychic powers.[96]

Jah Bones's teacher was an elder by the name of Bra P., born Carl Smith in Trelawny sometime around 1930. He was "a molder by trade, roots engineer by profession; he made aluminum pots but subsequently manufactured stoves, clothes irons, manhole covers, and casings." Bra P., Jah Bones says,

> served to steady my life as a ghetto youth in a very subtle but firm way. For starters he was a hard working man—honest, truthful, and ambitious. But what impressed me most about him was the way in which he lived for and in these qualities. Brother P. taught actions meant more than words. He never wasted words by repeating his points in an argument. He forced his listeners to use their ears, their eyes, and all their senses; he even compelled people to use their imaginations.[97]

From this important influence sprang a new culture. Jah Bones' generation, born (like Pinnacle) around 1940, developed the rhetorical blend of scripture and folklore that comprises the Rasta oral tradition.

The word *dreadlocks* is a good example. Until the end of the 1950s most Rastas were "beardmen," but they still cut their hair. Some took to growing uncombed locks, like the Indian *saddhus* or the Ethiopian guerrillas who took an oath not to cut their hair until Ethiopia was freed from the Italians in the 1930s. Howell himself, his son says, did grow his hair for a short period of time, but did not encourage his adepts to make themselves too conspicuous and subject to victimization. He had only three fierce-looking locksmen guarding Pinnacle; people called them "mountain lions," like the Ethiopian warriors. It wasn't until the 1960s that locks became a more common style. Jah Bones claims it was at Fire Key that the term *dreadlocks* came into being.

> Errol, Danny, Jimmy, Parker and I decided that Drednis was crucial to Rasta "developman." . . . Non Rasta Jamaicans would notice the new hairstyle of locks and became frightened and jumpy. . . . It was rather interesting to I and I that it was so. I and I felt that the new hair style should get a name. A man suggested fear locks and immediately the other four say no. I think it was

Danny who said why not call it dreadlock since that sounds better, and according to the dictionary it means fear. Straight away
the name was adopted and a big, strong bout of laughing interrupted the discovery for a while. . . . It wasted no time in catching on because I and I moved around and dropped it all the time
until all the dreads got the message. That was '59, closer to '60
than to '58. . . .[98]

Verbal cadences and rhythms became a crucial trademark of the
new Jamaican culture, a different kind of "talking drum" that energized the art of the original Kingston DJs like King Stitt and U Roy,
and then empowered I Roy and Big Youth, who in turn inspired
American rappers. "I and I realized that words are very powerful
and that this is made manifest by vibration. The rhythm of the
sounds was crucial to the pattern of the reasoning. Each word had
its meaning in relation to its specific context in social-human power
relationships."

Some see the influence of the old freemasons like Archibald
Dunkley and Hibbert, who talked about the symbolism and mystic
relationships of numbers and sounds, in the rhythms of Rasta dis-
course. But the Rastas of the new generation took this concept even
further, putting this codependence between language and society to
the test. Jah Bones and his brothers began to scrutinize the English
language. They changed "understand" to "overstand." For a people
marked by slavery, colonialism, and fascism, the idea of standing
"under" someone or something did nothing to uplift the community's morale.

Create also become *crelove*, as *hate* seemed antithetical to creation. Jamaican patois with its euphonic rhythms, simplified grammar, and colorful imagery had to be reclaimed from scorn and
dereliction. Rasta's new diction gave believers a sense of identity and
spiritual nationality. *God* became *Jah*, a word that Rastas pronounce
in a sincere and powerful exaltation. Some see a cabalistic influence
in the choice of *Jah*, almost certainly a shortened form of *Jehovah*,
but there's also a link to the Indian *Jai*, recalling that some of the

earliest Pinnacle prayers were inspired by mantras and contained Hindi and Urdu words.

But clearly the most cherished word of early Rasta lyric terminology was *I*. Deep, voluptuous, high-flying, *I* is associated with anything good and spiritual: *I-man* is I, *de I* is you, because *I* is straight and *U* is crooked. *I and I* is us, the community living in *Inity* (and not *unity*), etc. The *I* was a new game they used to question and dissect the English language, and to rebuild it to what sounded right. Soon all of Kingston was doing it. When brother met brother new words came into being, and if they sounded good, they were adopted right away. Bob Marley's song "Revolution" is almost a primer about the use of *I* as an affirmation of faith.

Rasta had become urban. New codes, new hairstyles, new languages, new colors, and, in everything, more wisdom. The new imagery spread through ghetto alleys like salvation-quality good news. Every day more of the city's young became attracted to it, and Rasta slowly began to appear on the fringes of the Jamaican middle and upper classes. All it needed now was a music to carry the swing. In the east, ska was already simmering.

At Bull Bay, on the coast east of Kingston, on Nine Mile Beach four or five wooden huts are scattered under the tamarind trees. This is a Nya-Binghi community, the Jahola Theocratic Government. When the sun goes down, Bongo Puru, Bongo Sheffan, Ras Porta, Ras Hill, and Ras Benjie prepare a chalice. "Jah Rastafari." Once the ritual is through, three or four wooden drums appear and the evening pulses along to the heartbeat Rasta rhythm. It's such pacifying music. I love to listen to it deep into the night, lying in my small tent by Bongo Sheffan's house. Old men's voices mingle with the children's, all fresh and sincere. The bass drum breathes out a slow, sleepy type of music. "The bass drum is the *first* drum," explains Harry T. Powell, one of the greatest Rasta drummers in

Jamaica. "We call it 'at-man,' which means that it goes at man, at the people. You can hear it for miles. You know-say, something is happening over there. The drum is the sound of the people. The repeater is now *the* solo drum. It is like the warrior who sneaks out from camp and comes back to warn the others when the attack is launched. The repeater is *on*. The repeater is the one who dances over there in the distance, and it makes the people dance. Among the drums he is the dancer. He plays the musical part of your heart while the *funde* keeps the tempo. The funde is the base, the rhythm of the heart."[99]

I love above all the quiet cardiac pulse of the *funde*, the heart-beat of ancient wise men looking at the world from above, free from fear. I had come to believe that this beat had been developed at Pinnacle, but knowledgeable people have convinced me that it was the faster Kumina drumming that the Howellites played at their celebrations. So where was the better-known Rastafarian "riddim" born?

27

Rasta Music — Kumina or Burru?

The day I met Miss Gertrude Campbell, leader of the Tredegar Park Howellites, she was wearing everyday clothes. Her worn-out old T-shirt and skirt were dazzling white, as was the cloth she wore wrapped around her gray country-woman plaits. She had given herself to Leonard Howell's cause the day she met him some sixty years before. She was his secretary and his accountant. She cared for Tyneth's children. She cooked for him when everyone else was on the run. It was Gertrude Campbell alone who looked after Howell in his last moments. Now about eighty years old, Miss Campbell welcomed me with curiosity and with a glimmer of humor in her slightly drooping eyelids. She hadn't been expecting my visit, as the world had forgotten that they were the ones who had started it all. But she knew that something was bound to happen someday. "One man soon coming here, Mr. *Time*! Well, dat man I'm waiting on. Nothing can come before the Time." She had erected her wooden tabernacle plank by plank, tin sheet by tin sheet, with the help of other Tredegar Park faithful just as poor as she. It is the seventh one they've built; the six previous had all been destroyed by fire or the police. On the day of our first meeting, Miss Campbell went into the corner where the drums are kept, and, bending down over the solo drum, began to play a call—pure Kumina! I had begun to come to terms with the fact that the Rasta rhythm, "Nya-Binghi" as most call it, had not originated at Pinnacle. But where had it come from?

Of the few things that Africans carried with them in their forced exile, there was one that survived, and gloriously at that—their music. Surprisingly, slavery might not have been the period in history that did the most cultural damage to this music. This was because some slave owners and overseers thought it convenient to let their workers have a good time if it kept their spirits up, which was crucial to production. In 1818 Matthew Lewis, the British author of the notorious (and bestselling) gothic horror novel *The Monk* and the owner of inherited sugar estates in Jamaica, allowed his slaves to hold boisterous evening dances in the parlor of his great house while he was in residence.

> "The chanting began at six o'clock and continued without interruption until two o'clock in the morning. Never in my life had I heard such incredible sounds! All the space in the house not occupied by dancers was occupied by men, women and children sleeping deeply. . . . At midnight, my manager wanted to get everyone home, but the company kept dancing and howling until two o'clock in the morning. It is around this time of night that people tend to reach their limits of kindness, but finally everyone departed and I was left to nurse a violent headache in bed.[100]

It's obvious that "Monk" Lewis—a friend of Shelley, Keats, and Byron—was not an ordinary slave owner. His horrified neighboring planters saw his Romantic curiosity and humanistic attitude as dangerous and subversive. Near the end of his stay on the island, he was confronted by an angry mob of local slave owners.

After Emancipation, planters saw little reason to further placate the Afro-Jamaican populace, and during the period between 1835 and 1865, the bosses were harshly repressive of slave culture. African cultural manifestations were, and still are, viewed as potentially dangerous. "[A Jamaican magistrate] found that up until January 19, 1848, no African had resumed work; their drums still resounded in the villages and in the mountains. These dances they do to the rhythm of the drums are the embodiment of all wickedness and debauchery known to the African race."[101]

In 1854, some twenty years after Emancipation, "a magistrate in Trelawney described the general laboring population as 'exhibiting lamentable behavior, their irreligious and immoral character serving as the basis of all their unworthiness. Their march back to barbarism had been rapid and successful.'"[102]

Many repressive decrees were subsequently enacted, including the banning of public Christmas celebrations as well as the popular New Year fife and drum parades. In December 1840, the dances were banned only five days before Christmas, which created a massive upheaval. Some children were playing a small drum, homemade fiddle, and tambourine in the streets of Kingston when they were seized by the police and taken before the magistrate for disturbing the peace. Even though these children pleaded their innocence, they were punished by the magistrate. This greatly angered the people, and a crowd of mostly women gathered around the courthouse. Mounted police attempted to disperse them, but were met with "a volley of brick bats. The police turned and fired. Five people were shot, two fatally."[103]

Nothing, it seemed, could "lessen the obstinate attachment of the population to their Christmas orgies." These were the times when people turned their backs on white churches and flocked to syncretic cults. After the Morant Bay rebellion, the new governor, Sir John Peter Grant, decided that the colonial budget would be better spent building schools and roads than in maintaining the prisons. But the colonial mentality remained entrenched. The specter of "barbarism" continued to feed Jamaican middle class paranoia, and even now, at the dawn of the third millennium, the Jamaican bourgeoisie is still wary of Africanism. Even reggae music was subject to semiofficial repression in the form of radio blackouts until Bob Marley's planetary recognition made it acceptable.

In 1940 at Pinnacle, African culture was still more of a concept than a reality. It was the migrants from India who provided attractively exotic models. The first Rastafarian hymns were taken from the Christian *Sankey Hymnal* (used by almost all the island's churches) with lyrics transposed to the benefit of Ras Tafari, or from familiar anthems by Arnold Ford, the UNIA composer. Howell did not incorporate the Kumina drums immediately. At first he was trying to establish a communal life free from imposed cultural associations or specifications. His Anglican background didn't predispose him to embrace "those religions that howl," as Garvey had once called them. It wasn't until Howell's imprisonment that an African revivalist aspect of Rastafari began to develop. Drumming up at Pinnacle became Kumina-based, since much of the community had come from St. Thomas.

Kumina is one of many African traditions in Jamaica, and later Rastas would have their choice of a few different styles. At Maroon funerals and festivals, one sometimes hears almost entirely intact African songs, unchanged for centuries. From the tin churches of the ghettos comes the sound of voodoo-like rhythms; the darkest of all is Kumina. After Emancipation, St. Thomas parish saw the arrival of eight thousand African contract workers, along with many Indian indentured laborers. Kumina is believed to derive largely from the religious practices of these first-generation Afro-Jamaicans. Other Africans came via a more complicated route: the Westmoreland Nagos (Yoruba) and the St. Thomas Kikongos were rescued from slave ships after the trade was outlawed by the British in 1808. As it was impossible to return them to their villages of origin, they were offered paid work on Jamaican sugar plantations. These Africans held onto their language and their music, and in certain areas Kumina drumming developed from their influence. In 1963, British ethnologist Madeline Kerr described the "kyando" and "plain case" drums still used by Kumina sects as built of hollow tree trunks and played by hand in the style of West African talking drums.

Since the first settlers at Pinnacle were from St. Thomas, it is only natural that Kumina musicians were prominent at the community festivities. Even today Kumina drums are brought out on certain high occasions, like the birthday of Leonard Howell. When the community scattered in the 1950s, they carried its Kumina tradition to their new yards in West Kingston. In 1953, G. E. Simpson, an American ethnologist, was going back and forth from Kumina to the Rasta yards, and he discerned no notable difference between the two types of music. It wasn't until five years later, at the 1958 Rasta Convention, that a differentiation was clearly defined. East of Kingston, things may have been slightly different, as the 1958 "grounations" at Rasta stalwart Issie Boat's camp already featured Count Ossie's Burru style of drumming.

There are two important African traditions in Jamaica linked to Christmas—Burru and Jonkunnu (John Canoe). Both have clear social functions—to purge society of evil spirits accrued during the year, and to start the new year with a clear heart and spirit. These traditions normally focused on the perfidy of the slave owners and contained barely disguised biting social commentary. The Rastas were attracted to these Christmas traditions for the opportunities of rebellion they provided. Of the two traditions, Jonkunnu is closest to traditional carnival. The origin of the name is disputed. An 1828 text states that it derives from the name of a rebellious Muslim slave who made himself famous through various "barbarous" deeds.[104] Accompanied by mock military bands, Jonkunnu processions still contain many starkly African elements. The Montego Bay parades in the early twentieth century featured rattle-shaking dancers wearing horse skulls on their heads (like the Dogon of Mali), spinning dancers covered head to foot with straw or cloth (like the Zangbeto of Benin), and mummers in horned masks waving long whips, like in Mali or Morocco.

But more than Jonkunnu, it was Burru, the other Christmas tradition, that attracted the Rastas.

Burru songs exposed the good and the evil aspects of a person or a village. The Burru people sang songs about current events and about individuals in the community who may have been guilty of some misconduct during the year. This reflects another African custom practiced among tribes on the Gold Coast . . . whereby at the end of the old year an ordained sect of the community would go from house to house singing derogatory songs. . . . [It was] a sort of purification rite which absolved the village of its sins before entering the new year.[105]

Burru songs let the slaves laugh at their masters without risking punishment, as the name of the mocked or parodied individual was always withheld. Burru musicians formed themselves into quasi-outlaw guilds (barely) tolerated by the authorities. They even got employment from some planters during slavery, but this didn't survive the period between 1835 and 1865.

Burru bands were allowed to play music in the fields; this buoyed the spirits of the slaves and thus they worked faster, speeding up production. After slavery, Burru drummers were without work. They had little experience as field hands [so] they flocked to townships, gathering mainly in the slums of Kingston and Spanish Town. During the first nine months of every year, Burru players eked out some sort of existence. From September on they met in groups and practiced their music for performance at Christmas time.[106]

It was on this occasion that Verena Reckord, the Jamaican ethnomusicologist, discovered the Burru drummers.

I remember as a child in the late '40s when I lived in Spanish Town and my grandmother would send me out to buy bread every morning. I took a shortcut through a slum lane called Sherwood Alley. Most of the year, my grandmother had no objection to my little shortcut, but beginning in September she would warn me constantly: "Don't yuh go t'ru Sherwood Alley. Ah doan able fi trust dem damn Burru man." . . . I never went the long way to the bread shop, especially not during the last quarter of the year. I used the time I had saved by taking the alley peeping through the nail hole in a dirty zinc fence at the Burru men playing their drums around a fire, singing and cursing all the time. It was the sweetest sound my child's soul had ever heard. I was incapable of resisting it. If, while I was passing, the drums went momentarily silent, I would dally, hoping they would begin again, so as to watch the animated faces and bodies, and most of all the nimble hands of those unkempt Burru men. Back at home, as my grandmother rocked my baby brother to sleep, it was not to European lullabies, but to the strains of Burru rhythm. I know that in trying to keep me from the Burru she was denying the part of herself that colonization had stamped evil, primitive, and wrong.[107]

There was a natural empathy between the Burru men and the Rastas. Both had, according to them, "conquered fear." Both had experienced harassment and had responded with humor and arrogance. "The Burru men of earlier times," Verena Record notes, "were regarded by the rest of the community, even in their social strata, as good-for-nothings and criminals." The Burru drums traditionally welcomed released prisoners back to their communities. The Rastas also took pride in the existential dread they inspired—better to frighten than to be frightened. Ghetto dwellers went back and forth between Rasta and Burru yards, and when they began searching for their African roots, Rastas went to the Burru drummers to learn. This is precisely how Count Ossie met Watto King. The rhythm born from their encounter is today called the "Rasta Riddim" or "Nya-Binghi," but Count Ossie drummers still call it Burru to this very day.

What is the difference between Kumina, the St. Thomas style of drumming played at Pinnacle, and Burru, the ancestor of Nya-Binghi and Rasta music? Reckord notes "the variation of tone effected on the third beat in each case. The *plain case* of Kumina and the *repeater* of Rasta and Burru music are characteristically the same; however the plain case's tempo is much quicker. The rhythms are very complex and almost impossible to notate. However, Burru's repeater rhythms can be transcribed with relative ease." Brother Royer, bass drummer of the legendary ensemble Mystic Revelation of Rastafari, Count Ossie's performing group, says that the real difference is more in the concept than in the actual playing.

> The Kumina and the Burru sound much alike. The difference lies in the continuous repetition of Kumina, while Burru tends to drop back into the repeater. With Burru you hear more of a funde going on instead of the repeater. Sometimes when the repeater comes up in Burru it sounds more like Kumina. We try to keep that trend of repetition [from] Africa. With Kumina, you are dealing with Africa. The man with Kumina, him just play. When you hear the Nya-Binghi drum, you may think it is the Kumina drum because it is actually the same style of playing. But we don't sit on the drum. They sit on the drum and use heel to make the sounds. We use our fingers and the stick for the bass drum. So it is really the concept we play with, that creates the difference. An *African* concept. The whole thing is from Africa—Ketu, Etu, Kumina, Brukkins—but there are some people who do it culturally and some people who really *do* it. You have Kumina men who think basically about their culture, and then you have another whole set of Kumina men who don't think about that; him play Kumina cause him can play it. Now with the man who play Burru drum all the time, you hear Rasta drum and you know this man is really dealing with Africa. So our whole inspiration has shifted from Jamaica to Africa. Jamaican people might not love it, because me don't know who is Jamaican still—you know? Cause *ninety five percent* of the people here is of African descent!

28

Count Ossie

Brother Royer told me that Kumina and Burru were "African t'ings" that survived the middle passage between Africa and the West, between freedom and slavery, and could be heard in similar form all over the Caribbean. "World music," the globalization of musical culture, unearthed hundreds of musicians in the last three decades, but few of them ever produced more than one or two recordings. Reggae's impact was clearly different. Who beyond Jamaica would ever have heard Leonard Howell's message without this sticky rhythm that undulated even in the most remote villages on five continents? Speedy Kumina, with its wildly complex, impossible-to-transcribe solos, could never have carried such a success around the world. Without reggae pulsing behind him, there would never have been an international champion of human rights named Bob Marley. Reggae was a hybrid that grew from the cross-pollination of western pop music and Afro-Caribbean rhythms. One man was responsible for this essential mutation—the legendary Count Ossie.

In Wareika, at the very end of Glasspole Avenue, beyond the small triangular park that displays a bust of Marcus Garvey, stands a two-story concrete building. Its front facade is adorned with naive murals whose colors have faded in the sun. One of the paintings shows Ras Tafari under a canopy, a lion at his feet, angels at each side. (Athlyi again!) Behind the building the gray-green hills of Wareika rise up, the notorious refuge of outlaws going back to Arawak times. In front of the building, on the other side of Glasspole Avenue, the Rockfort ghetto sprawls down through steep lanes ending at Windward Road and the sea. Several old beardmen are sitting on wooden benches in the corner of the building yard, taking in the evening breeze. A slow hypnotic rhythm flows gently from the windows. This is the Count Ossie Cultural Center, headquarters of the famous band of drummers known as the Mystic Revelation of Rastafari. Every Sunday for fifty years, the Saints, as the neighbors fondly call them, have met in the area to beat their drums. It is here that the canonical rhythms of the Rastafarians were codified.

There is a carved stone bust atop one of the gate pillars. The head has the regular features of a full-blooded African, and sinuous marks around its quiet eyes of the fingers that molded it. The figure wears a long tam pulled down halfway with the top standing up. This was the preferred style of the eastern Rastas, who declined to adopt the dreadlocks of their Trench Town brothers. The bust immortalizes the master drummer Count Ossie, who died on October 18, 1976—Jamaica's National Heroes Day.

Count Ossie, a key figure in the Rasta movement, was born Oswald William on March 26, 1927. Howell was then sailing around the world. Garvey was still in jail, soon to return to Jamaica. For Oswald's peasant mother, raising her three children in the hill village of Bito above Bull Bay, black nationalism was a remote concern. Oswald's mother came to Kingston in the 1940s looking for work. She settled on Slip Dock Road, at the eastern end of Windward Road close to the sea. The area was called Rockfort for the old bastion that defended the eastern approaches to the harbor. Back then, the area was still green and quiet, a country-like community of fishermen, housemaids, and laborers. Her son Oswald turned out to be a true-born drummer. Music was his passion. Every Sunday in

Mystic Revelation of Rastafari, Wareika, 1998. © HÉLÈNE LEE.

Bito he played fife and drums in the Boy's Brigade. He joined the local scouts' marching band, Mr. Barrington's Saint Savior Call Troop. The drums became the true expression of his soul.

"I would describe him as a 'cool ruler,'" recalled his son Time. "He rules real cool! Somehow he always knows what dem have fe do, him always get it done without saying much, you know. Them two sisters and the mother is the same, you have to juk them with a pin for them say a word. So boring, man! And Count could sit there and do the same thing all day and don't say a word. If you see him sitting there with a little fire going round, a little after that he is on the drum. If he is tuning up, or fixing something, he is always with it. Him really a quiet man." Though Count Ossie didn't talk much, he liked to listen in on discussions of the issues that distressed and agitated his generation. He went all over Kingston, listening to the people while he played.

Salt Lane is on the eastern border of a blasted rectangle, one of the most infamous ghetto zones in all of Jamaica. It lies between May Pen Cemetery (west), the harbor (south), and Spanish Town Road (north). Salt Lane, the Dungle, Back O'Wall, Ackee Walk—the very names send chills down one's spine. But Ossie William often visited Salt Lane to reason with a group of Rasta brethren there about Marcus Garvey, Rastafari, and black awareness.

Ossie to Verena Reckord: "Yah know, man was anxious, all o' them time, to know the answers to puzzles about himself and his race. Is during this time, down there at Salt Lane, under a tree where we generally met to reason, that the idea of the music came to me and I work at it, until we have what people call today Rasta music."[108] But besides reasoning, he also listened to a Burru master drummer, Brother Job, who would come by their meeting spot under a tree in Salt Lane. They noticed that the "Burru drumming remained one of the few undiluted African musical forms still alive in the late forties." For several months, in sessions that went late into the night, Count Ossie sat with Brother Job, learning to play the funde to Job's Burru rhythms on the repeater. Then, during the afternoons, Ossie practiced avidly on an empty paint can at Slip Dock Road, where his Rockfort brethren gathered around him with boxes and old cheese tins, wanting to learn the new style.

After a while he put away enough money to purchase a drum built by Watto King, one of Jamaica's greatest Burru masters and Brother Job's teacher. (Eventually Ossie's entire group would have a set of drums financed by Brother Filmore Alvaranga, the only man in the band to have a regular job. Brother Fill also owned the dairy truck in which the band traveled from venue to venue. It was out of gratitude for all his efforts that Count Ossie sent Brother Fill to Ethiopia in 1961, in his place.) Watto King was a legend in his own right, and his role in the development of Burru into Rasta was of great importance. He was a generous man, a spiritual leader, and very respected for his wisdom. He lived first at Ferry, halfway to Spanish Town, where he would welcome the refugees of hurricane destruction and keep them fed for weeks in his wide yard, as he did during the hurricane of 1951. He finally settled in Trench Town, where most of the Rastas got to know him. Jah Bones: "Brother Watto, who embraced the dreadlocks, had his camp at 9th street in Trench Town. He was *very* powerful. Bra Watto had a big yard with about four houses and a tabernacle in the middle. The camp was vibrant and alive—one of Jamaica's best-known yards during the late fifties and sixties. Bro Watto's spirit represented peace and love, and yet he was solid and firm, a father-figure for young men and women, and a counselor among his peers and elders. He taught everyone the discipline of the Rasta life. He was able to host the Nya-Binghi meetings in his large courtyard, which had room for many drummers to gather and play. He saw that everyone had something to eat and drink, [because] Bra Watto knew how to earn money. While most of his brethren were out hustling little jobs, the sisters were selling in the markets downtown."[109]

During the 1950s, Watto's Trench Town yard was Rasta Music Central. Most if not all of the Rastas' drums were built in Watto's workshop. Count Ossie's drummers still remember his tabernacle, decorated with dozens of drums hanging from the rafters. People sometime hired drums from him before ordering their own custom-made set. But the truth is that no one knows where Watto learned to make and play the drums. Which part of Jamaica did he come from? None of the Count's drummers were able to answer this question. But if Watto King was a Burru man (as described by V. Reckord) and a Rasta (as Jah Bones says), he should probably be recognized as the missing link between the two communities. Young Rastas gathered around him to learn his rhythms, then moved on to other yards or camps to scatter the seeds.

In his book, Jah Bones speaks of other Rasta drum masters, like Brother John in Rose Town. Bones describes him as "the greatest Rasta akete [repeater] drummer in the whole of Jamaica." At the 1958 convention, Jah Bones saw Brother John play with Brother Rubba, another musical genius. "Brothers John and Rubba frustrated Count Ossie, causing him to take his repeater and leave Ackee Walk." Annoyed by the aggressive style of Brother John, which reportedly was "loud, violent, and magnetic, Count Ossie caresses his repeater and assaults your ears with a cascade of sounds that are difficult to differentiate but easy to assimilate. Brother John fights with his repeater—clap, clap—and though he rarely fingers the rim, he creates thunderous, murderous sounds that make the heart quake . . ."

Count Ossie was introducing a new concept into Burru drumming. His music was still rooted in the old style but it had a new objective—to strengthen the acuteness of the Rastafarian "reasoning," the philosophical discussions that often followed the drums. "Count Ossie and the group at Salt Lane," Verena Reckord recounts, "discovered that after long periods of serious drumming, their reasoning became more intense; insights and the paths to answers became clear. It is for this reason that more and more emphasis was placed on drumming at meetings."[110] Under Count Ossie's direction, the Burru rhythm settled slowly into a softer pattern. The African pulse found its way back into the human heartbeat, at sixty beats per minute. This elementally peaceful rhythm can comfort a man —"as a maternal pulse would comfort a fetus," Reckord observes. Some Rastafarians suggest that there are healing powers in the music. They claim that after sessions of drumming and chanting, they have been rid of lesser discomforts like headaches, fever, and colds. Sometimes the rhythm speeds up as well, but this is due to the power of inspiration, not of irrational emotions. "Visions, not dreams," as the Rastas say. The Nya-Binghi Rastas mostly forgot those slightly faster Burru rhythms after becoming transfixed by the newer, calmer ones. But Count Ossie's drummers still practice them today. It was from these rhythms, in the beginning of the 1960s, that ska—Jamaica's first international cultural export— began to evolve.

By the late 1940s, Rockfort/Wareika youths were increasingly interested in Count Ossie's "grounations." Most of the youth in the eastern part of the city were not country folk, but the sons and daughters of workers and servants, rebelling against the petit-bourgeois ideals and customs of their parents. One of them, Brother Powdy, was thrown out of his house because he refused to go to church, and he found himself camping in the hills with other Wareika outlaws. "Our parents did not understand what was going

Two members of the Mystic Revelation of Rastafari at their "center,"
1996: Brother Royer (left) and Brother Powdy (right). © HÉLÈNE LEE.

on," he explains. "When I first told my father that all I wanted to
do was to follow the teachings of Jah, he told me to leave the house.
We all had to leave our families and go into the hills. We would
gather on the gullybank and reason until Count Ossie brought in
the drums. We started practicing on old cheese tins!"

Food was the number one problem. The youths went to the
beach to offer their services to the fishermen; sometimes they were
allowed to keep the small fish they caught and share it among themselves. They cultivated vegetables. Farther down the coast, hot water
springs flowed out from the ground at the bottom of a hill, form-
ing a pool of clear water where the brothers went to bathe and to
wash their only pair of pants and shirt. It was in 1951, after the hurricane, that things got worse. This was the era of Woppy King, the
legendary villain who didn't trim his hair, and who haunted the Palisadoes wilderness along the peninsula that connects Kingston to
Port Royal. He liked to rob swimmers who came to the bathing
beaches. One day while patrolling in his little canoe, Woppy spied a

pastor he knew. He had a girl from his flock, and was trying to take advantage of her on the beach. Woppy attacked the pastor, cut his throat, and raped the girl. But then she fought for her life and managed to swim away. Woppy King was tried and hanged, but the rumors began to fly that the dreaded "blackheart men" were at it again, killing and raping.

Woppy King was no Rasta, but his matted locks tarnished the movement. "People were scared of us; they refused to give us water," Powdy remembers. They were arrested, as they had been in the west, and beaten up. Their hair was trimmed. Police pillaged their villages and burned down huts. Powdy remembers being locked up for days without food or water. "When we asked for water, they came to us with a hose and spray we with it, so at night we have to sleep in the damp. . . . They said we were being subversive, but we had done nothing. We were just talking about love. But they did not like it, so they pressure we."

Meanwhile a different trend was developing in the east. Blackness of complexion became a nonissue (as Jah Beck, one of the oldest and best loved of Count Ossie's drummers, was nearly all white). More emphasis was placed on respecting other peoples' opinions. Some smoked the holy herb, some didn't. Some grew locks, but most didn't. Brother Powdy recalls that, in the old days, most Rastas wore beards, not locks. When locks became the fashion in the west, the eastern Rastas saw no reason to change their style, and so they kept their beards. It was at that time that Mortimer Planno was gaining support because of his strong contacts in the government, and because Bob Marley and the other young Trench Town singers were behind him. But "West Kingston people talk a lot and don't do much . . ."[111]

Up until this point, Wareika and Rockfort had been the towns of the free thinkers among the Rastas. According to Verona Reckord, the movement's "Big Three" were Count Ossie, his saxophonist friend Big Bra Gaynair, and Bro Filmore Alvaranga (today the patriarch of the Mystic Revelation of Rastafari). To those must be added Brother Love, a Rasta elder who used to preach in Mountain

View on the western slope of the Wareika Hills. The very first Rasta convention was organized there in the east, at Issie Boat's camp in Wareika, at Christmas 1949. Bro Sigismond remembers the thundering of drums pouring down from the top of the hill unto the city. The drumming could be heard all the way to west Kingston.

After Hurricane Charlie in 1951, not much remained of the gully bank near Slip Dock Road where Count Ossie used to practice. It was at this point that the drummer switched his grounations to Rennock Lodge, a building site where he found a job as a night watchman with his friend Bro Nya. This is where he met Alvira Sweeny, the mother of his son Time. After the project was completed, he went on to establish a new camp at Adastra Road, which soon became a famous meeting place. Hundreds of drummers came here to practice Burru. "Men would come and listen," said Count Ossie, "until they could memorize a riddim. Then they would go back to their group or them yard to practice drums or whatever, until they have some riddim under control. Then they would come back to the camp to learn something else."[112] These rhythms became the backdrop for the entire Rasta movement.

By 1958, Count Ossie was already working on something new. Garth White reported that Ossie was already so advanced in his technique and respected for his convictions that people had begun asking him to play at cultural events where the audience would listen to him instead of dancing. His fame was beginning to spread. His grounation now attracted certain intellectuals, professional jazz musicians, and people from the Alpha Boys School.

Alpha is another legend. This Catholic children's institution on South Camp Road in eastern Kingston was founded in 1880 by the Sisters of Mercy to care for orphans and troubled children. Meanwhile in Alabama, Booker T. Washington was establishing a similar project in Tuskegee, which even attracted Marcus Garvey to American shores. It was toward the end of the nineteenth century that humanists realized that equality for blacks before the law, as promised by Emancipation, was nothing more than empty rhetoric if the sons of slaves did not have any access to education. Until

African Americans were able to become educated, they were still, as Bob Marley sang, in mental slavery. Alpha School's founders, like Washington, argued that professional training was the only way for an ex-slave to become integrated in society. At Alpha, children were trained for different professions: printing, cabinetmaking, block molding, and music. Strict discipline and chores (cleaning, washing, cooking, gardening) taught the value of work. Some children complained or ran away, but relations between children and the sisters were generally good. Sister Ignatius, a beloved figure, kept in correspondence with many of the graduates. She was particularly fond of the musicians.

In early 1908, the bishop of Jamaica donated new horns to the school, with the idea of setting up a marching band. An army sergeant was hired to teach music. From this motley crew of orphans, abandoned children, and bad boys came some of the greatest names in modern music. Sister Ignatius proudly enumerated Leslie Thompson, the first black conductor of the London Symphony Orchestra; Oscar Clark, who played with Louis Armstrong; Bertie King, Joe Harriot, Little G. McNair, Eddie "Tan-tan" Thornton—all great names on the British jazz and reggae scene. Jackie Willacey (trumpet) and Wilton Gaynair (saxophone) spent the best parts of their careers in Germany, Charles Clark and Ron Wilson in the United States. Jamaican music was staffed mainly by Alpha veterans—Don Drummond, Cedric Brooks, Rico Rodrigues, Deadly Headley Bennett, Johnny "Dizzy" Moore, Ruben Delgado, Lennie Hibbert, JoJo Bennett, Babe O'Brien, and of course Leroy "Horsemouth" Wallace, star of the movie *Rockers* and an incredible reggae drummer (some think the best). At Alpha he gave the sisters a hard time and was eventually expelled.

The Alpha School was situated in the populous and churchgoing section of East Kingston, inhabited mainly by domestics and civil servants. Alpha's pupils were the children of these impoverished families, ripe to be enchanted by the Rasta message. Count Ossie's best friend was Wilton Gaynair, an Alpha student who hid on Friday nights to listen to jazz broadcasts on the radio. During rehearsal, pupils fought over the only horn, trying to reproduce the solos of their idols. Gaynair, a respected saxophonist, took his friends to Count Ossie's sessions, where they were entranced by his "African" rhythms. (The 1950s jazz scene in America was likewise Afrocentric, with Art Blakey's *Orgy in Rhythm*, Dizzy Gillespie's *Afro*, and Randy Weston's interest in African roots.) There were always famous musicians at Count Ossie's Sunday night sessions, many from Alpha—Rico Rodriguez, Bobby and Wilton Gaynair, Cedric "Im" Brooks, Dizzy Moore, and of course the jazz king of Jamaica—Don D!

Donald Drummond (or "Don D" and "Don Cosmic," among other names) was the most legendary Jamaican instrumentalist as well as a pioneer who opened the music profession to the Rastas. They played with him twice at the Carib Theater and three or four times at the Bournemouth club. "African drums at midnight!" the advertisement read, "with the haunted trombone solos of Don Drummond." It was Drummond who pulled people in, because when the drummers asked to be booked on their own, the owner of the Bournemouth scratched his head and said, "Bwoy, I would give you a night, but the beard business don't work." The social situation hadn't progressed much by the end of the 1950s, and Rasta music seemed doomed. Brother Royer from the Mystic Revelation of Rastafari remembers,

> All we used to do is go dance hall, because we used to have some likkle youth who keep bands in the ska era, you know? So we used to go dance to play. The only venues we used to go [were] at Tiverton Road, just around the corner here across Wareika Road. It was a big yard where the brother used to make coffins. He worked for a funeral parlor, so he made coffins there. It's a big place, and he has a place where he push them and lock them, so during the night you don't see them. So you keep dance there.

And that's where we used to go. We be there still, without Marguerita Mahfood! She was the one who really unleashed the whole business. She was so important, Marguerita Mahfood—our Helen of Troy.

It was a woman, and a half-white woman at that, who forced Rasta music into Jamaican pop and eventually around the world. Without her, it might have stayed hidden in the ghetto and withered. There might never have been a music called reggae. Her role has been ignored by the Rasta historians—as was the crucial role of the Indians. But Brother Royer, who took part in the legendary events and understands their importance, recounted the following:

Marguerita was an international rumba dancer, them call belly dancers in Jamaica. She is a Syrian you know, born in Jamaica. I hear her family come from Honduras. She married a boxer named Rudolph Bent, a good boxer from Aruba. And after she leave him, she have two youths for this brother Bent, one boy, one girl. The guy carry them over to Aruba. Now what was happening was that Marguerita danced at Vere Johns's [talent] show. She used to come to us because she liked the drums. When she heard us, she wanted to make a new dance. The African riddim had her doing a different thing. She *leaping* now, and making good steps, and *breaks*, so it's different now, those pelvis movements not going [so hard] anymore. You are getting African movement now, more cultural, just shape the whole thing. She created a new impact, and loved what she was doing. So she went and talked to [journalist] Vere Johns, who at the time is putting on *Opportunity Hour*, a show promoting young musicians that went from theater to theater all over Jamaica. [It later became *Opportunity Knocks*, and then *Singaree*.] It was a radio show where Jimmy Cliff and Bob Marley and almost everyone got their first on-air performances as youths.

So it was Christmas morning and Marguerita had two shows, one at Ward Theater and one at Carib. It was at that time that

Norman Manley had said, "Anywhere you see Rastaman, you have to lock them up." In the late 1950s, the show at Ward Theater was being conducted by Vere Johns's son, Vere Johns Jr. She told him that she wants to dance to Count Ossie. He said it would be kind of difficult, because his father doesn't work well with the Rastas. But because his father is over at the Carib Theater, he said maybe he could work something out at the Ward. So we all went to the Ward Theater, the best house in Jamaica, down in Parade, and let me tell you! It was like the revival of all the peoples' *souls*. It was like the whole place crashed! People got crazy about the new sound.

OK, so we supposed to leave from there now and go to Carib to do the other leg of the show. And when we get there, Vere Johns says no, it won't work. "Oh, you are going on with a whole heap of Rastaman? No, no, no Maggie, you can't do it!" So she says, "Mr. Johns, I done it already and it's the same we gone to play." And he says, "Sweet Jesus!"and him put a hand up over him head and said, "You are prepared to disgrace us, because, I mean, a lot of Rastamen and no one know how the crowd gone react!" She says, "But it's *alright*!" And he says no no no, he can't allow it. So she now, great girl, she says, "Mr. Johns if these people not going to play, I not going to dance." And he says, "Alright then, alright." And she says [to us], "Come, come," and we turn back [to leave]. And when we get to the car, him said, "Alright, alright, come Maggie, come and tell them fe come."

And when we go through the gate, him say we're going to play, but he is not going to put the light on the stage where we are. He put us in the corner, in the back. He's gonna tell the light man to put the spotlight on Maggie when she dance. One [of us] say to him, "Bwoy, once darkness should come to light!" And him just stand and say, "Well . . ." And then we go in to play. The exact same thing that happened at Ward Theater happened up here. Explosion! When the drums started to play, everybody in the crowd: "Wha? Who dat? We want to see the musicians!"

They were laughing. One man hollered out, "Is *Count* dat, you know!" People were howling, so then the man 'pon the light put the spotlight on our corner, and the whole thing *went up*. Maggie caused quite a stir, because, man—she could *dance*. Not many woman like her, I tell you.

Then a man came [backstage] saying, "Mi Gawd, who dat solo man? Bwoy, first I hear such a . . . Who is the manager, who is the manager?" But we didn't have no manager, because we are just a bunch of guys who play around the yard. That same man, that was Vere Johns! The same man who told us that we could not come in; now he was asking who was our manager. And Count say to himself, "What is dark must come to light!" And him laugh. I remember him using the very words. And later that evening Vere Johns went up to Count's yard to say that he wanted to be the manager. And this is how the Rasta fraternity began. From then on Rastas can go on stage and perform, even wear their beards. Marguerita cleared the way. And from there we started going from theater to theater, in competitions, putting on our show. Then one day [the great singer] brother Slim Smith came for the final, and we and him went on stage together during a competition—and we won. Then we won the National Jazz Festival competition. It was Marguerita who opened the door for us, not the jazz musicians. Great girl! Our Helen of Troy!

⟨⟨⟨ 29 ⟩⟩⟩

The 1960s

The years between 1958 and 1962 saw the consolidation of the political system that rules Jamaica today. The British West Indies decided
to create a federation to face the challenges of independence.
Jamaica's first federal elections gave victory to the Jamaican Labour
Party, which campaigned against the federation, but a year later, in
1959, the Peoples National Party regained the majority and took
over the government. Bustamante and the JLP continued to insist
that the federation failed to serve the best interests of the nation.
Manley put it to the test of a referendum. On September 19, 1961,
the federation was abandoned. Now Jamaica began reinventing itself
with music. Music was becoming the expression of the new national
consciousness.

With independence in 1962, Jamaica was no longer a sleepy
colony. It had strong labor and political institutions, a corps of com-
petent civil servants, a daring and well-informed press, and a progressive university that was the lone survivor of the defunct West
Indies Federation. A new and bubbling music called ska seemed
emblematic of the new nation's cultural vitality.

Although independence was celebrated with island-wide festivities, the island's general mood was more that of an irritated shrug,

as if to say "About time!" The Rastas thought independence was something of a joke. It was Africa they were searching for. "Dem exchange an island for a continent!" But the fact was that, since 1958, the movement had been suffering from the same east/west division that split the country's politics. The "country" Rastas resided on the west side of Kingston, in Trench Town and Back O'Wall. They saw themselves as pureblooded Africans who lacked formal education but not culture, who expressed a new confidence and identity with their long locks, "dread" fashion, and talk. They believed most strongly in their back-to-Africa vision; they were not interested in finding local solutions. The east, especially Wareika and Rockfort, bred Rastas of a more modern type of thinking, who avoided cabalistic, emotional, and racial simplifications. They too wanted to get back to an idealized Africa, but they also tried to better their living conditions through organization and education. The two groups grew side by side, respectful of each other but nonetheless competitive. Those in the west suffered in poverty and anger, while those in the east sought openings through new culture. Since there was a similar phenomenon going on in Jamaican politics, with Bustamante preying on popular emotion and Manley striving to evolve manageable compromises, it was not shocking to see that the PNP prevailed in the east, especially in Rennock Lodge (just behind Count Ossie's camp), while Bustamante was the hero of the western slum districts. Most Rastas still shunned political affiliation, but after independence they became more divided in their approach to their situation. Western Rastas were fascinated with the sixth and seventh book of Moses and other cabalistic mysteries, while Count Ossie's crew believed in education. Ossie's cultural center in Wareika started both a library and a school with more than two hundred pupils. Ossie believed in sharing the Rasta mentality with the rest of the world, and was working to this end through his music.

After their landmark Christmas triumph with Marguerita, Count Ossie's drummers quickly became folk heroes in Jamaica. Jazz musicians began falling in with even the fastest of the Burru rhythms. Not only could people dance to them, but the musicians could demonstrate their virtuosity playing them. In 1961, a youth in Spanish Town named Harry Moodie, the son of the owner of a hardware store, recorded some fantastic sessions of Count Ossie and the jazzmen playing together. The recording contains the seeds of everything that Jamaica would witness musically in the following decades. It was an explosion of ideas, the missing link between Burru drumming and R&B, jazz, and reggae. A handful of songs clarified everything; all that was missing was a name for this new style. It would later be called ska, a syllabic equivalent for the back-beat half of the rhythm: *ts-ḳa, ts-ḳa, ts-ḳa*. This rhythm, slowed to a more sedate, ganja-heavy tempo, later became the basis of reggae music.

Deploying the new rhythm, Count Ossie soon had his first hit record, "O Carolina," recorded in 1961 with the Folkes Brothers, a group of young singers from the neighborhood. Thus the once-despised Rasta musicians were making serious cultural break-throughs and giving a voice to their entire generation.

The 1960s began badly for the Rastas. Politicians had absolutely no use for them; repression of Rasta culture was in full swing. In May 1959, a "bearded" Coronation Market security guard fought with a policeman. What followed was a state-sponsored pogrom in which the police stormed and ravaged Rasta camps in West Kingston. The notorious Henry Affair followed in 1960, and churchgoing Jamaica plunged into a paranoid war against the Rastas.

Claudius Henry was born in 1903, and like Howell, he was raised an Anglican. He began having visions in his youth that led him to question the validity of church teachings. His first critique concerned the Sunday services, as the Bible explicitly stated that Saturday was the sabbath day that should be consecrated to God. This seemingly trivial question divided Jamaican churches, as for some this question put the entire European tradition under scrutiny. For whites, Saturday was a day of spending, of drinking, of vanities and profanities. Claudius Henry read Isaiah, one of the Rastas' favorite prophets, who fearlessly condemned the hypocrisies of the rich and powerful.

Behold, ye fast with strife and debate, and to smite with the fist of wickedness: ye shall not fast as ye do this day, to make your voice to be heard on high.

Is not this the fast that I have chosen? To loose the bands of wickedness, to undo the heavy burdens, and to let the oppressed go free, and that ye break every yoke?

Is it not to deal thy bread to the hungry, and that thou bring the poor that are cast out to thy house? When thou seest them naked, that thou cover them? And that thou hide not thyself from thine own flesh?

Then shall thy light break forth as the morning, and thy health shall spring forth speedily, and thy righteousness shall go before thee; and the glory of the Lord shall be thy reward . . .

And the Lord shall guide thee continually, and satisfy thy soul in drought . . .

And they that shall be of thee shall build the old waste-spaces; thou shalt raise up the foundations of many generations; and thou shalt be called the repairer of the breach, the restorer of paths to dwell in (Isaiah 58).

Like Athlyi, Balintine, and Howell, Claudius Henry had a millenarian view of religion. While locked up in an asylum in 1929, he had a vision of God speaking the verses of Isaiah. He decided that God had deemed him the "Repairer of the Breach," hence the letters R.B., which he added to his name. Like Howell he left Jamaica and spent thirteen years in the United States before being called back to Jamaica in 1957 by another vision. There he married Edna Fisher, a fish seller who was also president of the local chapter of the Ethiopian World Federation. From her yard on Rosalie Avenue, Henry preached the divine nature of Ras Tafari and repatriation to Africa. He had followings in Vere and Anotto Bay. He considered himself the brown son of Almighty Selassie, while Garvey was the black Holy Ghost. He predicted repatriation to Africa would occur on October 5, 1959, and sold hundreds of postcards as passports. But of course, the miraculous repatriation did not take place and many (but not all) lost faith in him.

A few months later the post office intercepted a letter addressed to Fidel Castro written by Henry, in which he told the Cuban leader that since "all their efforts for peaceful repatriation had proven futile, that Jamaica and the rest of the British West Indies were to be turned over to [Castro] and [his] government after the war for Africa's freedom was over." His language was unequivocal. "We want to go back home to Africa; if we are not welcomed back with love, we will go anyway, in hate, as we were brought here. If we cannot go in peace, then we must go in war."[113] The local branch of the EWF was then searched and homemade weapons found, together with dynamite and a box of fuses. Henry was tried for treason and sentenced to ten years at hard labor.

While he awaited his trial in jail, the matter developed into something far worse. His son Ronald, who lived in New York, dreamed of liberating Jamaica through violence. At the Bronx YMCA, Ronald recruited and formed a gang of youths he called the First Africa Corps. A young policeman of Jamaican origin helped them organize a holdup in order to gather funds. They then managed to get to Jamaica under false identities and linked up with Ronald's father's people. Among these was Ras Thunder, a Rasta the police had been looking for since the beginning of the Henry Affair. They set up a camp, ten huts in the Red Hills just above Kingston, where they intended to train Rastas in armed struggle. It was rumored that they had planned to poison the city water supply, but apparently the group was divided on the tactic, and three Rastas led by Thunder turned against the "foreign" terrorist/revolutionaries and let this information leak to the police. There was a raid on the camp, and the Americans started shooting. Two soldiers were killed, two others wounded. At the camp police found the fresh graves of the three executed Rasta "informers," who had been shot point blank. A few young rebels escaped, but they had nowhere to run. Their desperate flight can be compared to that of a defeated Che

Guevara in the mountains of Bolivia seven years later. Dirty, hungry, half-dead, they hid in the homes of poor peasants, taking the time to explain the meaning of their struggle, talking about Garvey, slavery, and the situation of black people all throughout the world. They carried pictures showing the kinds of tortures endured by Africans. They were eventually captured on June 27, 1960, hiding in a rum shop near Orange Grove—a property owned by Joseph Watt, just above Pinnacle. They had perhaps tried to find the famous caves into which the Gong had so cleverly disappeared, which, as the legend relates, allow for passage between them. Ronald Henry and three of his American comrades were tried and hung. Ronald climbed the steps of the gallows, saying, "I die in the name of Marcus Garvey."

This bloody affair did nothing but further discredit the Rastas in the eyes of the public. On June 16, after the shooting that cost the lives of two British soldiers, Prime Minister Norman Manley launched an appeal that newspapers reported under the headline:

REPORT UNUSUAL RASTA MOVES—MANLEY

. . . This wicked and mischievous activity must come to an end. These people—and I am glad that it is only a small number of them—are the wicked enemies of our country. They do great harm to your name; it is tragic that this sort of thing should be happening just when we are on the verge of becoming an independent people . . .

. . . I want to ask every citizen to assist our government in protecting the reputation and name of Jamaica. I ask you all to report any unusual or suspicious movements you may see pertaining to the Rastafarians. Make this your duty. Report whatever it is to the proper authority, and if need be, to the nearest police station.

This proclamation presented an open invitation to arbitrary detention and violence. Manley's intention was clear. He wanted to convince the British, whom he had been trying for years to let go, that he was ready to stamp out the Rastafarians the same way he had smashed the Communists in 1952 and suppressed the ganja trade in 1954. He did manage to convince the British of his firm intent, and won Jamaican independence two years later in 1962.

The spoils went, however, to his opponent, Alexander Busta-mante, who was Young Jamaica's prime candidate. Perhaps the per-secution of the Rastas wasn't such a good idea after all, at least for Norman Manley's political career. On July 20, 1960, with the coun-try still reeling from the Henry Affair, Norman Manley had on his desk the new University Report on the Rasta Movement, which intelligently pleaded for official indulgence toward Jamaica's spiri-tual nationality.

Mortimer Planno had invited three university researchers, M. G. Smith, Rex Nettleford, and Roy Augier, to spend two weeks with their students interviewing the Trench Town Rastas. They did remarkable and invaluable work. Notwithstanding a few short-comings, this report remains the key reference for all research on the Rastafarian movement. It concluded by warning the government to stop persecuting the Rastas because "the movement is large, and in a state of great unrest."

The PNP probably had nothing viscerally against the Rastas; in fact, the socialist political party and the Rastafarians both sprang from the same anticolonial struggle. There were even persistent rumors that Michael Manley, the journalist son of Norman Manley, did not refuse a spliff in private. The Rastas, led by Mortimer Planno, later met with Norman Manley, and he decided to give them a chance to put their dream to the test of reality by sending a delegation to Africa to study the possibility of "repatriation."

The 1961 Mission to Africa was a highlight in the Rasta saga. After endless discussions, seven movement leaders were selected to go. There was Planno, of course, and two of Count Ossie's close friends, Brother Filmore Alvaranga and Douglas Mack. Count Ossie, who did not like to make speeches, withdrew in favor of artic-ulate friends. The Back-to-Africa movement sent three envoys—M. B. Douglas of the Afro-Caribbean League, Monroe Scarlett of the Afro-West Indian Welfare League, and Cecil Gordon of the EWF. The UNIA sent Westmore Blackwood. A doctor and a journalist also joined the delegation. Leonard Howell, living quietly in Kingston, was ignored—possibly for the unsavory connection they suspected he had with the JLP.

The Jamaicans visited mostly English-speaking countries that shared Commonwealth ties—Nigeria, Ghana, Liberia, and Sierra Leone all accepted the idea of a return of the New World blacks with varying degrees of ardor. The more candid African functionaries, no doubt eyeing the Rastas, suggested that qualified professionals might be more welcome than other types of applicants.

The mission's pinnacle, at least for the three Rastas, was the visit to Ethiopia. The delegates went to Shashamani, the valley that Selassie gave to the New World blacks who had assisted during the Italian war. "Shashamani," the report says, "a beautiful rolling country that lies between the Malkoda and Shashamani rivers on the lower slopes of the Addis plateau, was designated by the Emperor as a gift-land to Western black people who desired to settle in Ethiopia." There the mission found a few black Jews of the EWF who had been living in Ethiopia for seventeen years.

> James and Helen Piper were originally from Monserrat. After living in New York for some years, where they became members of the Ethiopian World Federation Inc., they migrated to Ethiopia in 1948. James Piper taught carpentry in a technical school in Addis until 1952 before returning to New York. A year later he was back in Ethiopia having decided to take an offer to farm certain lands which had been made by the EWF. They farm and run a cornmill, grinding all the corn in their neighborhood for a certain fee. They are happy and prosperous. They own fifty cattle, fields of corn and sunflowers, and a herd of goats. Mrs. Piper served us *enjera* and *watt* (the Ethiopian national dish) under a sycamore tree.[114]

Word of Shashamani hit Jamaica like Paradise Found. Around logwood fires in the ghetto, the legends were told of the Rastafarian Shangri-La, a sort of new Pinnacle, and under the embracing wing of Ras Tafari himself, King Haile Selassie. Unfortunately very few Rastas ever made it there due to lack of funds, at least until the Jamaican reggae stars began visiting. Most who did get there left after a few years for various reasons. The dream became a reality for only a few hundred who settled there.

The other great moment of the mission was meeting with the Emperor. The three Rastas of the delegation had prepared presents for the monarch. Mortimer had knitted a red, green, and gold scarf. Selassie expressed his wish that the Rastas "should send the right people." In the past he had welcomed doctors and professors, had asked army officers to join his ranks, and offered university exchanges for teachers and students. He presented each delegate a white *chamma*, the robelike national dress, and a gold medal with his effigy, which would become the Rastas' most treasured talismans.

The mission stopped over in Nigeria, which had recently achieved independence under the leadership of Nnamdi Azikiwe.

Nnamdi Azikiwe?

It was the name on the cover of *The Promised Key*! "Editor in Chief of the *Morning Post*, Accra Ghana"—who became the first black governor-general of Nigeria. After independence he became president. He was a friend of Kwame Nkrumah, the pan-African leader who led Ghana to independence. Howell had somehow presciently singled out a future African leader. Had he met him while Azikiwe was studying and working in New York? Dr. Azikiwe, the report states, "spoke warmly of how indebted were the West African nations to the West Indian teachers, pastors, and settlers." He observed that he himself had been taught by West Indian teachers, and stated that the philosophies of the late Marcus Garvey were in large part responsible for his work toward the independence of Nigeria. He told the Jamaicans he hoped that the question of reverse African migration would be taken up at the official level.[115]

In Ghana, Kwame Nkrumah, a long-time Marcus Garvey fan, requested a bust of his hero from Jamaica, as well as pictures of him.

"How shall I put it?" Nkrumah told the delegation. "Our meeting is historic. It has historic significance not only because we're blood relations but also because many attempts were previously made and failed. Marcus Garvey tried but was prevented." Nkrumah, who was then facing the numerous problems that come with a country's first year of independence, renamed Ghana's national shipping company the Black Star Line in Garvey's memory.

Upon the arrival of the delegates in Liberia, President Tubman recalled that the establishment of the country was due in part to the American Back-to-Africa movement, and that it had stayed true to its principles. But in Sierra Leone, the welcome was by no means as warm. A local paper, the *Daily Mail*, reproduced an article from the London *Sunday Dispatch* that said that they "planned to send the bearded Rastafarians home in chains," a statement purportedly made by Dr. John Karefa Smart, Sierra Leone's minister of external affairs. The statement had him asserting that the government was aware of the nature of the West Indian Rastafarian movement and would be cautious in considering any application for immigration to Sierra Leone. This was quite an embarrassment to the Rastas.

The mission returned home on June 3, met by five thousand Rastas chanting and waving flags. When the delegates stepped off the plane in their African clothes, there was an explosion of cheers and Rasta hymns. But the mission had been the object of much criticism while abroad, and the government did not follow through on their promises. A second mission in 1963, sponsored privately, attempted to conclude what the first mission had started, but a divergence of opinion between the EWF and the Rastas prevented any further action. The Piper family stayed put at Shashamani. As Planno put it, "They were Jews. They didn't want no Rastas around." Not until the 1970s, when some Twelve Tribes Rastas with a bit of cash went to settle there, was the dream of Shashamani fulfilled for any Jamaicans.

The mission to Africa left little more than gold dust in the memory of the Rastas. And maybe it was better this way. What would have become of the Rasta message if it had changed its focus to Black Zionism, with all the antagonism and misunderstanding that any Zionist movement historically brings? On the other hand, it appeared that, once more, an open door had closed for the descendants of slaves.

Jamaica celebrated its independence in 1962. Again the peoples' choice swung from the PNP to the JLP. Bustamante finally had gained control over the executive, the police, and the army. And one of the first moves he made was to launch the Jamaica Defense Force (as the army was now called) against the Rastas, in an anti-Rastafarian campaign more bloody than any the colonial government had ever undertaken. This has gone down in history as the Coral Gardens Massacre.

Coral Gardens is situated on the north coast of Jamaica, a few miles from Montego Bay. Above it stands the famous Great House called Rose Hall, the home of Annie Palmer, the eighteenth-century "white witch" who, according to devoutly accepted legend, used obeah sorcery to murder her husbands one by one. The flat, mosquito-ridden coastline below was of little interest to anyone, and Rasta squatters were able to live there peacefully until tourists began to invade the area in the 1950s, changing its wild face with golf courses, hotels, and polo fields. The Rastas were, of course, in the way. Developers—"crooks with blueprints"—had trouble promoting their schemes with Rastas living on the land. The local authorities decided to wipe them out, and this first came down on the unfortunate head of one Rudolf Franklyn.

Franklyn, the son of an estate watchman, was a "beardman" who squatted in the hills above Coral Gardens. The story goes that he was cultivating his small garden, and one day on his way back from the field he stopped at a gas station to ask for a glass of water. Instead of giving him water, the attendant sprayed him with gasoline and threatened to light a match if he didn't leave.[116] Franklyn got mad and the attendant called the police, who arrived and shot him several times. They left him for dead at the Montego Bay hospital. But Franklyn wasn't dead, and the doctors did all they could. They even installed an intestinal prosthesis that saved him. After several months in the hospital, Franklyn was transferred to prison to serve a short sentence on a charge of resisting arrest. When he came out six months later, his level of anger and frustration was at the boiling point. Living with an artificial bowel was not a joyful prospect, and Franklyn felt he didn't have much to lose. He gathered five of his brethren, "sufferers," who were as frustrated by daily humiliations as he was, and they began preparing weapons— straight machetes sharpened on both sides, spears forged from concrete reinforcing rods, missiles made from shells filled with cement, cutlasses stolen from a banana plantation.

On Thursday, April 11, 1963, the six Rastas appeared at the gas station at dawn. The night watchman swore he was a Rastaman too, and gave them a spliff of herb, so they let him go. But they hacked to death a white driver who happened to stop, and then set the station on fire. They went to a nearby motel, murdered a hapless guest, and then retreated to the hills. The Rose Hall estate overseer was their next victim, having just put his goats to pasture. By that time police had sent three cars after them. Two cars of armed civilians joined the hunt for the Rastas, but their little safari went bad when the Rastas ambushed the convoy at a rock outcropping at White Gut Road, about two miles from Rose Hall. Two Rastas died in the fusillade of police bullets, but the others managed to slash two members of the police department to death, as well as one of the civilian vigilantes.

This was when the war really began. The Montego Bay police called in reinforcements from Kingston and put Superintendent Bertie L. Scott in command, a brute loathed by the poor people in the area. They described him as carrying a whip and a machete; he would catch your wrist or your ankle with the whip so you would fall to the ground, then he would cut up your back with the machete. But fate caught up with Bertie Scott at the bend in the White Gut Road. When he stopped his jeep by the bodies of the slain cops, a Rasta brandishing a machete jumped out of the bush. It was Franklyn, who, despite a head wound, had sent his troops away for his final suicide mission. The newspapers reported that Franklyn ran up to the superintendent and killed him with a gun that he had taken from one of the dead police before himself falling forever. But Rastas swear that Franklyn, already riddled with bullets, carried only a machete, which he held high in the air as he charged Scott. Cops started firing from all directions. In the ensuing frenzy, a policeman who had come to the scene accidently shot and killed Bertie Scott.

When he heard of the death of Scott, Bustamante didn't want to get into any details. Always prone to manipulating and capitalizing on the emotions of the people, he positioned himself as the bulwark against Rasta peril. Having just been elected prime minister of newly independent Jamaica, he wasn't about to let any opportunity to assert his new authority pass. The legend goes that he blustered, "Bring in all the Rastas; those that the jail won't hold, the grave will!" He then sent elite Strike Force troops to Coral Gardens, army commandos trained by John F. Kennedy's counterinsurgency Green Beret program and armed with the latest American-supplied assault rifles. David Elliot, a young Rastaman from the Rosemont ghetto in Montego Bay, saw these weapons for the first time on this occasion. Like many witnesses, he claims that there were hundreds of deaths in the ensuing suppression. "No one dared to wear red, green, and gold again. Just saying 'I' could lead to being accused of saying 'high' and imprisoned as a Rasta. If they didn't kill you, they would severely beat you, tie you by your hair to a rope and drag you behind a police car. Most 'beardman' had to trim their locks, or else run to the hills and hide." Some Rastas refused to cut their locks and went to Trench Town or Back O'Wall, where Rastas could hope to be protected.

At this time, the situation in Kingston had started to change. The University Report and the Mission to Africa had given occasion to many exchanges, and the Rastas now had an ear in cultural circles. Leaders such as Mortimer Planno in the west and Filmore

Alvaranga and Douglas Mack in the east were demonstrating that Rastas were wise, knowledgeable people. But even the aura of people like Count Ossie couldn't protect the brethren, and two months after his return from the mission Douglas Mack reported that "a large contingent of police led by detective Ted Ansel swooped down on the camp at Wareika Hills. They held us at gun-point while they burned our dwellings and all of our earthly possessions." These possessions included all the documents that he had brought back from Africa.[117]

But after Count Ossie won Vere Johns's competition and recorded several singles, his camp became a safe haven for some north coast refugees. Every night on Adastra Road the grounations turned into bubbling jam sessions, where the best horn players on the island took turns playing solos. This was when the young drummer Lloyd Knibbs was working on a new style inspired by the Burru rhythm. He would test his ideas at the nightclub where his drummer father played, taking over the drums while his father was out having a beer. Lloyd Brevette, who played bass, liked what Knibbs was doing and worked in a walking bass line halfway between jazz and reggae. Soon the horn player joined this drum and bass duo, and word of the new sound spread like a fever. The combo made it no longer necessary for jazzmen to bring the whole Count Ossie ensemble down to the studio when they wanted to capture the Wareika sound. At Vere Johns's shows and in the nightclubs, these young ska musicians became the new sensation; now all they needed was a name. One night late in 1963, while they were getting ready for a show at the Regal, at Crossroads, they discussed the idea of a name backstage. Trumpeter Johnny "Dizzy" Moore suggested "the Satellites" since the band was, like Sputnik, Telstar, and other orbitors, the newest craze. "Let's make it the *Ska*talites!" said Jackie Mittoo, the keyboardist.

And so were born the Skatalites. They would guide ska's first steps, even if they lasted only eighteen months together. This period, however, established the square root of the reggae instrumental arrangement—insistent rhythm guitar, airy repeater solos, nostalgic horns, dancing shuffles, a slight Latin tinge. A band without a singer or lyrics, the Skatellites were nonetheless "political." Every day, new stories of victimization, violence, and injustice against the Rastas and other "sufferers" cried for justice through their melodies. Their visions shone clear through their horns. The magical duo of Lloyd Knibbs and Lloyd Brevette answered the hatred and blood by creating one of the most peaceful musics of all time. It was soon to escape them, however, as it entered show business and became commercial.

How did the music of Jamaican outcasts, even at the height of anti-Rasta paranoia, become a cutting-edge sound of the era, even spreading via emigration to England, where ska was marketed as "Bluebeat"? Each musician has his own version of the story. Johnny "Dizzy" Moore, the Skatalites' trumpet player, contributed his:

> It had been awhile that I have refused to cut my hair. I was uncomfortable in the barber's chair ever since I was a child. I preferred to have my hair on my head than to see it on the ground. My grandfather was also like this, and I take after him. This is me. Sometimes I try not to be me, but it don't work out. . . .
>
> After I left the Alpha School, I joined a military band, but I was always up at Count Ossie's place, so when I would get to work in the morning I was never fresh. My eyes were always red, and they would say, "What is it with you, mon? Didn't you wash your face?" And I said, "Well, mon, I been drinking," and so in the end they kicked me out. But along the way the idea came to me that things would happen on the music front in Jamaica.
>
> So I went to [producer] Coxsone [Dodd] and we spoke on the issue. I mean prior to that there were other groups recording, but not like this stuff. There was maybe some mento and some American stuff like that, but it took him quite some time to accept the idea. At the time Coxsone was in the sound system business. He was going to America to buy records; he wasn't doing any original stuff at the moment. I think I was the one responsible for

getting him into that sort of thing. He let me know that if I could get the musicians and organize the sessions, I could receive ten percent of all that, but I don't see to sign no paper with people of my race. I thought it would not be necessary. So it took Coxsone some time, and eventually he decided to try it. This is what we have today. I see myself as one of the people who conceptualized the whole movement through the auspices of the Great Creator. I am only one of his messengers.

Early tracks? We had "Roll River Jordan," a Clancy Eccles song with instrumental solos, which was a huge hit in Jamaica. "Schooling the Duke" also came out of that era. Songs like "Little Willy" were instrumentals. The people of Jamaica were *elated* by the whole thing. It was kind of bluesy at first, moving away from the American stuff, but that is what we were being fed. Jamaica had its own [style] called mento; some called it calypso. The spiritual type of thing that we Rastas got into is one of the strongest because the roots of it are buried in Ethiopia by the divine love of Haile Selassie. Was Coxsone doing it for spiritual reasons? I don't know. He's a smart guy, and certainly the richest of all of us. He's got pearls and diamonds and sapphires, rubies, gold, silver, zinc, and copper. He's got it all! He has the whole thing. Did he pay the musicians? Not that I know of, but I don't like to put anybody down. That is a question you could ask him.

Recognizing that its musicians were having an impact in metropolitan markets, Jamaica decided to send two star singers to New York in 1964 for the Worlds Fair—Minnie Small, who had just hit it big on the pop charts in England and the United States with "My Boy Lollypop," and Jimmy Cliff. The Skatalites were asked to be the backing band. What revenge—Rastas going to New York to represent Jamaica. At the last minute, however, Edward Seaga, a former scholar and producer of Jamaican folk music, and then the JLP minister of development, decided that "those red-eyed savages" could not be allowed to serve as Jamaica's cultural ambassadors. He instead chose Byron Lee and the Dragonaires, a flashy hotel lounge calypso band. Today Byron Lee, a longtime friend of the JLP, argues that this only happened because he was already in New York at the time and that saved Seaga the price of transport. But the Rasta musicians were furious. Overcome with bitterness, the Skatalites soon broke up. Knibbs got a job on a cruise ship and left Jamaica, not to return for nine years. The others went to play on the north coast for the tourists. Some started solo careers in the recording studios of Kingston.

Although Brother Royer noted that approximately ninety-five percent of all Jamaicans came from African roots, Jamaican independence did not awaken much recognition of an African cultural identity among its citizens. This comes, unfortunately, as no surprise. The minister of development, Edward Seaga, who also served as official culture czar, was a "Syrian" (of Lebanese extraction, as are nearly all Jamaicans of Middle Eastern origin) and studied ethnology at Harvard, specializing in Pocomania and other Afro-Jamaican cults. His important field recordings were issued on disc by Folkways Records in America, and he also produced ska and mento records for local consumption. Bustamante gave Seaga the task of designing a manipulative program to channel the young country's cultural aspirations away from the artistically vital Rastas. Marcus Garvey's body was brought back to Jamaica in 1963 and was received with a great ceremony (as Leonard Howell had prophesied). In 1964, a religious radio program featured the Rasta drummer Ras Michael. Apart from playing and reading from the Bible, Michael was not given permission to speak about social issues. The program was soon taken off the air.

In 1968, the National Heroes Commission was established in order to select a few "National Heroes." The roster included legendary rebels Nanny and Paul Bogle as well as the nation's founders, Bustamante and Norman Manley. The government finally decided to extend an official state visit invitation to Haile Selassie, after years of pressure to do so by PNP stalwarts N. N. Nethersole and Michael Manley, Norman's son. It was said that the JLP was scheming to discredit the Rastas by publicizing Selassie's public denial of his supposed divinity. But it didn't quite work out that way.

Several weeks before the emperor arrived, the adepts streamed into Kingston. Thousands waited peacefully to greet him. A gentle rain was greeted by the faithful as a shower of benediction. When Selassie's plane finally landed at Palisadoes Airport on April 6, 1966, pandemonium broke loose when the Rastas beheld the rampant Lion of Judah insignia on the jet's tail. The official welcome was overwhelmed by the surging crowd, and a huge grounation started in the shade of the big jet's wings. Delirium. Joyful noise. There were chalices burning, banners waving, grown men weeping, hymns floating through the tropic air. The huge crowd milling around the plane was an unheard-of breach of royal protocol, and it annoyed the emperor. He stayed on his plane, refusing to come down, until Planno had fought his way up the steps and assured him that he was not in danger. There was one uncertain moment when the plane door opened and a tiny olive-skinned figure with an aquiline nose and thin lips, wearing a beribboned uniform, appeared at the top of the steps. "Get out of the way!" shouted some of the brethren. "Let us see His Majesty!" What a mistake. This little man was His Imperial Majesty Ras Tafari.

"Make way for His Majesty!" Planno shouted, and the crowd parted like the Red Sea before the Hebrews. During the days that followed, thirty-one Rasta leaders were granted audiences, and each received a gold medallion inscribed with the Lion of Judah. Selassie, a devout Christian, duly vouchsafed that he wasn't God, but this only made the Rastas smile. Was not his humility truly divine?

Years later, in the privacy of his office, Selassie would ask his Indian secretary to read him the letters written to him by the Rastas. "Selassie was moved by these letters," recalled Professor Ajai Mansingh, a friend of Selassie's secretary. "He was deeply touched."[118] The King of Kings took his role as the patriarch of his people very seriously. He thought he had been empowered by God to handle it wisely. Selassie's visit to Jamaica would become the greatest event in the Rasta saga, and would greatly benefit his main advocate Michael Manley, to whom Selassie presented an old, meticulously carved riding stick—a symbol of command in Ethiopia. This talismanic baton came to be called "the Rod of Correction," which legitimized Michael's political career in the eyes of the Rastas for many years to come.

After Haile Selassie, music served as one of the greatest inspirations for the Rasta people. Marley called Jamaican music "another bag," an alternate window into the way things are. Edward Seaga intended to capitalize on the island's new music and develop it into an export commodity. He encouraged all kinds of folkloric performers and created song festivals to promote Jamaica's R&B crooners. Some great talents surfaced, but it was still a reactionary, colonialist culture Seaga was selling. Bob Marley, Peter Tosh, and Burning Spear's chances wouldn't come until later. In 1968, while promoting folkloric culture, the government persecuted anyone who tried to teach a different context in Jamaica. Walter Rodney, a radical Guyanian professor at the university, was deported for having too many contacts with ghetto people and for attending grounations with Rastas. But the injustice of this deportation created an uproar, and from then on it would prove impossible for the ruling classes to silence the Rastafarian revolution.

Nineteen sixty-eight was a crucial year in this process. That was the year Perry Henzell wrote the screenplay to *The Harder They Come* as a showcase of the new and evolving modern Jamaican culture. That year the term *reggae* was coined by soul singer Toots Hibbert, of the Maytals vocal trio, in his song "Do the Reggay." The new reggae rhythm had a slower tempo than either ska or its "rock steady" successor, with a ganja-stoned bass line and uncompromising lyrics. It was barely played on the radio in Jamaica, but soon began to get widespread coverage on the international music scene.

The irony was that the image that international promoters chose to project was that of the dreadlocked West Kingston Rasta of the most "dreadful" and flamboyant sort, but soon another Gong was beginning his ascent to international stardom—Tuff Gong—Bob Marley.

The 1960s, by far the most dramatic and tumultuous era in the Rasta movement, ended with the death of Don Drummond. Ever since ska had exploded onto the scene, Don Drummond had become increasingly disturbed. A quiet boy in his Alpha School days, a genius ska trombone hero, and an amazing and revolutionary musician, Drummond began sinking deeper and deeper into schizophrenia. Returning from a Caribbean tour, he found that his beloved grandmother, who had bought him his first trombone, had passed away. Mad with grief, he went berserk, smashed his instrument, and was locked up in Bellevue Mental Hospital. When he got out, his friends gave a benefit concert in his honor in order to buy him a new trombone. But Donald had changed. He was seen walking in his socks up on Mountain View Avenue, throwing handfuls of coins to children in the streets and talking in tongues. He became pathologically jealous of his dance queen lover, Marguerita Mahfood. She found knives hidden under their mattress on several different occasions, but she refused to leave the handsome, dangerous, mysterious Don Cosmic, as he was called. Sister Sugus, another of Count Ossie's dancers, remembered her last night:

"The same night she died I was to go with her to dance up at Copacabana. She was going and she wanted me to come. Lloydie the drummer, who was living up here in the shop, told me, 'Don't go with her—she's gonna die tonight.' I didn't take him serious, but I didn't go either." Later that night, a stern Don D. came down to Lloyd Knibbs. "She's up there," he motioned. Lloydie went to their house; Marguerita was lying on the bed, the handle of the knife sticking out of her collar bone.

Since Don Drummond was a day patient at Bellevue Hospital, a registered lunatic, his lawyers pleaded unsound mind, and he was locked up at the asylum, in the same "N" ward where David Marchand was spending time. He died there two years later, under mysterious circumstances.

30

Reggae Stars

Picture this, an everyday scene in Kingston: a child is walking in front of me on Windward Road. A dread appears, walking in the opposite direction. As he passes the child he brushes her locks lightly, saying, "Hey, Rasta baby!" I smile. In two quick steps he is at my side, eyes shining. Suddenly his hand clasps mine. "True, it all depends on what you call Rasta," and he is gone.

What does it mean to be a Rasta? This is the inevitable question we outsiders asked ourselves when encountering Jamaica in the 1970s. There are as many answers as there are reggae singers. Most of the singers smoke the holy herb, and most abstain from alcohol, but many will not refuse the treat of a Guinness. Red meat is not a favorite, some don't even eat fish, but many eat chicken, and gladly, too, as protein can be scarce. Monogamy is advocated, but many individuals practice polygamy without apology. Africa is never far from a Rasta's consciousness, but a large portion of the community craves emigration to the United States. Race is a basic concept for some, and a mere cultural reference for others. My first perception of Rasta was the loose, "cool runnings" attitude of these guys, the direct street-side exchanges, and eyes that looked straight into mine. Jamaica came into my life, as it did for many of my generation, through Perry Henzell's movie *The Harder They Come*, which I saw in the States in 1976. When American immigration bureaucrats gave me problems shortly after, I jumped on a plane and "immigrated" to Rasta country.

After New York, where blacks and whites avoided each other's eyes, Jamaica was a welcome relief. Countless foreign pop musicians have fallen in love with the atmosphere while working in the Kingston studios. The list is impressive and eclectic—Paul Simon, the Rolling Stones, Paul McCartney, Serge Gainsbourg, Khaled, Manu Dibango. It isn't just the music and the marijuana that attract people to Jamaica, but also the magical feeling that turns clichés to dust and opens new doors in our minds. The Rastas I have met always have so many questions to ask me, and so much information to impart. No matter where you find yourself sitting, on the street corner or under a tree, the passionate reasonings of these folk resonate, carving new niches in your mentality, perception, and imagination. On Maxfield Avenue, where I found refuge when I had no money left to pay my rent, Winston and his friends didn't wear locks, yet Jah was always present when they sang their ballads and strummed their old guitars at night.

> *Take a ride, my brethren take a ride*
> *Take a ride in a prophetic land*
> *Never let the sad things get over you*
> *Don't allow devil thoughts to capture you*
> *Try to make a different move*
> *So you can see what you can prove*
> *And you can get the touch of something new*
> *And the old.*
>
> (AL CAMPBELL)

Sitting on the steps, I listened to their harmonies intertwining in the night. All of their suffering caught fire and burned as it was exorcized. Between the crumbling walls of their shacks, the brethren walked with measured tread, some slowed by ganja and malnutrition, but their movements were graceful and in perfect rhythm. One night while praying, they all exhaled "Jah Rastafari!" together, and I felt a breath on the back of my neck and I acknowledged His presence. The atheist that I claimed to be had sensed a spiritual force at work in this ghetto yard, something that allowed the people to endure the reeking slums with dignity, something that allowed them to be kings.

Through the medium of reggae, Rastas found new allies. The youth of the world, raised on "peace and love" clichés and reefer, were looking for new gurus. The hippies thought the Rastas were everything they wanted to be, and reggae music seemed to express their inchoate ideals. The reggae arrangement expressed its own ideals—moving straight ahead toward its vision, each musician taking his turn in a sequence punctuated by the discrete roll of the repeater. Each instrument respects the following instrument; there is always space for each musician to have his part. In this way the rock audience was seduced, and they didn't notice the ambiguity of black rebel bulletins broadcast and propagated by white capitalist machinary. Chris Blackwell, the Jamaican founder of Island Records, the man who made Bob Marley the first Third World superstar, is a white man with blue eyes (although he also claims African blood in his ancestry). Perry Henzell gives a very smart description of Chris (disguised as the record boss DeMalaga) in his novel *Power Game*.

His manner was that of a star in his own right. The strength of his personality was in its combination of opposites: he was a businessman with the lifestyle of an artist. He was rich but by no means entrapped by formality. He was a gambler but he was not reckless. He'd earn his money in the quicksand of show business, but he'd built his fortune on the rocksteady foundations of real estate. He was a sport but he was always working. He was physically at ease in the tropics because as a child he roamed his father's cattle properties on the island, barefoot with a band of peasant kids, before being shipped off to school in England, and he'd realized early that if he could combine the advantages of

being rich and white with the cool of being black and poor, he'd
have the best of both worlds.

Why did Chris Blackwell choose Bob Marley? "Because he was
the best," Blackwell says. "Nobody else in Jamaica wrote lyrics like
him. But if I hadn't done it, someone else would have." In fact, Bob
was already signed to CBS when Blackwell decided that he wanted
to work with him, and he was obliged to buy out the Wailers' contract. But only Blackwell understood the planetary relevance of the
Rasta message and put his resources behind it. Jimmy Cliff, already
internationally famous well before Bob, and also under contract
with Blackwell, was then growing dreadlocks. Everybody thought
that after the movie came out Cliff would be the top reggae star in
the world. But three years of financial problems held up completion
of the production, and by the time the movie eventually hit the the-
aters in 1972, Jimmy had left the Rastas, cut his locks, and become
a Black Muslim. "He let his chance pass," Henzell says. "The film
benefited Bob instead."

Bongo Sheffan, of the Theocratic Government's small community in Bull Bay, gave me another explanation for why Bob Marley
became "the First Third World Superstar"—"Is because him
white!"

Of course Marley was not white, but half-caste. In the eyes of
his black compatriots, though, Bob Marley's pointed nose and thin
lips looked white, and one must admit that there is ambiguity in the
fact that the modern hero of black identity was the son of a respectable white Kingston family. True, Bob's father was supposedly dis-
owned by them for having given his name to the son of a black
country girl. But if it is race that we are talking about here, then it
must be said that Bob Marley was both black and white. When he
came to Trench Town at the end of the 1950s, people proud of their
pure African blood made sure to remind him of this. The maledic-
tion "Mr. Brown" followed him around all of his life, from the
schoolyard to the ghetto yard. In bitter moments he would say, "I'm
not on the black side, I'm not on the white side. I am on the side of

God." But as his relationship with Chris Blackwell attests, Bob was spiritually above racial oversimplifications. Marley's message was universal, and Blackwell offered him the means to spread it throughout the world. Mortimer Planno, Bob's guru, encouraged him to take up this challenge. He showed him "on which triggers the empires are set," and helped him to negotiate some challenging political moves to keep as much independence as possible.

When Bob began working with Chris at the beginning of the 1970s, Jamaica was again at a historical crossroads. The PNP was on the verge of seizing power with charismatic Michael Manley in charge, wielding the rod of correction as he crisscrossed the island. The Rastas, although nominally advocating nonparticipation in politics, put their faith in him, and some hailed him as "Joshua." Michael had received most of the credit for Selassie's triumphant visit to Jamaica, and Manley did hold sympathetic feelings for the Rastas. He knew about Pinnacle when he was working at the Ariguanabo factory in Spanish Town, and he later met with Rasta leaders on several issues, including the legalization of ganja. Manley primarily appreciated the role the Rastas played in giving the island a national identity, something that many Jamaicans worried was severely otherwise lacking (and is somehow still lacking now; it only began to crystallize somewhat around the participation of the Reggae Boyz national football team in the 1998 World Cup). Manley realized the benefits to be drawn from the cultural and philosophical contributions of the Rastas—they knew emotionally what he was trying to prove intellectually, and with the help of the Rastas he could reach an audience he could not access alone.

"I could never pretend that the lyrics of protest music which motivated Reggae music taught me anything that I didn't already know," Manley later wrote. "From an intellectual point of view, these chants confirmed all that I believed as a socialist, and all that I have struggled against as a trade unionist. But I had not been born in the ghetto and was therefore never part of this experience. Reggae music influenced me profoundly by deepening my element of emotional comprehension" (*Reggae International*, 1982).

Bob Marley believed in Manley's sincerity, or he at least gave Manley the benefit of the doubt. At the end of 1971, with the new single "Trench Town Rock" in the shops, the Wailers decided to take part in "the PNP Musical Caravan," touring the country and performing on flatbed trucks. Although Marley left after only three shows, he would later pay a high price for his political flirtations. In 1976, just before the next elections were to take place, he offered to play a free concert in Kingston. The ruling PNP made it look like a concert in support of their party. A couple of days before the show was scheduled to go on, a gang of gunmen opened fire on Marley and his band with machine guns. It was perhaps a miracle that he wasn't killed. He was, however, grazed by two bullets, and both his manager and his wife were wounded. Who had ordered the raid? Manager Don Taylor guessed it was the CIA. Marley didn't want to make any public accusation, as he realized how naive he had been to think he could challenge in song the destabilizing agency that had overthrown Salvador Allende in Chile and supported the JLP's ongoing violent opposition to Michael Manley.

But it was no accident that the Manley years, 1972–1980, saw the recording of the most inspired and powerful reggae music in the history of the movement. Manley's quasi-affiliation gave Bob Marley a near-immunity against the establishment, a tacit payback for forty years of victimization against the Rastas. When Blackwell loaned Marley his local headquarters, Island House, near the prime minister's official residence on wealthy Hope Road, the singer brought his Trench Town style and entourage uptown. "I want to disturb my neighbor—in a rub-a-dub style." They planted calaloo where the flowerbeds had been, and sheltered gangster friends wanted by the police. Once a week Marley gave talks, like Selassie had done, to dozens of ghetto youth, and remained available to them even at the height of his fame. For thousands he was seen as a street bank, a resource to finance a business deal or to take a kid to the hospital, and nobody ever had to pay him back. The weight of this vaguely anonymous burden was probably heavier on his shoulders than he would have wanted to admit. (Marley's accountant estimated that in his last years as many as four thousand people depended directly on him for their daily bread.) It was certainly more difficult than writing songs. He even tried to stop the suicidal political war in 1978 at the famous Peace Concert. Bob Marley the ecstatic Rasta—the soul of the nation—joined the hands of Manley and Seaga, the two rival party leaders, above his head on stage. It was a legendary gesture for a short-lived truce. In 1980 he offered to give a concert in Zimbabwe in honor of its independence, paying for the transport of his band and the PA system from Europe out of his pocket. He never stopped working for the unification of the Rastas, presiding over stormy conferences at Tuff Gong, trying in vain to unite factions, sects, and gangs in a common line of action. He did all this while working madly on his music, giving Island Records ten faultless albums in ten years. He held the weight of two worlds, the black and the white, but it was too much for human shoulders. He developed cancer and passed away in 1981, just after the JLP had once again seized power. His death represented the tragic end of a classic era.

The white promoter and the brown singer had conquered the media, bringing in journalists from America, Europe, and Japan, who would dutifully sell Rastas to the world. Reggae records started to sell, but most of the time their message was blurred by misunderstandings and romanticized, picturesque exaggerations. The spasms of violence then shaking Jamaica, which was so much a part of the Rasta problem, were rarely analyzed, and then only as tabloid fodder. It seemed to me that the national dialogue was the most clear, lucid, and sophisticated in the ghettos. My friends referenced three continents—Africa, Asia, and Europe. They caught the main lines of Marxism, Garveyism, animism, Christianity in its various permutations, Buddhism, ecology. They didn't claim to weave all these thoughts and influences into any coherent intellectual system. They trusted the individual, once informed, to find his own way out. They identified with Bob's warning: "Life is one big road with lots of signs, so when you're riding through the ruts, don't you complicate your mind." The Rasta called this worldview "livity"—a huge cognitive reservoir of popular wisdom and social rules, where Garvey quotations and Bible quotations mingled with proverbs and songs and with the occasional line from a western movie. They took the calm of Asia, the rhythm of Africa, and the European dialectic and made their own thing. No church, no pope, no guru. "Politricks" hadn't yet penetrated Rasta. Each and every one was free to think by himself, was advised by the elders to take orders only from Jah.

In August 1975, upsetting rumors began to reach Jamaica that Haile Selassie had died. Deposed in a 1974 military coup, the emperor had reportedly been poisoned after two years of house arrest in Addis. "Show us his body, show us his grave," the Rastas challenged. In one of his most powerful performances, Burning Spear affirmed the Rasta truth: "Jah no dead!" Ever defiant, ever sure, unshakable in his root beliefs, Bob Marley sang, "Jah live, children—yeah! Fools saying in their heart, 'Rasta, your god is dead.' But I and I know—dread shall be dread-a-dread . . . *Jah live!*"[119]

But the end of the 1970s was inexplicably hellish, with the rise of factional violence and street crime and the systematic decline of Jamaica's economy. With the arrival of crack cocaine on the market in the 1980s, the Rastas became bitter as their illusions burned. The gap between them and the new dancehall-style reggae stars was widening. When the JLP regained power in 1980, "conscious" reggae began to fade into the obscene "slackness" style, the heavily promoted, cocaine-fueled music of the Kingston dancehalls. The question on everyone's mind was whether the Rasta movement could survive the precipitous, decadent decline of spiritual reggae.

31

Twelve Tribes

So what became of the Nya-Binghis, the Howellites, the Emmanuelites, and the other Rastas in the 1970s, while the reggae stars rode around in BMWs, basking in international glory?

After doing seven years of his ten-year prison sentence, Claudius Henry founded a community at Greenbottom. He ran a bakery (like Howell had), and a concrete block factory (like Tuskeegee). He built houses for his people and, unlike Howell, took care of his childrens' education, running a school for more than a hundred pupils.

But the Nya-Binghis were still extremely poor and isolated. Their small camps and yards across the country squatted illegally on "captured" Crown land, and constantly risked expulsion. Once or twice a year they met for a "Nya-Binghi" in a remote location, where they would throw up huts and spend a few days drumming and praying, celebrating, for example, Selassie's birthday in August. Their quasi-independent communities lacked any sort of central organization that could speak for them and defend their interests.

The Ethiopian World Federation also tried, without success, to gather the Rastas under one umbrella. L. F. C. Mantle had created the unofficial Jamaican "Local 17" in 1938, but another officially recognized branch was founded in Kingston in 1955 when the New

York EWF sent Miss Maymie Richardson to Jamaica as its legal delegate. Selassie had given control over all Ethiopian relations in the New World to the New York EWF. This irritated the Jamaicans, who thought themselves livelier and more numerous than the New York branch. It was a time of tragic "ism and schism," as Bob Marley later sang. The New York people didn't worship Selassie and didn't get the Rastas. The New Yorkers called themselves Black Jews, and many worshiped in the ancient Ethiopian Orthodox Church. They controlled the Shashamani valley in Ethiopia, which Selassie had deeded to them, stymieing any Rasta designs on the land. In the end the New York EWF declared the Jamaican Rastafarians to be "pagan" and their leaders to be "unscrupulous, artless, godless, and self-styled."[120]

Meanwhile, Count Ossie's community at Wareika survived many police raids and vandalism. In the early 1970s this band of drummers fused with the Mystics, Cedric Brooks's horn section. The Mystics were, at the time, one of the most progressive jazz bands in Jamaica. With the addition of Count Ossie's drummers, they became the legendary Mystic Revelation of Rastafari. The PNP was in power, and Jamaica's African identity was finally acknowledged. The Mystic Revelation was often invited to perform at official occasions such as state visits. They received two successive gold medals for percussion at CARIFESTA, the pan-Caribbean music festival. Count Ossie was able to purchase a piece of land above Adrasta Road on Glasspole Avenue, and he begun to build a cultural center. The library began to fill with biographies of great black men, with books of history and culture, self-sufficiency, folk medicine techniques, and trades.

While other Rasta camps were closing in on themselves, Count Ossie's camp thrived and stayed open to everyone in the area. No one was forced to wear locks or take part in any ceremonies or prayer, and everyone in the district sent their children to its school. This was the time when "university intellectuals and taxi drivers, novices and virtuosos, saints and charlatans, professionals and ne'er-do-wells, all gathered under Saint Ossie in the spirit of peace and mutual respect."[121] But the community would lose its leader on October 18, 1976, National Hero's Day. Count Ossie was killed while driving home from a show in his truck. A drunk driver, at the wheel of a bus with faulty brakes, crashed into him, killing Count Ossie and two band members. Despite his tragic death, Ossie's seminal repeater style lives on in the records he made with the Mystic Revelation of Rastafari, especially *Grounation* and *Tales of Mozambique*, much venerated by fans of Rasta music.

What happened to Prince Emmanuel, leader of the Rasta Convention of 1958? After his camp in Ackee Walk (Back O' Wall) was sacked by police in 1959, and his people thrown in jail, a renowned lawyer, who had previously defended the Mau Mau in Kenya, took up their case. The adepts were freed and the community benefited from the publicity. Prince Emmanuel lacked the charisma of Howell or Henry, and his pamphlet *Black Supremacy*, which advocated a sort of Christo-Rasta faith, was really of little interest. But he did have a sense of ritual and costume, and his strict moral rules appealed to the Rastas' innate Puritan fundamentalism. Prince Emmanuel wasn't invited to the Mission of Africa, but he was one of thirty-one elders who met Selassie in 1966, and he received his gold medal with the Lion of Judah at long last.

In the 1970s, chased from ghetto to ghetto, he ended up in the hills of Bull Bay, in a beautifully constructed longhouse village decorated in red, gold, and green, with an inspiring view over the bay. There they lived by manufacturing brooms and straw mats. Visitors were not welcome, and for many years the outside world was entirely ignored. All Jamaica was familiar with the ubiquitous Emmanuelite broom vendor, always dressed in khakis with a high turban atop his head. They were in fact the only sect of Rastafari to have developed a strict set of social and liturgical rules. They said prayers three times a day, first on bended knee, and then lying flat on their bellies facing toward the east. The sabbath was observed meticulously. Women were separated from men for twenty-one days of every month for "purification purposes." This was considered a "natural method of birth control which the Father has shown us,"

Priest James explained to *Outlook* on August 20, 1995. It is possible that this segregation was supposed to ensure that women were not unfaithful while the men were away selling brooms. The result of this tactic was a small number of children for each family, two or three at most. As of 1978, the village listed "fourteen priests, sixty prophets, and fourteen empresses."

The Emmanualites, or "Bobos," remained for thirty years the most despised of the Rastas, even among the movement itself. Their blind obedience to rule and their absence of worldly ambition was repulsive to younger, more militant Rastas fighting for a cause. But everything changed with the death of Prince Emmanuel in 1994. The community opened to the outside world, and suddenly the Bobos appeared as new ghetto saints in the midst of a Jamaica wracked by corruption, violence, and moral decay. Hot young reggae deejays like Sizzla now sported the turban, and youths in the ghettos began declaring themselves Bobos, adopting the turban as well as a racist, sexist, and homophobic interpretation of the Bible. The original community then imploded into enemy factions; one was helped by longtime neighbor Rita Marley, who in turn exercised some sort of control. But the dispute turned ugly, and Rita's "traditional" Bobo villagers torched a new rival village built on the neighboring hill. The matter went to court, and the culprits were sentenced to jail.

But there was one particular branch of Rastafarianism that benefited greatly from the reggae movement. The Twelve Tribes of Israel was founded in 1968 by an ice cream vendor named Vernon Carrington, on the principle that not everyone had been created to fill the same part in the world. When Jacob called his sons to his deathbed, he assigned to each a different role. Twelve Tribes Rastas read this part of Genesis as a kind of horoscope —but which tribe was theirs? Twelve sons, twelve months—this was the key idea. Following your date of birth, you belonged to one of twelve tribes. January was Naphtali, February was Joseph, etc. Vernon Carrington himself was "Gad." Burning Spear was "Benjamin." Bob Marley, born February 6, was a perfect "Joseph," the beloved son sold into slavery by his jealous brothers, who would later become a mighty man and his family's savior when hunger forced them to flee from Egypt. There was even the parallel story of the shooting on Hope Road. "Joseph is a fruitful bough, even a fruitful bough by a well; whose branches run over the wall: The archers have sorely grieved him, and shot at him, and hated him: But his bow abode in strength, and the arms of his hands were made strong by the hands of the mighty God of Jacob" (Genesis 49:22–24).

It was their more inclusive vision of identity that allowed the Twelve Tribes members to open the Rasta "livity" to new blood, the half caste, the reggae stars, emancipated women, the sons of the bourgeoisie. The children of the ruling class had studied abroad, in California and in Europe, where they smoked marijuana and listened to reggae music. When they came home, they sought the company of Rastas. David Marchand remembers this period. "It was a time when even the big families in Jamaica were beginning to worry because their children were turning Rasta. It was an exciting period, a revolutionary wind was blowing; many good society children were at the Twelve Tribes. Cat Coore of the Third World [band], son of the Minister of Development, David Coore, was one of the leaders. Errol Flynn's daughter was one of them too, and spent her days smoking joints at her property on the north coast . . ."[122]

The Twelve Tribes became the most influential and active sect of the Rasta movement in the 1970s. Bob Marley attended Twelve Tribes meetings and probably gave money to the organization. They organized sound systems, opened vegetarian restaurants, and even sent a few colonists to Shashamani in Ethiopia. Their vision of an integrated world replaced the old Manichean idea of Black against White, spinning off the imagery of Joseph's technicolor dreamcoat—the world as a marvelous patchwork of cultures, so much like Jamaica, the island that was their home.

But the force and influence of the Twelve Tribes was due in great part to the status, education, social connections, and actual money of some of their elite members—resources that other Rastas did not possess. It was because of this that bitterness began to grow among the ranks of the poorest Rastas. Mortimer Planno, a sophisticated Rasta strategist, urged Bob Marley to use his authority to unite the Rastas. But the several Rastafarian conclaves that Bob sponsored at Tuff Gong in the late 1970s didn't lead to the vision he had been imagining. By 1979 the overworked singer was already sick with cancer. In 1980, in a state of collapse and afraid he was about to die, Bob Marley was baptized into the Ethiopian Orthodox Church in a New York hotel room. He had been its secret benefactor in Jamaica for years, financing the construction of its church on Maxfield Avenue. When he died in 1981, the Ethiopian Orthodox Church was to preside over his burial in a gorgeous ceremony of Coptic chants in Amharic and Geez, streaming incense, and rows of priests holding beautifully carved silver crosses. Marley's old friend, the Jamaican soccer star Alan "Skill" Cole, had to shoulder aside an EOC priest to get a word in edgewise for the Twelve Tribes at Marley's state funeral.

Why did Bob Marley turn his back on the Rastas? Some say he had been so aware of his death that he no longer cared for denominations, and who else could have baptized him, to prepare him for death? In front of whom could he have bent his head, when each and every Rasta leader sought nothing but favors? Marley had been received in London by Selassie's grandson, the Crown Prince Asfa Wossen, and given a black onyx ring with a rampant gold Lion of Judah. The Ethiopian church, the most ancient in all of Christianity, had a mystical authority that attracted the reggae king. In a world where he sang about "burning all illusions," he could still find in the Ethiopian church a profound sense of mystery.

But one can only guess what was going on in the mind of this man, only thirty-six years old and aghast at his fate, as he was so weakened by disease and then crucified by the immense suffering of cancer. Perhaps he wanted to please his mother, who had been trying for years to bring him back to Christianity. For the Rastas, however, it was a blow. Their ambassador, their prince, had gone to die in the arms of Jesus.

32

The End

So where was Leonard Howell while reggae conquered the world? He seemed to have disappeared. In 1958 he wasn't present at the Back O'Wall convention. The team of university-affiliated researchers preparing the report on the Rasta movement in 1960 didn't deem it necessary to consult its founder. They reported that Howell was either dead or locked up in an asylum without checking to verify the facts.

It isn't easy to recount the Rasta leader's last twenty years. The world's eyes were focused elsewhere. The twenty years spanning Jamaican independence to the death of Bob Marley were so crucial that the movement seemed to have forgotten its patron, even if he had formulated the message for which Jamaica had become so famous. Howell had lost the power to protect his people when he lost his political connections; he lost his connections to politics when he lost Pinnacle and its prosperous ganja farm. The little money he had put aside didn't allow him to play Santa Claus as he had wished. Those who had thought of Howell as God began to look elsewhere for inspiration and an invitation to paradise. The Leonard Howell of the 1970s seemed to have shrunk down to human proportions. This old man with silver hair doted upon his blue-eyed granddaughter Gillian, who had been born to the elder of the two princes, Monty, before his departure to England in 1961. He picked her up at school with pockets full of sweets. Her mother, Yvonne, began to grow worried. "We were afraid he might take her away," she confessed. So Gillian was put in another school.

In 1971 Blade, the younger of the princes, also left Jamaica to go to the United States. His Chinese Jamaican wife was ignorant of her husband's lineage. "He never introduced me to his father," Curlyn says. "Too bad! It must have been a good life up there at the big house!" And then Blade explains, "Deep down we were proud of him, but sometimes we wished we had a father like anyone else's."

With his princes gone and everybody else turning their backs on him, Howell didn't have much to do in town. He went back to Tredegar Park, where the faithful Howellites had gathered to build yet another "tabernacle." What role was there for him to play? He didn't have many left to choose from, but when all else failed, he could still play Christ. He said his various defeats were successive crucifixions, six in all. He told his people that after the seventh, he would not go underneath anymore, but would remain alive. Hostile local police promised to give him all the martyrdom he deserved. They raided his cottage and burned it down. Canute Kelly, one of the young adepts from St. Thomas, remembers visiting him in Tredegar Park once, and finding Howell hiding out in a cave. "Such a great man he was," Canute sighed sadly.

Twenty years passed in a desultory fashion, and not one journalist or researcher approached the first Rasta. Professor Barry Chevannes of the University of the West Indies tried to see him at the beginning of the 1970s while conducting research on Bedward, but Howell declined to be interviewed. In 1979, only two years before his death, the Gong broke this silence for a Japanese ethnologist doing field research on reggae music. She was invited to visit him in his small house behind a brook (she remembers having to ford it on foot). He was an old man of eighty-one, but he fondly recalled his stopovers in Japan and the beautiful women he had enjoyed in Nagasaki—or was this simply again his ability to spin his legend one more time?

In 1980, Howell's last crucifixion took place. On a Thursday night his adepts were gathered as usual at the Tredegar Park tabernacle when they heard voices shouting in the night, "Ketch 'im! Cut 'im tongue and kill 'im! Trow 'im in May Pen cemetery!" They didn't realize that their leader was the object of all this shouting. But a few nights later Howell was attacked by a gang of thugs who held him down and actually tried to cut out his tongue. The old man kept his jaws clenched shut and caught the blade with his bare hands. He got home with one cheek sliced open and his hands deeply cut. The next morning, having cleaned and treated his wounds, he explained to the Howellites that this never-explained outrage was the seventh crucifixion.

At eighty, there was almost nothing left of the Gong but a withered old man hiding in a remote cottage. Was he destined to die in such shabby conditions? Would he be forced to end such an extraordinary life in such an ordinary fashion? Never. Leonard Howell still had a trick or two up his sleeve. At the end of 1980, sensing the end was near, he moved into the Sheraton Hotel in uptown Kingston. It was one of the most expensive hotels in Jamaica, where a night's lodging cost more than the monthly salary of a cane worker. He paid for his room daily, in cash. Miss Gertrude Campbell took care of him in the hotel until February 12, 1981. That morning he asked Miss Campbell to squeeze an orange for him. As he drank the fresh sweet juice, he closed his eyes, and was gone.

Many of his children gathered for his burial, flying from Canada, the United States, and Great Britain. Daphney Howell says that his will was read at the Pegasus Hotel. Blade flew in from New York and took charge of the funeral. Miss Campbell gave him a little gray cardboard suitcase containing Leonard's notebooks, a few documents, and a bundle of pictures of Ras Tafari, reproductions of the cards he had handed out during the 1930s. What was his legacy? His bank statement showed that there was some money left, enough to help Blade pay the funeral expenses. But when the prince tried to withdraw the money, another one of Howell's children contested his right to it. Blade, in the true manner of his father's spirit, decided to let the matter lie, as he had no use for the money. Leonard Howell's money is supposedly still in the bank.

Miss Campbell seemed indifferent to Howell's death. Her thoughts were that the Counselor could not really be dead, only absent. Once his body was washed and dressed, the undertakers turned to her as she sat quietly in the corner and asked her to tie his necktie in the way he liked it to be tied. For the last time the old lady approached her god-man, and, bending over his sleeping body, she tied the black silk tie the way she had seen him do it so many thousands of times before. She did it exactly the way he always had done it, "never lower than the third button!"

In Runaway Bay, in 1999, David Marchand is watching the sky. A purple bank of clouds on the western horizon has swallowed up the sun, and the first pale stars have appeared. David is perplexed. He is looking at an unfamiliar constellation. One of the stars isn't supposed to be there, but it's still early and the sky remains too transparent to be sure of this celestial apparition he thinks he sees. David waits on the shore, his copper features shining in the orange light under a halo of crazy hair. Maybe he's mistaken, but . . . *this strange star*!

Today I went to see Leonard Percival Howell's grave in Dove Cot. Tomorrow I leave Jamaica. It is always at the end of a trip that time becomes distorted and things seem only half real. A taxi, and the usual scramble to get inside one. I am not sure which line I am supposed to take to get to Dove Cot cemetery, and there are so many people waiting for cars at the Spanish Town bus terminal that even before I am able to ask their destinations, the taxis are full and gone. Eventually I am crammed inside a Lada with six big market women. It is suffocating, hot and tight. I try hard not to pay any attention to the thick air and clinging garments, as I am not really in my body. Leonard Howell is dead, and tomorrow I fly away.

The taxi leaves me in the open countryside. Fields. Bare expanses of grass. More fields and trees. The trees seem to be cypresses. This should be Dove Cot, but I see no tombstones. Getting a closer view I realize that the field is punctuated with a regular pattern of brass plates the size of cake boxes. A name, two dates, a number. Thousands of them are lined up in this soccer pitch of a graveyard. I walk sideways between them, reading the names. Here it is, number 563, Leonard Percival Howell. The line underneath reads, "No man is indispensable but some are irreplaceable."

I sat on the grass in front of the brass square. Am I sitting on his grave? It's hard to tell, as the grass evenly covers the ground. But I feel nothing. My heart is as empty as this football field. I head back toward the road, crossing the open field and looking up at the sky.

I go to Tredegar Park and say goodbye to my friends Amy and Vinette. I tell them I have been to Dove Cot. "So what?" is their response. They never bothered. I tell them that I sat on a grave, but

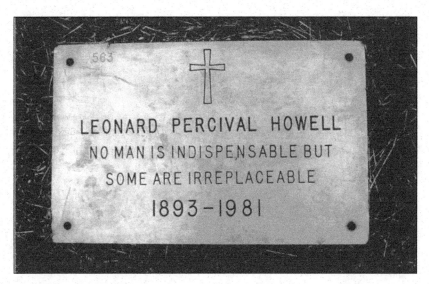

Leonard Howell's grave in Dove Cot (birth date is erroneous).
© HÉLÈNE LEE.

that it didn't feel like Howell's. Amy and Vinette look at each other and then burst into torrents of girlish giggles. "So you never believe what we tell you? *Him not dere!*"

Vinette lowers her voice. "Of course him not in Dove Cot. *Is we carry the coffin.* It was *empty!*"

David gets up from the armchair. He walks to the terrace overlooking the sea. In just a few hours, the strange star has grown into a comet. It is already bigger than the biggest planet. It has blossomed in the Jamaican night sky like a hot flower. Down below and through the waves, underneath a flood of fluorescent plankton woken by the comet, tongues of light roll out and flash white neon liquid sparks at the base of the black sea-worn rocks.

Paris, 1999
Bamako, 2002

Notes

1. M. G. Smith, Roy Augier, and Rex Nettleford, *Report on the Rastafari Movement in Kingston, Jamaica* (Mona, Jamaica: University of the West Indies, 1960).
2. A. Johnson, *JAG Smith* (Kingston, Jamaica: Kingston Publishers, 1991), 165.
3. *Daily Gleaner*, November 23, 1940.
4. J. A. Somerville, *Man of Color* (Kingston, Jamaica: Pioneer Press, n.d.).
5. Robert Hill, "Leonard P. Howell and Millenarian Visions in Early Rastafarianism," *Jamaica Journal* (February 1983).
6. Claude McKay, *Banjo* (New York: Harper, 1929), 200.
7. Ibid.
8. Claude McKay, *Home to Harlem* (New York: Harper, 1928), 293.
9. James Weldon Johnson, "The Making of Harlem," in *Harlem, Mecca of the New Negro* (Black Classic Press, 1925).
10. McKay, *Banjo*, op. cit.
11. Langston Hughes, *The Big Sea* (New York: Thunder's Mouth Press, 1986).
12. Hill, op. cit.
13. Ibid.
14. *La Guardia Report*, 1938, cited in Dennis Forsythe, *The Law Against Ganga in Jamaica* (Kingston, Jamaica: Zaika Publications, 1993).
15. Leonard Howell, *The Promised Key*. Passage inspired by Balintine's "Royal Scroll of Black Supremacy."
16. Pinnacle Papers, Jamaican National Archives, Spanish Town.

17. J. Szwed, introduction to *Black Gods of the Metropolis*, by Arthur Huff Fauset (Philadelphia: University of Pennsylvania Press, 1971).

18. Hill, op. cit.

19. Marcus Garvey, *Philosophy and Opinions* (London: Cass, 1967).

20. Hill, op. cit. "Gaathlyi" is a contraction of "Garvey" and "Athlyi."

21. *Holy Piby* (Woodbridge, NJ: Athlican Strong Arm Company, 1924); reprinted by Headstart Publications, P.O. Box 2967, Kingston 8, Jamaica.

22. B. G. M. Sundkler, *Bantu Prophets in South Africa* (London: Lutterworth, 1948).

23. *Daily Gleaner*, August 15, 1934.

24. Ras Miguel Lorne, foreword to *The Royal Parchment*.

25. A. A. Brooks, *History of Bedwardism* (Spanish Town, Jamaica: National Archives of Jamaica, 1917).

26. K. J. King, *Journal of Ethiopian Studies*, January 1932.

27. Roi Ottley, *New World A-Coming* (Boston: Houghton Mifflin, 1943), 108.

28. Rev. Lloyd Cowell, "Color Blind," a sermon.

29. Annie Harvey to the Secretary of State, March 31, 1946, Back-to-Africa Movement Archives, Jamaican National Archives.

30. Cited by Robert Hill, op. cit.

31. Cited by Claude McKay in *Home to Harlem*, op. cit.

32. Canute Kelly, interview with the author, 1997.

33. Pinnacle Papers, op. cit.

34. Ibid.

35. Ibid.

36. Ibid.

37. Ibid.

38. *Daily Gleaner*, March 14, 15, and 16, 1934.

39. Ibid.

40. *Daily Gleaner*, August 20, 1934.

41. Pinnacle Papers, op. cit.

42. Melrosa Francis statement, Pinnacle Papers, op. cit.

43. Marcus Garvey, *Philosophy and Opinions*, Vol. I, 34.

44. *Daily Gleaner*, August 20, 1934.

45. Ibid.

46. *Daily Gleaner*, August 15, 1934.

47. Cited by J. A. Rogers in *Real Facts About Ethiopia* (Kingston, Jamaica: 1936).

48. Letter by Timothy Heath and Puerto Cortez, Back-to-Africa Movement File, Spanish Town Archives.

49. *Jamaica Times*, December 7, 1935.

50. *The Beat*, December 1985.

51. Laxmi and Ajai Mansingh, *Home Away from Home* (Kingston, Jamaica: Ian Randle, 2000), 53.

52. Ajai Mansingh, "Rastafarianism: The Indian Connection," *Sunday Gleaner*, July 18, 1982.

53. Dale Bisnauth, *A History of Religions in the Caribbean* (Kingston, Jamaica: Kingston Publishers, 1989).

54. Ibid.

55. Ajai Mansingh, "Rastafarianism," op. cit.

56. Ibid.

57. Ajai and Laxmi Mansingh, "The Indian Presence," *Caribbean Quarterly* 41 (March 1995).

58. Ajai Mansingh, "Rastafarianism," op. cit.

59. *Daily Gleaner*, February 18, 1933.

60. Pinnacle Papers, op. cit.

61. Ibid.

62. *Daily Gleaner*, January 18, 1937.

63. Pinnacle Papers, op. cit.

64. *The Negro Worker*, June 1, 1930.

65. Ken Post, "The Bible as Ideology: Ethiopianism in Jamaica 1930–1938," in *African Perspectives* (Cambridge: Cambridge University Press, 1970).

66. "Lest We Forget," *Newsday*, October 1958.

67. Perry Henzell, interviewed by the author, 1997.

68. *Daily Gleaner*, January 18, 1940.

69. Director of Medical Services to the Colonial Secretary, January 16, 1941, Pinnacle Papers.

70. *Jamaica Times*, July 19, 1941.

71. W. F. Elkins, *Street Preachers, Faith Healers, and Herb Doctors in Jamaica 1890–1925* (New York: Revisionist Press, 1977).

72. Pinnacle Papers, April 1944, op. cit.

73. Indian Hemp Drug Commission, 258.

74. Marcus Garvey, "Do Your Work Without Fear," *The New Jamaican*, March 18, 1933.

75. Police report of March 1, 1939, in *Ganga Growing: A Report to the League of Nations*.

76. Police report of June 3, 1938, in ibid.

77. The "chalice" was and is the water pipe that Rastafarians craft from coconut shell and rubber tubing.

78. Ethiopian Salvation Society regulations, Spanish Town Archives.

79. Back-to-Africa Movement File, October 9, 1939, Spanish Town Archives.

80. Ibid., April 28, 1942.

81. Ibid.

82. Ibid.

83. *Jamaica Constabulary Force Magazine*, University of the West Indies Library, 1955.

84. Ibid.

85. *Strange man, Rastaman.*

86. *Memorandum on the Dangerous Drug Law*, in the "Ganga Growing in Jamaica" file, Jamaican National Archives, Spanish Town.

87. Elkins, op. cit.

88. Ibid.

89. Letter from the Citizens of Smith Village Association, May 12, 1936, Spanish Town National Archives.

90. Elkins, op. cit.

91. Stephen Davis, *Bob Marley* (Cambridge, MA: Schenkman Books, 1990).

92. G. E. Simpson, "The Rastafari Movement in the 1950s," *Jamaica Journal* (December 1994).

93. Smith et al., op. cit.

94. William R. Scott, in *Ethiopia Observer*, vol. 2, 1972.

95. Jah Bones, *One Love* (London: Voice of Rasta, 1985).

96. Ibid.

97. Ibid.

98. Ibid.

99. Harry T. Powell, interview with the author, 1980.

100. Lewis, Matthew Gregory, *Journal of a West-India Proprietor* (London: J. Murray, 1834).

101. Carr, cited in Lorna Simmonds, *Post-Emancipation Protest in Jamaica* (Kingston: University of the West Indies, 1983), 11.

102. Emery, cited in ibid.

103. Ibid.

104. Bridge, *Annals of Jamaica*, 1928.

105. Verena Reckord, "Rastafarian Music: An Introductory Story," *Jamaica Journal*, 11:1, 2 (1977).

106. Ibid.

107. Ibid.

108. Ibid.

109. Jah Bones, op. cit.

110. Verena Reckord, op. cit., 9.

111. Brother Powdy, interview with the author, 1997.

112. Verena Reckord, op. cit.

113. Barry Chevannes, *Daily Gleaner*, October 19, 1986, 9.

114. Mission to Africa Report, 3, and Minority Report, 8.

115. Mission Report, 6.

116. David Elliot, interview with the author, Montego Bay.

117. Douglas Mack, *From Babylon to Rastafari* (Kingston, Jamaica: Frontline Books).

118. Professor Ajai Mansingh, interview with the author, 1997.

119. Bob Marley, "Jah Live," 1975.

120. EWF document, University Report, 31.

121. Verena Reckord, op. cit.

122. David Marchand, interview with the author, 1995.

Index